# As Equals
# and As Sisters

**Feminism, the Labor Movement, and the
Women's Trade Union League of New York**

Nancy Schrom Dye

University of Missouri Press
Columbia & London, 1980

Library of Congress Cataloging in Publication Data
Dye, Nancy Schrom, 1947–
    As Equals and As Sisters.

    Bibliography: p. 185
    Includes index.
    1. Women's Trade Union League of New York—
History. 2. Women in trade unions—New York (City)—History. 3.
Feminism—New York (City)—History. I. Title.
HD6079.2.U52N483      331.88′3      80–16751
ISBN 0–8262–0318–3

Portions of Chapter 2 were originally published in *Feminist Studies* 2 (1975):
24–38, as "Creating a Feminist Alliance: Sisterhood and Class Conflict in
New York Women's Trade Union League." Portions of Chapter 3 were
originally published in *Feminist Studies* 3 (Fall 1975): 111–25, as
"Feminism or Unionism? The New York Women's Trade Union League and
the Labor Movement."

All quotations from the letters of Pauline Newman are reprinted by permission of Miss Newman.

To
Molly and Michael

# Acknowledgments

Many people were generous with their time, their knowledge, and their friendship while I was researching and writing this book. While the work was in its dissertation stage, Paul Glad provided much scholarly assistance and enthusiasm. Milton Cantor, David Thelen, Mari Jo Buhle, Maureen Greenwald, Jim O'Brien, and Daniel Rodgers read the manuscript and went far beyond the call of duty in offering useful criticism and suggestions and in lending encouragement and help. I am enormously grateful to them. Edward James provided me with much useful material and was always generous in sharing his knowledge of the Women's Trade Union League. Pauline Newman, former Educational Director of the International Ladies' Garment Workers' Union Health Center, took the time to read parts of the manuscript and gave permission to quote from her personal letters. Many librarians assisted me while I was researching this book. Special thanks go to Gloria Weinrich at the New York State Labor Department Library and Dorothy Swanson at the Tamiment Institute Library, New York University. I am also grateful to the directors of the University of Florida Library, which holds the Margaret Dreier Robins Papers, and the Schlesinger Library, Radcliffe College, which holds the Leonora O'Reilly Papers, for permitting me to make use of and quote from those collections. A Ford Foundation Women Studies Dissertation Fellowship helped support me for a year while I was working on this study. A faculty research grant from the University of Kentucky gave me a summer free to write. My family has been helpful from the beginning. My parents, Ned and Betts Schrom, have always been interested in my work. My children, Molly and Michael, have been sources of joy. My husband, Griff, has been an unflagging source of loving support and good humor. Without him, the book could not have been written.

N.S.D.
Lexington, Ky.
28 June 1980

# Contents

# No Place, No Power, No Voice

Late in 1903 a small group of social reformers and settlement house residents, working in the belief that "the non-industrial person could be of service to her industrial sister in helping her find her way through the chaos of industry"[1] founded the Women's Trade Union League of New York. From the first months of 1904, when the league began active work, through 1955, when it closed its doors, the organization's membership dedicated itself to improving the conditions of New York's women wage earners and elevating their status in the labor movement. Several hundred women joined the New York WTUL during the first two decades of the twentieth century—the period in which the league, like other progressive reform organizations, accomplished its best and most productive work. Together these women forged a unique coalition of women workers and wealthy women disenchanted with conventional philanthropic and reform activities. The women wage earners and reformers who made up the WTUL defined themselves as both feminists and trade unionists. As unionists, they worked to integrate women into the mainstream of the early twentieth-century labor movement. As feminists, they sought to create an egalitarian alliance of working-class and upper-class women and to make the early twentieth-century woman movement relevant to working women's concerns.

This book is the story of the New York Women's Trade Union League's efforts to reach New York City's working women and interest them in unionization, to create an alliance of upper-class and working-class women, and to synthesize unionism and feminism into a viable program for improving the lives of New York City's women wage earners. It is an attempt to delineate the cultural, ideological, and tactical difficulties the WTUL encountered in its efforts to organize the city's working women and its ultimate disillusionment with the strategy of integrating women into male-dominated unions. Finally, this work is concerned with the league's transformation from a self-defined labor organization that downplayed women's special concerns in the work force into a women's reform organization that emphasized specifically female demands, namely, woman suffrage and protective labor legislation.

When they began their work, New York WTUL members

1

believed that women of all classes, working together, could organize women into trade unions and persuade the labor movement to integrate women into its ranks. They devoted the better part of ten years—from early 1904 through 1913—to a grass-roots campaign among New York City's women workers. In this work, the New York league could point to substantial accomplishments. The league established several dozen unions of women garment workers, hat trimmers, milliners, buttonhole makers, overalls workers, textile operatives, paper-box makers, retail clerks, waitresses, and laundresses. The New York WTUL introduced thousands of such women to the labor movement, despite the fact that labor organizers often deemed such unskilled, poorly paid, and temporary workers incapable of unionization. The WTUL did particularly important work in the women's garment trades—the largest of New York City's industries. In late 1909, nearly 30,000 New York City shirtwaist makers, more than 85 percent of them women, launched the largest women's strike in the history of the American labor movement. In the following four years, tens of thousands of women in other branches of the city's women's clothing industry also struck for standardized contracts and better working conditions. The New York league played a central role in the 1909 shirtwaist strike and in organizing several International Ladies' Garment Workers' Union locals, as well as in helping to put the ILGWU itself on a stable footing. By 1913, thanks in good part to league efforts, the number of female unionists in New York City had increased almost ninefold since 1900. More than 71,000 women belonged to unions in 1913, as opposed to fewer than 8,000 at the turn of the century.[2] The league also served as an important training ground for working women. At a time when trade unions gave women virtually no opportunities for leadership, the WTUL enabled women to gain experience as organizers and business agents. A number of women prominent in the twentieth-century labor movement—Rose Schneiderman and Pauline Newman, for example—began their careers in the New York Women's Trade Union League. Dozens of other members went from the league to important positions in labor unions and public administration.

WTUL members, however, were disappointed in their organizing efforts. Although many more women belonged to New York City unions in 1913 than did when the league began organizing in 1904, union growth was confined to a few industries, most notably the women's garment trades. Furthermore, league members became increasingly critical of New York unionists' sexist attitudes and discriminatory practices. League efforts to persuade union men to regard women as "their equals and their sisters"[3] seemed doomed to failure. As one WTUL leader declared in 1912, women had "no place and no power and mostly no voice" in union affairs.[4]

The New York WTUL's difficulties in changing women's status as unionists and its disillusionment with organized labor are central themes in its history. Accordingly, much of this study examines the problems the league faced in unionizing New York City's working women.

The league began its work just as the American Federation of Labor was consolidating its control of the American labor movement. Understandably, the WTUL's founders decided to adhere to the policies and organizing methods of the AFL. Members worked hard to win the cooperation and support of both the national AFL leaders and local union officials. The organization's devotion to the federation, however, prevented its members from realizing how inappropriate craft unionism was for unskilled, poorly paid, and irregularly employed female industrial workers. Although the league gradually became aware of the limitations of AFL-style unionism, most members could envision no viable alternatives.

In addition, the New York league dealt primarily with young Jewish and Italian immigrants, and the problems involved in making contact with young immigrant women and interesting them in trade unionism often proved insurmountable. Inability to deal with the cultural, social, and language barriers between league members and the women they tried to organize helps explain these difficulties. Despite good intentions, upper-class members were often naive about class and ethnic differences. Finally, WTUL members were unable to formulate an analysis of working women's situation that took both their status as women and their status as workers into account. In keeping with the league's goal of integrating women into the labor movement, official policy throughout the early years was to consider women as workers, without regard to sex. This policy sometimes blinded league members to the ways women's experiences as workers were different from men's and weakened the organization's effectiveness.

By mid-1913, after the series of major strikes in New York's women's garment industry, members were disillusioned with the labor movement and frustrated with women workers. Although the New York league never abandoned organization, it increasingly put its faith in woman suffrage and in protective labor legislation as ways to ameliorate women's working conditions. From 1913 through the 1950s, WTUL members emphasized their role as feminist social reformers rather than their identity as trade unionists. This crucial shift from direct organization to an emphasis on political and legislative activity heralded a change in the way WTUL members regarded working women. Rather than continue to stress the commonality of male and female experience in New York City industry, they began to emphasize women's special needs and problems.[5]

League members were unable to resolve the question of how working women's oppression as unskilled immigrants related to their oppression as females in a male-dominated society. Their solutions were fragmentary and never embraced the totality of working women's situation. In short, the WTUL was never able to synthesize feminism with unionism, or its commitment to sorority with its commitment to class solidarity. Nor was the WTUL able to confront the labor movement on its own ground. The league's difficulties were not unique. Feminists have yet to formulate an analysis that comes to terms with working women's dual status, and feminism has yet to make a significant impact on the American labor movement. In the 1970s, only about 12 percent of the female work force was unionized and very few women played significant roles in union affairs.[6] Organized labor has rarely addressed itself to problems such as child care that confront female members. Women, then, are still largely without power, position, or voice.

The league also ran into difficulties in its attempt to form an egalitarian alliance of working women and upper-class women. Like other early twentieth-century feminists, the league's founders believed in the ability of women to relate to one another across class lines. More than any other women's organization, the WTUL tried to put the ideal of sisterhood into practice. Creating such an alliance, however, proved more difficult than anticipated. Despite careful provisions to guard against upper-class domination, the fact remained that in the years before World War I, wealthy, well-educated women determined the league's cultural atmosphere and often exerted a disproportionate influence in establishing the organization's policies. Then, too, social and cultural conflict between upper-class and working-class women was not uncommon. The two groups came to the league with different cultural backgrounds, different attitudes toward work, and different definitions of social class. Here, too, the league's difficulties were not unusual. Although American feminists in the 1970s continued to stress the importance of developing a movement that would reach women of every social class, American feminism has always had a clear middle-class orientation. The Women's Trade Union League went further than any women's organization in grappling with the problems a cross-class alliance posed.

The Women's Trade Union League of New York was one branch of a larger organization, the National Women's Trade Union League of America. Founded during the American Federation of Labor convention in 1903 and headquartered in Chicago, the national WTUL launched organizing campaigns among women throughout the country, attempted to persuade AFL officials to make unionizing women a federation priority, and worked to educate middle-class Americans to the necessity of trade unions for all American workers, male and female. The national league also played an important role in the suffrage movement by representing the needs of wage-earning women to middle-class suffragists, and it lobbied extensively for protective labor legislation.

Within a few months after the establishment of the national league in November 1903, social reformers and women workers formed local leagues in New York, Chicago, and Boston. In January 1904, Hull House residents Jane Addams, Mary McDowell, and Anna Nicholes and Ellen Henrotin, former president of the General Federation of Women's Clubs, founded the Chicago WTUL; in April 1904, Mary Kenney O'Sullivan, formerly an AFL organizer, Mary Morton Kehew, president of the Boston Women's Educational and Industrial Union, and Emily Balch, a Wellesley professor and settlement resident, established the Boston league. Over the following fifteen years, women started smaller leagues in at least a dozen cities. Hannah Hennessey, a garment worker, formed a vigorous WTUL branch in St. Louis late in 1907. Louisa Mittelstadt, a Kansas City brewery worker, established a small local in that city in 1910. Smaller, more ephemeral leagues were established in Baltimore; Philadelphia; Cleveland; Los Angeles; Denver; Milwaukee; Springfield, Illinois; and Madison, Wisconsin.

In many respects, the histories of the national WTUL and its other local branches run parallel to that of the New York league. Like the New York WTUL, the original goals of both the national and local leagues were to organize women wage earners into unions and to win acceptance of women from established male labor organizations. Under the leadership of Margaret Dreier Robins, the indominable individual who served as the national league's president from 1907 through 1922, the WTUL vigorously pursued these objectives. The national WTUL dispatched organizers and provided funds and favorable publicity to women on strike throughout the country. Shirtwaist makers in New York and Philadelphia; cloakmakers in Cleveland; men's clothing workers in Chicago; corsetmakers in Kalamazoo, Michigan, and Aurora, Illinois; textile operatives in Fall River, Massachusetts; collar starchers in Troy, New York; pearl-button makers in Muscatine, Iowa; and overalls workers in Sedalia, Missouri, were among the thousands of women workers who were aided by the national WTUL. In the 1920s, the national league ventured south, opening a regional office in Richmond, Virginia, to launch an organizing drive among southern textile operatives.[7]

The national organization also provided experience for a generation of women labor leaders. Mary Anderson, of the Boot and Shoe Workers' Union, Agnes Nestor and Elisabeth Christman of the International Glove Workers' Union, and Bessie Abramowitz of the Amalgamated Clothing Workers were among the women labor leaders who came of age in the WTUL. The national league fulfilled a more formal training function as well. In 1914, it established a training school for women organizers.

Local organizing efforts also flourished during the years before World War I. Chicago WTUL members conducted organizing drives among the city's women garment workers, stockyard workers, and waitresses and played a leading role both in conducting the massive Hart, Schaffner, and Marx strike in 1910 and in negotiating the settlement. In St. Louis, the league initiated organizing campaigns among women brewery, shoe, and garment workers. Boston league members, unable to raise funds or attract working-class members, were less successful than the other major local leagues in their early organizing efforts, but they did assist striking textile operatives, garment workers, and telephone operators.[8]

Like the New York league, however, other leagues ran into difficulties with the male-dominated labor movement. As one Boston WTUL leader stated, "In years past, prejudice against the League has been so strong and so bitter as to seriously handicap our work."[9] The national WTUL worked hard to win the support of American Federation of Labor officials and to convince them that women were a permanent factor in the labor force who needed to be unionized. Despite the wholehearted support the league gave the federation, however, the

national league's relations with the AFL were always conflic-
tual, and efforts to make the federation leaders responsive to
the needs of women workers never succeeded. Samuel Gompers, the hardheaded and practical president of the AFL in the
early twentieth century, never committed himself to unionizing women despite his protestations to the contrary. Gompers
was also perpetually suspicious of the WTUL, in part because of
the upper-class backgrounds of many league leaders, in part
because of the organization's association with the feminist
movement. Thus, despite league efforts, the AFL remained a
conservative bastion of male craftsmen, unwilling to respond
to the needs of women workers.

The national WTUL, like its New York branch, eventually
became disillusioned with the labor movement and turned to
protective legislation as a way to improve working women's
conditions. Together with the Consumers' League and the
American Association for Labor Legislation, the WTUL played
a central role in the passage of state ten-hour- and eight-hour-
day bills for women and of women's minimum wage legislation. The national league began to emphasize legislation as
early as 1909, when it presented its first legislative program
calling for an eight-hour day and the elimination of night work
for all working women, a legal minimum wage in "sweated
trades," seats for women in factories and stores, and the appointment of women factory inspectors. Finally, the national
league's legislative platform called for the prohibition of preg-
nant women's employment for two months before and after
childbirth and a system of maternity pensions.[10] In later years,
the national WTUL expanded its demand for a minimum wage,
calling for a state-regulated "living wage" for all women wage
earners. In addition to drafting a legislative program, the
WTUL also formulated a rationale for applying such laws to
only one sex, arguing that women needed the protection of the
state because they suffered both social and biological handicaps in the labor force.

This book concentrates only upon the New York Women's
Trade Union League rather than on the national organization
or other local branches. There are a number of reasons for this
local emphasis. The most significant and interesting work the
WTUL undertook was trade union organizing. The New York
league was considerably more active in this work than any
other local or the national. In the years before World War I, the
New York WTUL was the only league to maintain a continual
organizing drive. With the exception of the Chicago league,

which also launched vigorous organizing campaigns during these years, other local leagues' accomplishments in this area were more limited. The Boston league, for instance, was unable to attract a sizable contingent of working-class members, and its upper-class allies could not make much headway in their organizing efforts. Although the national league encouraged women's unionism by spearheading organizing drives and by providing organizers and funds to help women on strike, it did not maintain the same continual involvement with union organizing that the New York league did. Then, too, the New York WTUL was the only local league whose records have survived. It is only with the New York league, then, that one can follow the day-to-day process of organization—the recruiting efforts, the slow process of building unions, and the organizing tactics. Reconstructing the history of the New York league provides a case study of the experiences and difficulties involved in unionizing women early in the twentieth century.

My second reason for concentrating upon the New York WTUL is the fact that over the years its membership was more evenly balanced between upper-class and working-class members than were the memberships of other league branches or of the national. The New York league worked harder and had considerably more success than any other league save perhaps Chicago in establishing an alliance across class lines. The Boston league was heavily dominated by allies. The St. Louis league's membership was predominantly working class. Very little can be learned about the composition of the other small leagues or the relationships their members established. By looking at the relationships New York league women formed with one another and at their efforts to reach women workers, it is possible to gain some insight into both the possibilities and difficulties involved in women's relationships across class lines and the process by which female support networks are formed.

To understand this unique feminist labor organization, we must know something of the social context in which it originated. By the turn of the twentieth century, the United States was in the midst of its massive transformation from a rural, agrarian society to an urban, industrial nation. The industrial revolution dramatically altered the status and roles of American women. As a direct result of industrialization, more than 5 million women became wage earners. By 1900, women made up nearly one-fifth of the labor force. What was more, a fifth of the adult female population was gainfully employed.[11] One visible symbol of the dramatic changes in American society was the sight of factory girls trudging to work early each morning and swarming out of factories and shops at closing time. For millions of American women, the industrial revolution meant arduous toil for long hours and little pay.

For the wives and daughters of manufacturers, businessmen, and the new middle class of salaried professionals, however, industrialization had very different effects. The industrial revolution spawned a value system that fostered female idleness and delicacy. Women, as Thorstein Veblen concluded in his economic analysis of American society, were important primarily as consumers. Their clothes, their furnishings, their households, and their leisure itself were tangible evidence of their husbands' ability to make money. Women, in short, were ornamental anomalies in a society that glorified productive work.[12]

Trapped by a social definition of femininity that defined them by their leisure, many middle- and upper-class women felt frustrated in the safe but stifling world of the household. They complained of feeling childish, parasitical, restless. As journalist and WTUL member Rheta Childe Dorr described her life as an idle upper-class matron, "I made something like fifty calls a month on women who differed from one another no more than peas in a pod. . . . The men who came to our house . . . treated me like a nice child. They themselves and their womenkind were children. . . . We all lived in dolls' houses and I for one wanted to get out into the world of real things."[13]

The woman movement arose in good part out of this restlessness and desire to feel socially useful. The most publicized demand of the movement was, of course, the vote. But political equality was only one issue that concerned women. What women demanded above all was the right to meaningful work. Sentenced to what they viewed as a life of parasitical and oppressive leisure, affluent women often looked with fascination, even envy, at women who worked for a living. As radical feminist and WTUL member Henrietta Rodman declared, "Our sisters of the poorer class have the most fundamental right for which we are struggling—the right for economic independence, the right to continue their chosen work after marriage."[14] However much Rodman distorted the nature of working women's situation, the fact remains that many women viewed work, in and of itself, as liberating.

Significantly, when upper-class women began to leave their homes to find meaningful work in their communities, many turned their attention to working women. Women who joined the women's clubs in the 1880s and 1890s made investigations of social and economic conditions. Club women inspected local factories. Were there seats provided? Was there clean air? Clean water? How many hours a day did women labor? How much money could they earn? Popular magazines such as *McClure's*, *Everybody's*, and *Cosmopolitan* frequently carried narratives of factory life. Some affluent women assumed working women's identities and investigated their lives firsthand. Marie and Bessie Van Vorst, for instance, took positions as factory girls in canneries, shoe factories, garment shops, and southern textile mills.[15] Fascination with working women's lives permeated such endeavors. How did working women live? What were their aspirations? Then, too, such work was prompted by middle-class reformers' realization that for millions of women work had become a permanent and necessary part of life, despite the popular ideology that defined the ideal woman as leisured and secluded within the private world of the household.

By the mid-1880s, a definite movement to ameliorate working women's conditions was underway. In New York City, three organizations, the Working Girls' Clubs, the Working Women's Society, and the New York City Consumers' League, dedicated themselves to improving women's situation.

The Working Girls' Clubs were part of a movement that developed from a small group for "study and socializing" that philanthropist Grace Dodge established for New York City silk mill operatives in 1884. By the early 1890s, the clubs constituted a national network. Working Girls' Clubs did not encourage their members to unionize. Instead, the wealthy women who led discussion groups and financed the club boardinghouses were concerned primarily with imbuing young working women with good work habits and genteel notions of femininity. The clubs' names—"Endeavor," "Enterprise," "Steadfast"—offer a clue to their orientation, as does a collection of essays entitled *Thoughts of Busy Girls, Who Have Little Time for Study Yet Find Much Time for Thinking*. Young essayists discoursed on such topics as"What Constitutes an Ideal Womanhood and How to Attain It" and "Purity and Modesty: Two Words of Value." The essays emphasized self-sacrifice and gentleness. Very few essays dealt with work, though their authors spent the better part of their waking hours in factories and department stores. Wealthy club leaders saw themselves as bearers of culture, bringing some beauty into the drab lives of their charges.[16]

The Working Women's Society was formed in 1886 by a retail clerk, Alice Woodbridge. Unlike the Working Girls' Clubs, its specific purpose was to improve working conditions, particularly in department stores. Convinced that retail clerks could not better their conditions alone, Woodbridge appealed to Josephine Shaw Lowell, a reformer well known for her sympathy to labor causes, for help. Together, they appealed to women consumers to refuse to patronize stores that treated their employees unfairly. The society also convinced the New York State legislature to make the first systematic investigation of working women's conditions and lobbied successfully for legislation providing for female factory inspectors.[17]

The New York City Consumers' League grew directly out of the Working Women's Society. Consumers' League members stressed that women would naturally sympathize with their sisters in factories and stores once they knew about the deplorable conditions under which goods were manufactured and sold. The Consumers' League White List was an effort to inform women about the industrial world around them. Consumers' League leaders believed that once women were informed, their natural altruism would lead them to insist upon better working conditions.[18]

The women who joined these organizations, like the women reformers who later joined the WTUL, grew up in a culture that put great stress on the emotional differences between men and women. Men, according to nineteenth-century popular ideology, were naturally aggressive, businesslike, strong. Women were naturally sensitive, altruistic, maternal. For the most part, the woman movement did not challenge these stereotypes. Turn-of-the-century feminists believed that women possessed specifically feminine sensibilities. "Men are such strange creatures," a leading WTUL member reflected, "they seem to enjoy such questionable things—it seems so queer to me and one more convincing argument that women must enter public life."[19] Many women reformers believed that because women were instinctively nurturant, they had special responsibility for social welfare. As the president of the National Women's Trade Union League, Margaret Dreier Robins, expressed this sentiment,

> The nature of the attack of modern industrial despotism upon the integrity and promise of our individual and national life is such as makes a special call upon the women of our country, and it seems to have been reserved for this generation to work out a new basis for our industrial civilization. Free-

dom, maternity, education, and morality—all the blessed and abiding interests of childhood and the home—are at issue in this supreme struggle. All women who honor their sex and love their country should unite with us and our working sisters in the struggle for industrial freedom.[20]

Because women were brought up to believe that they were naturally more sensitive than men, they could often relate most comfortably to other women. Throughout the nineteenth century, women were socialized to form many of their most significant personal relationships with other women. They bonded together in female networks that provided mutual support, advice, assistance, and companionship. Women's reform organizations such as the Consumers' League and the Women's Trade Union League were in good part outgrowths of these female networks.[21] These support networks, the belief that women shared distinct feminine qualities, the conviction that the feminine values embodied in the home clashed with the values of emerging industrial capitalism, and fascination with their working-class sisters provided much of the impetus behind women's social reform activity at the turn of the century.

The Women's Trade Union League differed significantly from its predecessors. Its commitment to trade unionism was unique among both feminist and progressive social reform organizations. What was more, the WTUL was unique in its insistence on an egalitarian cross-class alliance in which working women rather than affluent philanthropists were to play leading roles. Nevertheless, in its concern for working women's situation and in its belief in women's ability to transcend class lines and understand one another on the basis of their common femininity, the WTUL was very much a part of the turn-of-the-century woman movement.

## CHAPTER 1

# Working Women's Situation

Every year the American Federation of Labor passed resolutions at its convention expressing solidarity with women workers. Since 1892, the AFL had called for women organizers, for women's participation in the labor movement, and for woman suffrage. The November 1903 convention was no exception: the delegates passed the customary four or five resolutions urging the executive council to appoint women organizers and to make unionization of the ever-increasing numbers of working women a federation priority. And, as usual, the convention endorsed woman suffrage.[1]

The resolutions were meaningless. The AFL had not hired a woman organizer since the early 1890s; its executive council was not to hire another until 1908. And woman suffrage was a simple matter to endorse, for it required neither effort nor money on the federation's part. The small number of women at the convention provided additional evidence of the resolutions' emptiness. Only 5 women mingled among the 496 AFL delegates, and one of these, a fraternal delegate from the Church Association for the Advancement of the Interests of Labor, could not vote. The 4 women unionists were all but invisible in the assembly.

That the American Federation of Labor would pay scant attention to the nation's 5 million working women was not surprising, given the organization's philosophy and tactics. By the turn of the century, AFL leaders had painstakingly forged a labor movement that could demand and defend good working conditions, decent wages, and job security for a small fraction of the country's working population—6.8 percent of the men and less than 1 percent of the women.[2] Members of AFL unions were the elite of the American working class: native-born craftsmen with a vested interest in protecting their skills and their status in an economy increasingly characterized by mass production and an unskilled immigrant work force. The AFL rejected women on three counts: they were unskilled, they were immigrants, and they were female. As unskilled workers, according to AFL reasoning, women threatened the job security and wage standards of traditional craftsmen. As immigrants, they disrupted the essential homogeneity of the skilled work force in which laborers had developed common values and

production standards. And as females, according to craftsmen's values, they belonged at home, not in factories or union
halls. "Do not they [unions] tend to defeminize and unsex
them?" a leading AFL official wrote Agnes Nestor, president of
the International Glove Workers' Union.[3]

Nevertheless, the small number of women at a convention
purporting to represent the entire American labor force, in
which one out of every five workers was female, did not fail to
impress a wealthy young social reformer, William English
Walling. Barely twenty-six, Walling was a resident at University
Settlement on New York's lower East Side. He had come to New
York from the Midwest where, after graduating from the University of Chicago, he had worked for a year as an Illinois state
factory inspector.[4] Through his experiences as an inspector and
his association with Hull House residents and the unionists who
held their meetings at the settlement, Walling became committed to the labor movement and aware of the special problems of
working women. In 1902, Walling moved to New York's University Settlement, where he quickly established ties with the local
labor movement. The city's Central Federated Union and many
small Jewish labor organizations held their meetings at University Settlement, and Walling was soon well-acquainted with
East Side trade union officials. Before his trip to Boston, Walling
had been trying to formulate some way to improve women's
situation in the work force. In 1903 he traveled to England to
observe the work of the Women's Trade Union League of Great
Britain, established in 1874. One characteristic of that organization that he found particularly impressive was the cross-class
nature of its membership: both upper-class and working-class
women strove to organize women and to integrate them into
established male unions. Late in 1903, Walling decided to
attend the AFL convention to determine whether a similar
organization could be formed in the United States.

Mary Kenney O'Sullivan was the first person Walling contacted in Boston. Ten years earlier, O'Sullivan had worked as an
AFL organizer. A bookbinder, she began her labor career as a
teenager by organizing the women in the Chicago bindery
where she worked. Her local became part of the Chicago
Ladies' Federal Union, an organization of women bookbinders,
seamstresses, candy workers, and laundresses that met regularly at Hull House. There, Kenney became friends with Jane
Addams and Mary McDowell. Her work with the federal union
brought Kenney to the attention of AFL leaders, and, in 1892,
the AFL executive council appointed her as part-time orga-

nizer. In her brief tenure as the federation's women's organizer, Kenney traveled up and down the East coast, working with New England textile operatives, Troy, New York, laundry workers, and New York City garment workers. She had little time to prove her worth, however. Barely five months after they hired her, federation officials decided that there was no need for a woman organizer and terminated her appointment. Shortly thereafter, in 1894, Mary Kenney married John O'Sullivan, a Boston streetcar workers' organizer. Marriage ended her active work in the union movement, but she maintained contacts with Boston labor organizations and settlement houses.[5]

Greeting Walling's proposal enthusiastically, O'Sullivan suggested an open meeting to discuss plans while the AFL was in session. The two arranged for a meeting room in Fanueil Hall and invited AFL executive council members and convention delegates whose trades included women to attend. Both O'Sullivan and Walling knew that male trade unionists would not be interested in creating and maintaining such an organization by themselves, so they also invited women settlement residents and reformers. They envisioned an organization in which "women of social influence who were interested in economics join hands with the progressive women in the trades and work to organize various branches of industry."[6] In short, they proposed a fusion of the labor movement and the woman movement.

The idea that women of all classes could cooperate to ameliorate women's working conditions was not without precedent. Mary Kenney O'Sullivan had had the help of Jane Addams, Mary McDowell, and other Hull House residents in her work with the Chicago Ladies' Federal Union. In Boston, O'Sullivan was active in the Women's Educational and Industrial Union, a cross-class organization similar to New York's Working Women's Society that was devoted to investigating and publicizing the conditions under which women worked. She and her husband lived at Dennison House, a settlement known for its sympathy to organized labor and its residents' concern for working women. Walling knew that in New York residents of University Settlement and the Henry Street Nurses' Settlement had assisted women workers occasionally in forming small unions. They were also familiar with the working girls' club movement, the consumers' leagues, and the New York Working Women's Society, all organizations that based their work on a sense of sisterhood, on the conviction that women could relate to one another across class lines.

A few AFL delegates, most from the Retail Clerks' Protective Association and the United Garment Workers, attended the three meetings on 14, 17, and 19 November 1903 that launched the Women's Trade Union League of America. With the exception of a delegate from a Boston federated women's union, the labor delegates were men. By contrast, nearly all the participants from Boston settlements and reform societies were women. After three afternoons of discussion, the organization that had existed only in the minds of Walling and O'Sullivan had a name, the Women's Trade Union League of America; a clear purpose, "to assist in the organization of women wage earners into Trade Unions"; and a constitution that embodied the ideas of the labor representatives, social reformers, and settlement residents who had attended the first meetings. The league's charter members established the WTUL's two basic principles: commitment to an egalitarian, cross-class alliance and allegiance to the American Federation of Labor.

The league's constitution stipulated that the organization's membership should include both women workers and *allies* — individuals outside the working class interested in unionizing women. To ensure the participation of working women and to prevent upper-class domination, the constitution specified that the majority of executive board members were to be female trade unionists. The others were to be "earnest sympathizers and workers for the cause of Trade Unionism."[7] From the beginning, then, WTUL members explicitly tried to avoid patronizing women workers. Ideally, theirs was to be an organization in which policymaking was largely in the hands of working women.

Participants in the Boston meetings were also unanimous that the WTUL should cooperate fully with the American Federation of Labor and adopt the philosophy and organizing tactics of AFL leaders. In an effort to avoid animosity between unions and a group that had no official connection with the labor movement, the first members insisted that the league always gain permission from the appropriate union before organizing women in a trade. Highly self-conscious about their status as "outsiders," they shied away from asking for the convention's endorsement, despite the fact that the federation annually endorsed the work of the Church Association for the Advancement of the Interests of Labor and the Women's Label League. As one reformer expressed WTUL members' sentiments, it was best to wait until they had "accomplished something" before asking for the federation's recognition and approval. For its part, the American Federation of Labor paid little attention to the new organization. An AFL executive council member proferred a few polite words of welcome, emphasizing that the federation stood firmly for the solidarity of all workers regardless of sex, but refrained from committing the AFL to any involvement.

Before the Boston meetings adjourned, the league elected officers. To lend prestige to the organization, Walling suggested that nationally known reformers serve as leaders. Members agreed that Mary Morton Kehew, a wealthy Bostonian long known in social reform circles and the president of the Boston Educational and Industrial Union, should serve as president and that Mary Kenney O'Sullivan should serve as secretary. Walling recommended Jane Addams for the vice-presidency, a post she immediately accepted. An AFL delegate from the Amalgamated Cutters and Butcher Workmen nominated Mary McDowell for the executive board in recognition of her organizing efforts among women in the Chicago packinghouses. The United Garment Workers' president recommended Lillian Wald in appreciation of her work with New York City's garment finishers and buttonhole makers. After the Boston meetings, the WTUL's charter members returned home to organize local branches: Mary Morton Kehew and Mary Kenney O'Sullivan in Boston, Jane Addams and Mary McDowell in Chicago, and William English Walling in New York.

Walling returned to New York late in 1903 to begin the work of organizing that city's Women's Trade Union League. He and the "small band of enthusiasts" who joined the new organization over the following months faced a formidable task. When the New York league began its work, more than 350,000 women were employed in the city. The majority of these women, like the majority of the nation's female wage earners, worked in service occupations. Nearly 150,000 were personal servants and domestic workers. More than 56,000 labored as retail clerks, waitresses, and laundresses. Increasing numbers of women were entering New York's industrial work force. In 1900, 132,535 women worked in the city's manufacturing establishments.[8] As a center for the manufacture of nondurable goods and as the capital of the men's and women's clothing trades, New York employed more women industrial workers at the turn of the century than any other American city.[9] It was to these semiskilled and unskilled female industrial laborers that the New York Women's Trade Union League devoted most of its organizing efforts.

The typical female industrial worker in early twentieth-century New York City was a young, single, Jewish or Italian woman who lived with her family. Women usually began work in their midteens and remained in the labor force until they married in their early twenties.[10] According to a federal investigation of woman and child wage earners, 87 percent of New York City's female industrial workers lived with their parents. Of these, 88.1 percent gave their unopened pay envelopes to the head of their household.[11]

Women factory workers in New York City labored in a large number of industries and performed a wide variety of work processes. They stripped, rolled, and packed cigars, assembled paper boxes, dipped and wrapped candies, trimmed hats, bound books, and made artificial flowers and feathers. The heaviest concentration—about 40 percent of women industrial workers—was in the needle trades. In 1905, approximately fifty thousand women were engaged in the manufacture of clothing; more than twelve thousand were employed in the men's garment industry, and over thirty-six thousand in the women's ready-made clothing trades.[12]

Because the majority of the women the league organized in the first years of its history were garment workers and because the needle trades dominated the city's economy, it is necessary to look at the industry in some detail. By the turn of the twentieth century, the term *garment industry* and the title *garment worker* covered a complicated variety of work places and work processes. The industry itself was a heterogeneous combination of several dozen trades, including not only the men's and women's ready-made clothing industries but also the millinery, men's hat and cap, neckwear, children's garments, and corset industries. The appellation *garment worker* described highly skilled craftsmen such as cutters, semiskilled sewing machine operators, and unskilled manual workers such as button seamstresses.

The industry's complexity resulted not only from rapid expansion as the nation's demand for ready-made clothing increased, but also from its decentralized system of manufacture. Few items of ready-to-wear clothing were made under one roof. Rather, three types of workplaces were found: the inside shop, or factory, the contracting shop, and the home. A manufacturer owned the inside shop; the making of a garment began and ended there. The manufacturer bought cloth and hired skilled cutters to cut it into patterns. Cutting was the inside shop's primary operation, although by the early twentieth century an increasing number employed sewing machine operators as well. The manufacturer sent bundles of cut cloth to contractors who agreed to perform additional operations on the garments to complete them. The contractor then hired his own workers to perform these tasks.

The contracting business was easy to enter: all a man needed was a workplace and a labor supply. In the years around the turn of the century, particularly before the passage of effective tenement-house legislation, both were easily attainable. The contractor's tenement flat could be converted readily into a sweatshop, and workers were recruited easily from the throngs of recent immigrants who crowded into the *Khazar Mark*[13] each day. Capital requirements were minimal: workers had to pay for their electricity and supplies and sometimes had to provide their own sewing machines as well. Rose Schneiderman, later a leading New York WTUL member, recalled that as a cap seamstress, "I had to furnish my own sewing machine. . . . I also had to furnish the thread I used. And not just one color either. You had to have several colors handy to match the colors of the lining. The cost ran up to at least fifty cents a month."[14] For workers, the contracting system was invidious. Because entry was easy, the business was highly competitive. Manufacturers awarded their business to the contractors who agreed to the lowest prices. As a result of competitive underbidding, contractors hired as few workers as possible, required them to labor unlimited hours, and set miserably low piece rates.

Other work processes involved in making clothing, particularly unskilled, unmechanized operations, were performed by women at home. No one in the early twentieth century knew exactly how widespread the homework system was. Although dwellings in which homework was performed were required to be licensed by the state factory inspector, there was no reliable way of estimating the number of men, women, and children who toiled in them. In 1901, the New York State Department of Labor put the number of homeworkers at thirty thousand, of whom the great majority were Italian women.[15]

Within the industry, there was a clear pattern of occupational segregation by sex. Men were the skilled workers, women the semiskilled and unskilled. Tailoring was a male occupation. Jewish tailors brought their skills with them from eastern European cities and, in turn, trained other men in New York.[16] Since women had few opportunities to learn tailoring skills, men dominated the men's clothing industry, which manufactured suits, jackets, trousers, and coats, and also held the skilled tailoring positions in the women's trades that manufactured cloaks, suits, and skirts. In addition to tailoring, men monopolized cutting, the industry's central craft. Cutting cloth into patterns was not only a skilled occupation that required a lengthy apprenticeship; it also constituted a bottleneck in the industry: without cutters' labor in the inside shops, manufacturing came to a halt.

Excluded from the skilled and relatively stable occupations of tailoring and cutting, women filled ancillary positions, performing unskilled tasks such as finishing, tucking, felling, basting, and turning. Such work was simple and took only a few hours to learn. Also, the majority of the semiskilled sewing machine operators in the women's garment industry were women. The waist, children's dress, wrapper and kimono, and white goods industries were known as the "women's trades." From 85 to 95 percent of the work force in these branches was female.[17] Several weeks were needed to learn to operate a sewing machine and to pick up speed, but operators usually learned to make only one part of a garment or to perform only one work process. While a skilled male cloakmaker or cutter could exercise a certain amount of control over the conditions of his work, manufacturers and contractors could easily replace Jewish and Italian unskilled and semiskilled women during a strike.

The garment trades provided seasonal employment. Because demand for ready-made clothing fluctuated throughout the year, most workers suffered periods of forced idleness that often lasted several months. The seasonal character of the industry created a mobile labor force particularly among women. A manufacturer would often keep a good cutter or tailor but lay off his female operatives, knowing that they could be easily replaced. A woman who worked on waists in the fall and early winter, for example, might turn to white goods or dresses when the waist season ended. Or she might leave the industry for another trade or to marry. The work force in individual shops often turned over completely from one season to the next.[18]

Wage rates, shop conditions, and work processes varied from shop to shop. In an industry as complex and fragmented as the garment trades, contractors' sweatshops that employed five or six workers and factories that employed several hundred existed side by side on lower Broadway, the lower East Side, and the Brownsville section of Brooklyn. A woman who worked at home making buttonholes or embroidering cuffs had little in common with one who toiled for a weekly wage as a factory sewing machine operator. In turn, the inside shop worker perceived few similarities between herself and a worker in a contractor's shop. A woman neckwear worker explained that it was "impossible for the workers of the warehouses [inside shops] and the workers of the contractors to belong to the same local, the prices, conditions, and hours are absolutely different as if they were entirely different trades."[19]

On the average, a woman sewing machine operator could expect to make about $6.00 for a sixty-hour week, working by the piece.[20] This figure, however, tells us little about the wages most women actually earned. A homeworker probably worked longer than sixty hours and received considerably less than $6.00 for her efforts. According to a state investigation early in the century, women home finishers earned approximately $175.00 a year—little more than $3.00 a week.[21] A learner apprenticed to an experienced operator usually earned nothing during the weeks or months of "learning." Unskilled trimmers and finishers in the women's trades could be found earning as little as $2.00 and $3.00 a week.[22] Nor does the $6.00 a week average figure reflect the fact that often a woman was unemployed or earned substantially less than this amount for several months of the year. The New York Women's Trade Union League discovered that 50 percent of New York City's working women lost from one to three months of employment during slack seasons and 12 percent lost as much as four to six months.[23] If a young woman earning $6.00 a week maintained year-round employment, her annual earnings would have been $312.00. A woman's real earnings were approximately 20 percent less than the full employment figure, however.[24] Thus, a woman's annual earnings were probably about $250.00.

The great majority of New York City's women wage earners used this income to help support their families. Working-class families required from $650 to $800 a year as a minimum income. Contemporary studies of the incomes of New York City working-class families concluded that their average income was in that range.[25] Thus, a young woman's contribution to her family's support was substantial.

A minority of New York City female laborers were self-supporting, or, as early twentieth-century social investigators called them, "adrift." By careful scrimping, a woman could subsist on $5.00 or $6.00 a week. On the average, she spent $3.30 a week on food, shelter, heat, light, and laundry. Clothes, transportation, medical expenses, emergency expenditures,

and amusements had to come out of the balance.[26] "What is so
discouraging," one self-supporting woman told a state investigator, "is . . . to know no matter how long or how hard I
work, at no time do I make enough to wholly support myself or
tide me over for a rainy day."[27]

Just as the average $6.00 a week figure tells us little about
women's wages, the average sixty-hour workweek tells us little
about working conditions. In contractors' sweatshops, a worker's hours during the "rush season" often stretched to eighty a
week. In the inside shops, where foremen could regulate hours
by turning the machinery on and off, working longer than sixty
hours a week during the busy season was common. By contrast,
the slack season brought little or no work.

Psychological pressure also varied from shop to shop. Oppressive as the contractors' sweatshops were, workers sometimes had a personal relationship with the "boss" based on
family, geographical, and cultural ties. Customs such as the
observance of the Sabbath and holy days were sometimes continued. Wages, hours, and conditions in the contractors' shops,
however, were totally unstandardized, while factories were
characterized by impersonality, ethnic discord, and strict work
discipline. "In the shops we don't have names, we have numbers," one young woman told the league. "We work so steadily
that in most cases we do not know the girl who works next to
us."[28]

Harassment—fines for lateness, for talking, for singing, and
verbal abuse for mistakes—was also a common experience in
the shops. After a few years of work, the New York Women's
Trade Union League cited the "tyranny of the foreman" as an
omnipresent reality in working women's lives.[29] Harassment
was a common experience for both men and women, but
sexual exploitation was a factor that distinguished women's
experience in the workplace from that of men. Pauline Newman, an International Ladies' Garment Workers organizer and
a WTUL leader for many years, described the situation in a
letter to Rose Schneiderman:

> You know as well as I that there is not a factory today where the
> same immoral conditions does [sic] not exist! You remember
> your factories where you have worked and so do I, and both of
> us know that the cloak factories and all other shops in the city
> of New York or Chicago, every one of the men will talk to the
> girls, take advantage of them if the girls will let them, the
> forman [sic] and superintendents will flirt with the girls, and it
> is nothing new for those who know that this exists today

everywhere. . . . You find the same old story, that the forman [*sic*] asked a girl to come into his office and hold hands, etc.[30]

Speed was also an omnipresent and harsh reality. In the early twentieth century tasks that had once been performed by hand, such as buttonhole making, were being mechanized. As more tasks were mechanized, work processes became subdivided and the manufacturing process was sped up enormously. From 1900 to 1905, for instance, the speed of sewing machines required for simple seam stitching doubled. Machines carried as many as ten needles and turned out several thousand stitches a minute. Physical fatigue and nervous strain were common complaints of women operators.

Working conditions were much the same for women in industries outside the garment trades. They could rarely earn more than five or six dollars a week or advance beyond repetitive, unskilled and mechanized work processes. Most important, every industry in New York City was characterized by clear occupational segregation patterns in which men held the central, skilled positions and women the poorly paid unskilled jobs. Even in the traditional crafts such as printing and bookbinding, which employed considerable numbers of women, the same situation prevailed. In the printing trades, a small number of women worked as typesetters and compositors. Unlike male printers, however, who underwent a four-year apprenticeship, women acquired their training on the job or in a few weeks' course on typesetting. The same situation held in the binding trades. Skilled bookbinders were highly trained males. Although women made up nearly half of the trade's work force, they received, at most, a few weeks' instruction in one or two simple processes such as sewing or folding. Thus, although both men and women were listed as bookbinders by occupation, in reality their work was very different.[31]

As a group, then, New York City's women industrial workers shared several characteristics. They were young, unmarried, usually lived with their families, and were temporary workers. Their wages were low and their chances for economic mobility through their own efforts severely restricted. The great majority of the city's female industrial work force were immigrants or daughters of immigrants, primarily from south Italy and eastern Europe. Finally, nearly all of the city's female workers were unorganized.

In 1904, the Women's Trade Union League estimated that with the exception of domestic servants, whom members considered unorganizable, the great majority of the city's female workers came under the jurisdiction of AFL unions. Of garment workers, almost 27,000 came under the jurisdiction of the International Ladies' Garment Workers' Union and 10,000 under that of the United Garment Workers. Of other industrial workers, nearly 9,000 women came under the jurisdiction of either the International Cigar Makers' Union or the International Tobacco Workers; some 6,400 came under the jurisdiction of the Neckwear Makers, and almost 5,400 under the jurisdiction of the United Textile Workers. The Boot and Shoe Makers could claim some 1,600; the United Cloth Hat and Cap Makers' Union, 1,400; the International Brotherhood of Bookbinders, over 3,000; and the International Typographical Union, almost 4,000.[32] In addition, women in the marginal trades of confectionary and paper-box manufacture had unions to which they could turn. According to the league's sanguine initial estimates, large numbers of nonindustrial women workers also came under the jurisdictions of AFL unions. The WTUL estimated that 27,500 women could be organized by the Retail Clerks' Protective Association and more than 18,000 by the Shirt, Waist and Laundry Workers' International Union. Only a minority of the city's "organizable" work force, according to the league, worked in trades without unions. These included hand garment workers, artificial-flower and feather makers, and fur and leather workers.

In reality, the situation was quite different. Trade union membership figures paint a dismal picture of women's participation in the New York City labor movement in the first years of the century. Industrial prosperity during the years 1900 through 1903 spurred dramatic union growth in the city, but women did not take part in this general increase. As the number of women workers increased steadily and as the number of male unionists increased, the percentage of women unionists fell each year from 1900 through 1908. In late 1903, right before the New York Women's Trade Union League was founded, women made up only 3.7 percent of New York's unionists.[33]

When the league began its work, fewer than 10,000 of the city's 350,000 female workers were organized. The WTUL found significant numbers of women in the garment, cigar, bookbinding, and printing unions. Several thousand women in the tobacco industry belonged to Cigar Makers' locals. About 600 women printers belonged to the International Typographical Union. About 3,000 women bookbinders were organized.

Approximately 1,000 women belonged to small, unstable organizations in the women's garment trades. Of these organizations, only one, Bookbinders' Local No. 43, a female local of the International Brotherhood of Bookbinders, was a stable and powerful organization. Early in the century, it organized the principal New York binderies, restricted entry into the trade, raised weekly wages, and managed to enforce an eight-hour day.[34]

Outside these industries, however, only a handful of women was organized. A few factory laundresses, electrical workers, and paper-box makers belonged to small unions. The situation among paper-box makers was typical. In 1904, the Paper Box Makers' Union president reported to the New York league that the women in the trade were poorly organized and that any efforts to organize them usually had disastrous results. During a recent strike, for example, 800 of the 3,000 women in the trade briefly joined the union. But the strike failed and the employers compelled the women to sign "iron-clad oaths." As a result, only 80 women members remained. "The bosses forced them to resign from the union," the president stated, "with the instruction never to set their foot up there if they wanted to continue to work in the shops."[35]

New York City's hotel and restaurant workers, retail clerks, and candy and confectionary workers were totally unorganized. International unions existed in these trades and organized women successfully in upstate towns, but they did not organize in New York City.[36] Unions seemed to be "an entirely new thing" to retail clerks, a University Settlement worker reported to an investigating commission from the state assembly. "You ask them if they belong to any kind of a girls' club and they seem very much surprised if you mention any trade union or club for the raising of wages." Working women's organizations, she went on, "seem to be largely social; they belong to little societies; they tell me they belong to a 'Heart and Hand Club,' a social club; nothing for the study of their own wage conditions at all."[37]

No single factor explains why so few women were unionized in early twentieth-century New York City. Instead, the difficulties involved in integrating women into the city's labor movement resulted from several interrelated factors involving ethnicity, skill levels, and sex roles.

In part, women's poor showing in the city unions' membership rolls reflected their immigrant status. Immigrant men also experienced great difficulty entering the city's labor movement.

The strong unions in New York City, as elsewhere, were those of highly skilled craftsmen in the building, printing, cigar, brewery, and machine trades. These crafts were not only exclusively male or nearly so; they were also made up almost entirely of native-born workers of Irish or German descent. These stable, affluent AFL craft unions commanded considerable bargaining power and were strong enough to win closed shop contracts. Jewish and Italian men, however, were excluded from the elite trades and their unions and worked in immigrant industries and occupations. When they organized, as Jews did in the garment industry, they did so without the AFL craft unions' interest or help.[38] In the first decade of the century Jewish unions were generally weak and unstable.

Trade union membership figures also reflect the fact that the overwhelming majority of women workers were unskilled or semiskilled and therefore rarely eligible for membership in AFL unions. Women who belonged to the Cigar Makers' International Union or the International Typographical Union, for example, were among the small minority of female workers who were skilled and who earned sufficiently high wages to qualify for membership in AFL craft unions. Thus, women cigar makers, although less skilled than their male counterparts, could sometimes qualify for membership in the AFL union. Other women who worked as unskilled cigar packers, tobacco strippers, and bookers could not.[39] The same situation prevailed in the immigrant unions: skilled male cutters and tailors organized early in the century; women were not included.

But to say that most women were not organized because they were unskilled immigrants is to overlook the importance of traditional notions about women's roles in influencing the course of women's unionization in the early twentieth century. Employers' attitudes toward their female laborers, women's perceptions of themselves as workers, and male trade unionists' conceptions of a woman's proper place help explain the difficulties involved in organizing women.

Many women were indifferent to the appeals of union organizers. One woman's efforts in the 1890s to organize shirtmakers illustrate some of the difficulties involved in reaching New York City immigrant women and interesting them in organization—difficulties the Women's Trade Union League would face throughout its organizing campaign. In 1897, Leonora O'Reilly, later a leading WTUL member, recorded that a United Garment Workers organizer boasted that he could organize twenty-five men's shops in a day "while the women laugh at him or refuse point blank to attend [meetings]." She visited sixteen of the shops in an effort to interest women in joining the United Garment Workers' Union Local No. 16, a women's union of shirtmakers. "All of them were given the cards asking them to attend Wednesday night meetings. Some of them responded; others looked as if they feared even to touch the foreign thing: the ticket." The following Wednesday evening O'Reilly and several residents from the Nurses' Settlement reached the meeting hall at eight o'clock. "Then we sat and waited. Neither of the two women who had promised me faithfully that they would come to help organize put in an appearance. . . . By 9:30 we had seven women in the hall. We resolved to talk to these women and do what we could. It was of no use, only as a figurehead . . . not more than two out of the seven understood English."[40]

In part, women's apathy may have had to do with their attitudes toward work. Young women frequently viewed their years in the labor force as a short interval between girlhood and marriage. Understandably, many saw matrimony as liberation from the harsh, exhausting conditions of the workplace. Marriage did terminate New York working women's labor outside the home. Despite the fact that Jewish women in the Russian pale and eastern Europe frequently played central economic roles in their households, married women did so less frequently in America. Once a Jewish woman married, she devoted herself to her home and family. In 1905, only 1 percent of Jewish wives worked outside the home. "No matter how great the poverty," one investigation concluded, "the Hebrew men seldom allow the women of the family to do the [clothing] work at home, even though they may have been shop-workers before marriage."[41] Italian women were somewhat more likely to continue as wage earners after marriage, in part because of the prevalence of the custom of taking in industrial homework and in part because the economic need of Italians was probably greater. Nearly 5 percent of Italian wives worked outside the home in 1905—a figure that does not include married women who took in homework.[42]

Women's day-to-day experiences at work no doubt reinforced their disinterest in unionizing and their anticipation of liberation through marriage. Patterns of occupational segregation locked women into low-paying, low-status, unskilled female jobs in which they could exercise virtually no control over wages, hours, or work discipline. In the power hierarchy of the workroom, visible authority figures—foremen, supervisors, factory owners—were male. "The workroom," historian Leslie Woodcock Tentler writes, "represented a social world where one's sex mattered more than one's intelligence, personal resourcefulness, or physical attractiveness. . . . In sum, women rarely possessed power in the work situation, and they saw at work virtually no avenues for achieving power, individually or collectively. But women, unlike men, were permitted by the culture an acceptable personal and occupational identity entirely independent of paid employment."[43]

Then, too, women's reluctance to organize may have reflected very real fears of reprisal. Manufacturers often hired women because they regarded them as more tractable than men.[44] They were also cheaper and, in the competitive economic life of New York City, employers depended upon women's cheap labor. For these reasons, they often strenuously resisted women's efforts to organize and frequently intimidated their female employees. As one union leader told the WTUL, "We have done everything possible to make the women interested, but the bosses have compelled them not to go to the union."[45]

Other factors also made organization difficult. The question of a meeting place, for example, was a serious problem for would-be women unionists. Many male unionists liked to hold evening meetings in saloons. Respectable young women, however, could not attend meetings in beer halls or walk the streets alone at night.

But women's resistance to unionization, although one factor that helps explain why so few women were organized, was not as important as the fact that male unionists usually manifested little interest in recruiting women. Although a number of the weak organizations among the city's marginal industries, such as the paper-box makers, worked hard to organize the women who made up the majority of the trades' work force, they were exceptional. Especially important to a discussion of New York City women was the fact that garment workers' unions at the turn of the century often did not consider women fit subjects for organization. "The East Side Jewish tailor refuses to regard the industrial activities of the Jewish girls as worthy of serious attention," one contemporary study concluded, "and thinks it is hopeless to expect the women employees to be unionists."[46] Despite the fact that unions in the needle trades organized semiskilled male workers such as pressers, they did not extend their attention to women.

Women often described shops in which men were unionized while they themselves were not. As a result, women worked longer hours and took wage reductions every time the men won improved conditions and wages. In her autobiographical novel, *Out of the Shadow*, Rose Cohen recalled such a situation in an 1890s cloakshop:

> I had no idea what a union meant or what all this trouble was about. But I learned a little the next day. When I came in a little after six in the morning, I found only the three girls who were at my table. Not a man except the boss was in the shop. The men came in about five minutes to seven and then stood or sat at the presser's table talking and joking quietly. The boss stood at his table brushing coats furiously. Every minute or so he glanced at the clock and his face looked black with anger.
>
> At the first stroke of seven the presser blew a whistle and every man went to his place. At a minute of twelve the presser again blew the whistle and the men went out to their noon meal. Those who remained in the shop ate without hurry and read their newspapers. The boss kept his eye on us girls. We began last, ate hurriedly, and sat down to work at once. Betsy looked at the men reading their newspapers and grumbled in a whisper, "This is what it means to belong to a union. You get a time to straighten out your bones. . . . "
>
> The men returned a little before one and sat waiting for the stroke of the clock and the presser's whistle. At seven in the evening when the presser blew his whistle the men rose almost with one movement, put away their work and turned out the lights over their tables and machines. We girls watched them go enviously and the boss turned his back toward the door.[47]

Trade unionists' attitudes toward female workers were rooted both in the traditional animosity of skilled craftsmen toward unskilled laborers and in men's conceptions of femininity and sex roles. Women workers were daughters, sisters, and future wives, not fellow workers. As the United Garment Workers' newspaper editorialized, "They are good citizens now, good workers, and we sincerely hope that they may all be good wives and mothers before very long, for better wives and mothers could not possibly be found."[48] Male unionists often viewed women as flighty nuisances who lowered hard-won wage gains and conditions. "It is the men who suffer through the women who are employed in the manufacture of clothing," one member of the United Garment Workers complained. "While the men through long years of struggle have succeeded in eliminating the contracting evil and the rotten system of piece work the girls . . . are now trying to deprive the older

members of the Garment Workers of the benefits because [they]
. . . can afford to work for small wages and care nothing about
the conditions of the trade."[49]

The frequent refusals of unionists to acknowledge women as
workers in their own right is well illustrated by the contention
that women could afford to work for small wages. Throughout
the early twentieth century, trade unionists as well as employers argued that women worked for "pin money" rather
than from economic necessity. Because the overwhelming
majority of New York City's working women were unmarried
and lived with their parents, this argument went, they had no
financial responsibilities and were free to spend their wages on
clothes and entertainment. Despite the critical importance of
women's earnings to the support of others, the pin-money
argument persisted with remarkable tenacity. The use of it by
trade unionists indicated their refusal to take women seriously.

The difficulties that New York City women faced with organized labor can be illustrated by looking at their experiences
with the United Garment Workers of America, an AFL affiliate
that organized workers in the men's clothing trades. Unskilled
and semiskilled women constituted a substantial portion of the
union's national membership: by 1902, 8,000 of the UGW's
25,000 members were women. In the same year, 96 of the
union's 179 locals either included women or were segregated
women's unions. The picture, however, is misleading. The
UGW was a conservative labor body that rarely sanctioned
strikes. Instead, it used the union label as an organizing tactic.
An employer could use the label if he agreed to employ only
union workers, maintain minimal sanitary standards, comply
with labor legislation, and "regulate hours and wages in accordance with union standards maintained in the locality."[50] Because many manufacturers found it to their advantage to use
the label, they "unionized" their employees. In reality, then,
many of the locals were company unions. In other instances,
corrupt UGW officials made a lucrative business of selling the
label to manufacturers.

The national statistics are particularly misleading when
compared to the UGW's record in New York City. In 1902, only
two New York locals had women members. One was a German
union of Brooklyn tailor shops; the other was a women's local of
overalls makers with about 90 members.[51] Union officials interpreted women's poor showing in the city as a sign that
immigrant women were incapable of organizing. One study
noted that women UGW members were "practically all girls

born in America, frequently of Irish or German parentage; the majority, perhaps, of American parents." There was no more than a "slight sprinkling of Jewish and Polish women, probably not more than one percent of the total."[52] In part, the UGW's lack of interest reflected that union's prejudice against immigrants from southern and eastern Europe. But it also resulted from an unwillingness to organize women. This indifference was particularly noticeable in label policy. In theory, any manufacturer who used the UGW label had to maintain a union shop. In New York City, however, employers frequently hired nonunion women. Although the union occasionally threatened to withdraw the label from New York, this was never done. Instead, the UGW continued to negotiate contracts with employers who hired unorganized women.[53]

The history of Leonora O'Reilly's unsuccessful shirtmakers' local, UGW Local 16, illuminates the indifference of UGW leadership to women's efforts to organize. In June 1897, O'Reilly noted that the local had met, although the "meeting was not as large as it ought to be. The men sent word that, as yet, they are too busy with contractors to spare a minute to strengthen the organization of either men or women, but this week will end the strike and then the regular business of organization will begin."[54] Somehow Local 16 never seemed to be included in the regular business of organization. When O'Reilly spoke to the UGW organizer, he agreed that it was important to organize women but never offered tangible assistance. O'Reilly could organize women if she pleased, but without financial or organizational help from New York's UGW leadership. In the late 1890s, Local 16 filed a formal protest at the UGW convention, stating that "the female garment workers have not been given the necessary cooperation by the other tailor unions" and asking that the UGW organize the women in union shops, but the resolution had no effect.[55] Without assistance, Local 16 failed. Although the WTUL revived it for a short time, this women's union could not maintain itself without cooperation from the national body.

The International Ladies' Garment Workers' Union proved more responsive than the UGW to women workers. The ILGWU originated in 1900 as a union of male cutters and pressers. From the beginning, the organization marked a departure from the "pure and simple" unionism represented by the American Federation of Labor. A union of Jewish immigrants, it was not characterized by the anti-immigrant prejudices that marked the United Garment Workers and the AFL as a whole.

Most of the Jewish men who founded the ILGWU were committed socialists; counter to AFL policy, the new union encouraged workers to engage in political activity and saw no reason to separate political involvement from union organizing. Thus, the ILGWU early established for itself a reputation for political radicalism. Although ILGWU leaders were skilled craftsmen, the union pioneered a modified form of industrial unionism. Cutters maintained their own powerful locals in most branches of the women's clothing industry, but all other workers in a given branch organized together.

Because women made up a much larger percentage of the work force in the women's garment industry than in the men's clothing trades, any strong union would have had to include women. By 1902, President Herman Grossman was attempting to affiliate with organizations of waistmakers, wrapper makers, and other trades that fell under ILGWU jurisidiction.[56] These organizations were small unions that appeared and disappeared sporadically as the result of spontaneous strikes in the women's trades. Next to nothing is known about them. Only two left any records. One, Local 12, was a waistmakers' union that affiliated with the ILGWU in 1901. Reefer makers also organized and amassed a large if temporary membership as the result of several general strikes early in the century. Because the memberships of these unions were transient and their treasuries were small, they could not weather slack seasons and usually failed within a season or two.[57] The ILGWU, unlike the UGW, made some effort to give these small unions some financial assistance and encouraged their organizing efforts. Nevertheless, the ILGWU did not undertake any significant organizing efforts itself. Provided that the shirtwaistmakers, the white goods workers, or other workers in the women's trades could organize themselves, the ILGWU would accept them as members. It is this theme that dominates the discussion of unionizing women in New York City at the turn of the century. Once organized, women would be incorporated into a union, but established unions would spend little time, effort, or money organizing them. If women were to be organized, they would have to do the job themselves.

The Women's Trade Union League began its work in a difficult time and place. It would have to devise ways to reach and organize young women who were unskilled, poorly paid, and temporary. Its members would have to learn to communicate with immigrants who spoke no English and who knew little about American industrial society. Finally, its members would have to find ways to adapt union structures created for skilled men to unskilled women and to convince indifferent or hostile trade unionists to organize and accept women as their sisters and their equals.

## CHAPTER 2

# The League Begins Its Work

The New York Women's Trade Union League was slow to begin unionizing women. Meeting first at University Settlement and, by the spring of 1904, in its own tenement headquarters on the corner of East First Street and Second Avenue, the individuals who formed the WTUL devoted nearly two years to recruiting allies, trade unionists, and women workers and establishing a viable cross-class coalition. Realizing that the success of the New York league would depend upon its ability to appeal to both workers and allies, William English Walling recruited its first members carefully. He envisioned an organization in which "women of college education were to give ideas, women of social position to use their influence to create a social sensitiveness and the women in the trades to supply the practical information."[1]

Two working women, Margaret Daly and Leonora O'Reilly, were Walling's first recruits. Daly, an overalls worker, an officer of the United Garment Workers' Overalls Makers' Local No. 92, and a national organizer for the UGW, served as the league's president in 1904. One of the few women at the turn of the century to build a successful career as a union organizer and business agent, Daly traveled throughout the United States negotiating union label agreements with men's clothing manufacturers. From the outset, however, Daly was ambivalent about the goals and membership policies of the WTUL and, despite her office, rarely took an active role in the fledgling organization. Despite WTUL attempts to keep her by supplementing her UGW salary, she decided to stay with her union. Daly resigned the presidency in 1905 and played virtually no role in league activities thereafter.[2]

Leonora O'Reilly, however, became one of the New York league's most influential members. When Walling contacted her about the WTUL she was thirty-three years old, a resident of Asacog House, a Brooklyn settlement, and worked as a sewing instructor at the Manhattan Trade School. An outspoken individual with a keen sense of humor and quick temper, O'Reilly grew up in a desperately impoverished Irish working-class family. She began work in a New York City shirt factory when she was eleven. O'Reilly's introduction to trade unionism came through the Knights of Labor. Her mother, a seamstress "passionately devoted to labor,"[3] was active in the Knights and took her daughter to their meetings. In 1887, when Leonora was sixteen, she, too, was initiated into the order.

After the Knights' decline in the early 1890s, O'Reilly, still a factory operative, was active in a variety of women's and reform organizations. Throughout the decade she worked sporadically with a struggling union of women shirtmakers, United Garment Workers Local No. 16. Although she came away from this initial organizing experience frustrated by male unionists' attitudes toward women, she wholeheartedly supported the league policy of cooperating with the labor movement. "Keep at it until we get the best Trade Unionists believing in us," she penned on the back of Walling's letter inviting her to join the league.[4] O'Reilly was also active briefly in the Working Girls Clubs, which she hoped would take the lead in unionizing female wage earners. Only organizations such as the clubs, she maintained, could break down the "false pride, the shrinking into their narrow customary sphere, and the fear of foolish strikes which keeps working women from any kind of large industrial union."[5]

O'Reilly came to the WTUL already familiar with the ideal of sisterhood: cooperation between working-class and upper-class women was a reality for her. "Are we not all sisters of one another," she asked in an early speech, "and should not a woman's heart thrill at being called upon for help?"[6] In her attempts to organize shirtmakers, O'Reilly had had the support of Lillian Wald and Lavinia Dock of the Henry Street Nurses' Settlement. Through her involvement with the Working Women's Society, which she helped found in 1886, O'Reilly became a friend and admirer of Josephine Shaw Lowell. Most important in shaping O'Reilly's views was a close and long-lasting friendship with Louise Perkins, a wealthy Boston teacher interested in labor and reform causes, whom O'Reilly came to know through the Working Women's Society. Throughout the last decade of the nineteenth century and the first years of the twentieth, Perkins, whom O'Reilly addressed as "Big Sister," served as her mentor and benefactress, helping direct O'Reilly's personal goals and social concerns. In 1897, Perkins provided O'Reilly with a personal income that enabled her to leave her job as a shirt factory forewoman, take up residence at the Henry Street Settlement, and embark on an industrial education course at the Pratt Institute. Once she had finished the Pratt program, O'Reilly directed her interests to vocational

education, opening a model sewing shop at the nurses' settlement and helping to establish the Manhattan Trade School.[7]

In 1901, when O'Reilly was head resident at Asacog House,
she became friends with Margaret and Mary Dreier, who served
on the settlement's board of directors. Among her first suggestions to Walling was that the Dreier sisters be invited to join the
league. From early 1904, they offered their time and generous
financial backing to the organization.

Margaret and Mary Dreier grew up in Brooklyn Heights,
daughters of a German-American businessman who had made
a substantial fortune in the English iron industry. His wealth,
which the five Dreier children inherited upon his death in 1897,
enabled them to live independently, pursuing their individual
interests in the arts and social reform. The Dreiers' German
Evangelical household was an affectionate and happy one, in
which the children were imbued with a strong sense of discipline and individual moral responsibility.

Margaret Dreier, the eldest daughter, was thirty-six when she
joined the New York WTUL. Until her late twenties, "Gretch-
en's" life fit the conventional pattern of a young woman of
leisure—traveling abroad to visit relatives in Germany, study-
ing history and philosophy with tutors, and "seeing friends,
going to luncheons, receptions, dinners, and a round of parties,
concerts, and opera."[8] Her first ventures in social service as a
volunteer for Brooklyn Hospital's Women's Auxiliary and as a
member of the State Charities Aid Association's visiting committee for state insane asylums fit the pattern of genteel philanthropy. Seeing the effects of poverty firsthand in the Brooklyn
Hospital's wards prompted Margaret Dreier to question the
value of conventional charity. It was all very well to see that the
poor were comfortable and cared for in hospitals, but such
work did not touch the causes of poverty.

In 1903, Margaret joined the Women's Municipal League and,
with social investigator Frances Kellor, conducted an exhaus-
tive investigation of employment agencies. After months of
painstaking research, the two women systematically documented the connection between organized prostitution and the
agencies that placed young immigrant and southern black
women into domestic service. As chairwoman of the Women's
Municipal League's legislative committee, Margaret Dreier
traveled frequently to Albany to testify about her findings and
to lobby for new legislation that would regulate employment
agencies' practices. The investigation proved to be a turning
point in her life. It helped channel her heretofore unfocused

interests into a specific concern for women workers. Equally important, Dreier learned through her successful investigative and lobbying work that she possessed gifts for organizing, for persuading, and for communicating her knowledge and her concern to others—in short, she learned that she could accomplish significant work.

Leonora O'Reilly persuaded Margaret Dreier to join the WTUL in the spring of 1904. Early in 1905, Dreier became the New York league's president. A dynamic, vital individual, Margaret undoubtedly would have been the driving force behind the New York branch. Early in the spring of 1905, however, she met and fell in love with Raymond Robins, a Chicago-based political reformer, settlement house worker, and Social Gospel preacher. A few months later, they were married. The couple returned to Chicago, where they set up housekeeping in a cold-water flat on the west side and immersed themselves in the exciting reform activities of the city. While her husband devoted himself to municipal reform, Margaret joined the Chicago WTUL. In 1907, she was elected president of both the Chicago and the national branches of the Women's Trade Union League. As president of the national league, an office she held until 1922, and through her close, affectionate relationship with her younger sister Mary, Margaret Dreier continued to influence the policies of the New York WTUL.[9]

Mary Dreier was twenty-nine when she joined the league in 1904. She and Margaret were a study in contrasts: Margaret was assertive and confident; Mary self-effacing and quiet. A beautiful, gracious woman with striking blue eyes, Mary Dreier had occupied herself with family affairs and social life and had dabbled in a variety of philanthropic activities before she joined the WTUL. In 1904, she was a student at the New York School of Philanthropy. After Margaret married, Mary Dreier became the New York league's president. Assuming leadership was very difficult at the beginning. Public speaking, in particular, was terrifying. "I am going to make my maiden speech tonight on 'The Value of the Union Label from the Point of View of the Consumer' and I am scared stiff," she confided to Margaret Robins. "[I] worked 4 or 5 hours over this foolish little address which lasts 6 or 7 minutes and still I am scared."[10] Quickly, however, Dreier gained confidence and learned to be a capable speaker and organizer. "How Mary has developed and 'come out' without losing any of the gentler more lovable qualities," one observer noted, "she is the dearest of people, as well as being so much besides."[11]

Both Margaret and Mary Dreier were strangers to the labor movement in 1904. Neither had had any direct contact with working women. Nevertheless, both immediately embraced the cause of trade unionism with almost religious fervor. For both women, the labor movement came to hold immense personal and social as well as economic significance. Unions were agencies for personal development and self-expression, for education in democratic ideals, and for a "sense of fellowship." As Margaret Dreier Robins explained, "The chief social gain of the Union Shop is not its generally better wages and shorter hours, but rather the incentive it offers for initiative and social leadership ... and the sense of fellowship, independence, and group strength it develops."[12] Once committed to organized labor, the Dreier sisters never hesitated to lend their support to labor causes in the early twentieth century. In 1906, both women publicly demonstrated against the forced extradition of leaders of the Western Federation of Miners in the murder trial of the governor of Idaho. Both took a vigorous stand against the use of judicial injunctions to break strikes and boycotts. Unlike many progressive reformers, they never wavered in their support of the closed shop.

Throughout 1904, the Dreier sisters, Walling, O'Reilly, and a handful of additional members publicized their work among social reform organizations, settlement houses, socialist women's groups, and suffrage societies. They formed a speakers' bureau with lectures on such topics as "Trade Unions and Public Opinion," "Organize or Perish," "Club Women and Working Women," and "The Settlement and the Working Woman." This recruitment campaign met with enthusiastic responses among upper-class women. As one early league member concluded, "I look about me here in New York and see hundreds of energetic enthusiastic earnest young women of independent means who are positively zealous to do some real practical commonsense work for humanity. In the League we furnish ... a field for work and for study without that condescension which is the curse of most altruistic work."[13] Early league meetings were especially popular with settlement residents. Women and men from the College, Henry Street, Greenwich, University, and Normal College Alumnae settlements attended early league gatherings. Well-known settlement residents Lillian Wald, Lavinia Dock, Mary Simkhovitch, Elizabeth Williams, and Jane Robbins and reformers Walter Weyl and Robert Hunter were enthusiastic participants. Contacts with socialist women's organizations led to a working relationship with the Women's Committee of the New York Socialist party. Speeches to women's clubs, charity groups, reform associations, and suffrage organizations attracted such women as Mary Beard; Henrietta Rodman, a radical feminist; journalist Rheta Childe Dorr; suffragist Harriot Stanton Blatch; and social investigators Mary Van Kleeck, Kate Claghorn, and Frances Kellor.

Gertrude Barnum and Helen Marot were among the individuals who attended early meetings and stayed to play important roles in the league. Barnum was the national WTUL's first organizer, and Marot worked for nearly ten years as the New York league's permanent staff secretary.

Gertrude Barnum had come to New York from Chicago, where she had been active in the settlement movement and had helped establish the Chicago WTUL. Like most early members, she was in her midthirties and independently wealthy. In the early 1890s, Barnum, the daughter of a prominent Chicago attorney and federal judge, spent a year at the University of Wisconsin. She found student life in Madison unappealing, however, and returned home, where she rebelled against her parents by refusing a debutante ball. Chicago society, she decided, like university life, was unfulfilling and divorced from reality. At Hull House she found meaningful work and the company of other young women who rejected traditional roles. Barnum devoted herself to the settlement movement at Hull House and at Henry Booth House through 1903. Gradually, however, she became impatient with settlement work, deciding that only through a career in the labor movement could she attack poor working conditions in a direct and effective fashion. Early in 1904, she helped establish both the Chicago and the New York leagues.[14]

Helen Marot was living in Greenwich Village and working as a child-labor investigator for the New York Child Labor Committee when she learned about the WTUL. A forceful, serious woman, she was thirty-five when she joined the league. Marot, the daughter of a well-to-do publisher, grew up in a Philadelphia Quaker family. When she was in her late twenties, she and her lifelong companion, Caroline Pratt, opened a reading room that stocked socialist and labor literature. The small library soon became a popular gathering place for Philadelphia reformers and socialists. Pratt, also an active WTUL ally and a progressive educator who later founded the New York City and Country School, recalled that "people of all shades of radicalism came there—Single Taxers, Socialists, philosophical anarchists—attracted by the unusual books and periodicals, and no less by the opportunity for discussion."[15] In 1899, Marot's interest in labor and social reform took a more active turn. She and Pratt carried out an investigation of Philadelphia tailors' working conditions for the United States' Industrial Commission. The investigation marked a watershed in her career. As one biographer stated, it "transformed her from a studious librarian of pacifist tendency into a belligerent activist."[16] Marot became a socialist, moved into a Philadelphia settlement, and took on a new assignment investigating child labor for the Association of Neighborhood Workers. Her work with the Child Labor Association brought her to New York, where she soon gained a reputation as an efficient and thorough social investigator. After she became the league's secretary in 1906, Marot promptly spearheaded a drive to organize the city's office workers. She was one of the founding members of a union for bookkeepers, stenographers, and accountants.[17]

As a group, WTUL allies shared a number of characteristics.[18] Without exception, they were wealthy. Just how wealthy they were cannot be determined, however, for their family backgrounds are often impossible to trace. Several, like Margaret and Mary Dreier, were affluent, indeed. But, with the exception of Irene and Alice Lewisohn, daughters of the copper magnate, and Carola Woerishoffer, daughter of an exceedingly wealthy investment banker, allies did not come from the families of major nineteenth-century industrialists. Many allies were exceptionally well educated. Of twenty-seven allies active in the organization before World War I, twelve were college graduates and at least two others had attended. Several held law degrees. Almost all were single. Finally, by early 1905, virtually all allies were women. Although nothing in the WTUL's constitution or policies specified a female membership, male reformers did not stay to assume permanent roles. Even William English Walling lost interest in the league. In 1905, fascinated with the Russian revolutionary movement, he left for two years of observing the revolution firsthand. After he returned to the United States, a new commitment to socialism led to active involvement with the Socialist party, and a new interest in race relations led him to help found the National Association for the Advancement of Colored People in 1908. Both concerns eclipsed his involvement with the WTUL.[19]

Virtually every ally came to the WTUL with experience in

social reform or philanthropic activities. Most of the older members had been active in charity societies as friendly visitors. Some had belonged to the New York City Consumers' League or the Women's Municipal League. Others had coordinated activities of working girls' clubs, employment bureaus, and trade schools. Others, such as Mary Van Kleeck and Louise Odencrantz, both of the Russell Sage Foundation, had already established reputations as social investigators. A few, such as Harriot Stanton Blatch, already noted for her suffrage work when she joined the league in 1904, came directly from feminist organizations.

The involvement of the allies in philanthropic and reform activities followed a common progression. Genteel charity work such as friendly visiting usually provided their initial experience in social service. Friendly visiting supposedly provided moral uplift among the poor by encouraging habits conducive to hard work and clean living. Despite charity societies' condescension and their limited understanding of the causes of poverty, friendly visiting was a valuable experience for many allies. It exposed intelligent, sheltered, upper-class women to living and working conditions they would never have seen otherwise, and it fostered the beginnings of their discontent with American society. Charity work also enabled allies to realize the inadequacies of traditional nineteenth-century explanations of poverty as the result of individual moral failure and led them to question American social and economic institutions. As Elsie Cole, a young Vassar graduate who joined the WTUL in its first years, stated, her work as a placement secretary for the Association of Working Girls' Societies was "a great opportunity for an interested observer of the actual workings of this blessed old capitalistic system of ours."[20]

Once a woman became disenchanted with traditional welfare work, she often turned to a settlement house. Because settlements frequently sponsored industrial investigations, allies were often knowledgeable about working conditions. But settlements offered no solutions to the problems that confronted the urban poor. Gertrude Barnum explained in 1905,

> I myself have graduated from the Settlement into the trade union. As I became more familiar with the conditions around me, I began to feel that while the Settlement was undoubtedly doing a great deal to make the lives of working people less grim and hard, the work was not fundamental. It introduced into their lives books and flowers and music, and it gave them a

place to meet and see their friends or leave their babies when they went out to work, but it did not raise their wages or shorten their hours.[21]

Personal considerations also influenced upper-class women to join the WTUL. Restless and discontented, they, like many middle- and upper-class women, were searching for meaningful work in a society that offered them few opportunities for vocational expression. A conviction that their lives were essentially childlike was a theme that dominated allies' comments about themselves and their backgrounds. Part of their motivation for joining the WTUL was an intense desire to experience "real life" by vicarious, empathic identification with working women. Mary Dreier, for instance, wrote her sister Margaret about how important it was to her to complete her thesis at the New York School of Philanthropy. "I shall feel real satisfaction in doing that, which may seem very childish to you two who have done so many real things but to me who have so seldom gone through with things begun it will mean a lot."[22] Mary Dreier also reflected upon the differences between her life with the league and the lives of her older sisters Dorothea and Katharine. They "should just once get into a strike and forget themselves," she decided. "If they could only once be made to endure hardship and discomfort for a cause of someone else they would understand."[23]

The backgrounds of three New York allies, Maud Younger, Elizabeth Dutcher, and Carola Woerishoffer, illustrate allies' personal motivations for joining the WTUL and their progression from charity work to trade union organizing.

Maud Younger was an early executive board member and the chairwoman of the league's waitresses committee. She grew up in San Francisco and, until she was thirty, lived with her parents, occupying herself with music, travel, social gatherings, and charity work. In 1903, while passing through New York on her way to Europe, Younger visited College Settlement. The visit apparently tapped a wellspring of discontent with her life as an aging debutante. Within a few days she cancelled her European trip and moved into the settlement. Once a settlement resident, Younger began to take an interest in women workers on the lower East Side, which led her to undertake an independent investigation of waitresses' working conditions. By taking a series of positions as a waitress and keeping a detailed journal of her experiences, she constructed a valuable, albeit romanticized, documentary.[24] During her investigation,

Younger met women interested in forming a union of restaurant workers. Although she was dubious at first about trade unionism, the conditions she encountered in New York City restaurants and hotels persuaded her of the necessity for organization. In 1905, she joined the WTUL and helped organize a small, independent waitresses' union.[25]

Elizabeth Dutcher also served on the league's executive board and was active in WTUL efforts to organize retail clerks. Dutcher grew up in Brooklyn, graduated from Vassar in 1901, and spent the years immediately after graduation engaging in a variety of philanthropic activities. She conducted sewing and cooking classes for immigrant children, worked for the Charity Organization Society, and did friendly visiting for the Brooklyn Bureau of Charities. Gradually she became involved in trade union activities as an outgrowth of her charity work in factory neighborhoods. She joined the league in 1906 and the Socialist party a short time later.[26]

Carola Woerishoffer, one of the wealthiest New York league members, grew up in a progressive family: her grandmother, Anna Uhl Otterndorfer, was editor of the *New Yorker Staats-Zeitung*; her mother took an active role in organizations working for protective labor legislation and a progressive income tax. Carola graduated from Bryn Mawr in 1907 with a combined major in philosophy and economics. Immediately after graduation she moved to Greenwich House and joined the New York City Consumers' League. During the summer of 1907 Woerishoffer conducted an investigation of conditions in New York City steam laundries for the Consumers' League. "I undertook when I began working in laundries," she wrote to Florence Kelley, "to find out as nearly as I could how it would feel to have the amount of money that I could earn with my strength, without skill."[27] The laundry investigation prompted her to join the WTUL.

Allies were crucial for the league's daily functioning. Originally, Walling had hoped that the labor movement would help defray the league's expenses, but the city's unions never gave substantial assistance. The league soon became solvent, however, thanks to the contributions of affluent individuals. Among the most generous were Irene and Alice Lewisohn, who played little role in day-to-day activities but could be counted on to help finance activities. When members decided that they needed a full-time secretary, for instance, the Lewisohn sisters paid Helen Marot's salary. They underwrote the expenses of a "model" unionized laundry in a campaign to organize the city's

laundry workers. Margaret and Mary Dreier and Carola Woerishoffer also made frequent contributions to the New York
league. When Woerishoffer joined, she presented a check for
five thousand dollars instead of the customary two-dollar initiation fee. In 1910, she donated ten thousand dollars to establish
a permanent strike fund. During strikes, allies met bail and
legal costs. Few financial records survive from the WTUL's early
years, but those that are extant illustrate the importance of
wealthy sympathizers. From March 1906 to March 1907, the
league's expenses totaled $3250.55. Two-thirds of that amount
came from allies. Most of the rest came from dues, initiation
fees, and room rentals. Only $61.00 came directly from city
labor unions.[28]

In addition to their financial contributions, many allies provided useful services. Bertha Rembaugh and Madeline Doty,
feminist attorneys, provided free legal counsel to women workers. Louise Odencrantz and Mary Van Kleeck, carried out detailed investigations of industrial conditions. Rheta Childe
Dorr, had valuable contacts with the local press. Then, too, a
significant number of allies remained in the organization for
many years, thus providing continuity and stability.

Trade unionists were the second group the league worked to
recruit. Late in 1903, Walling sent letters to every union in
trades that included women, urging them to send representatives. He scheduled the first meetings for late Sunday afternoons, at the hour when the New York City Central Federated
Union's sessions adjourned, in the hope that CFU delegates, who
also met at University Settlement, would participate. The first
meetings attracted a small group of unionists from trades with
large numbers of women. Men from the International Ladies'
Garment Workers' Union and its waistmakers' local, the
paper-box makers' union, the Shirt, Waist, and Laundry Workers' International Union, the Cigar Makers, the United Cloth
Hat and Cap Makers, and the United Garment Workers attended.

Unlike prospective allies, unionists were wary about the
league's purpose, methods, and usefulness. The most vocal
participants in the first meetings, they voiced reservations
about an organization composed so heavily of outsiders and
stipulated that the WTUL was not to interfere in the unions'
internal affairs. Despite the fact that the unionists who attended early WTUL meetings represented trades made up almost entirely of unskilled workers, they were adamant about
adhering to American Federation of Labor principles. As the

president of the paper-box makers' union stated, "If this is a pure and simple trade organization, I am willing to support it, but I could not take part with anything that is going to be detrimental to the organization. We expect to control."[29]

The league's first members, allies and unionists alike, were united in the opinion that the WTUL should defer to labor movement policies and decisions. From the start, the New York league assumed a subordinate stance. The league's deference to the AFL and its New York City affiliates derived in part from allies' sensitivity about their own class backgrounds in a period marked by distrust between the labor movement and the public. But the WTUL's initial identification with the AFL indicated more than a desire to please labor leaders and to establish a good working relationship. Despite the members' belief in sisterhood, official league ideology stressed that the problems women faced in the work force were to be attributed more to their economic role as workers than to their social role as women. Thus, the best way to improve women's position as workers was to integrate them into the established labor movement.

League members discovered that establishing relations with trade union men was easier than recruiting the women workers who surrounded the WTUL in East Side factories and shops. Few women wage earners took a sustained interest in the league during its first years. From late 1903 through 1906, when the league rarely had more than fifty members, uppper-class women dominated numerically. With the exception of Margaret Daly, who never assumed an active role, all of the first officers and a small majority of the original executive board members were allies. Sometimes places on the executive board and committees were left vacant because no working woman could be found to fill them. As Mary Dreier summarized the situation as late as 1907, "The allies . . . control because the unionists are not as regular and not as active in the work."[30]

The league's first members established vague guidelines for recruiting women workers. They stressed that their work should be "personal," from "girl to girl in the shops."[31] They were determined to shed any vestige of what Leonora O'Reilly described as "the attitude of the Lady with something to give to her sisters."[32] But such advice provided little concrete guidance.

Allies, however, anticipated no difficulties in recruiting working women or in relating to them once they were members. Women could, they believed, surmount social and ethnic differences and unite on the basis of their femininity. In this respect, the Women's Trade Union League embodied the principles of early twentieth-century feminism. A conviction that women could relate to one another across class lines in the spirit of sisterhood and an emphasis on the special qualities that women shared linked the league to the larger woman movement. One of the major ideological themes of early twentieth-century feminism was the notion that women were different, emotionally and culturally, from men. As Rheta Childe Dorr expresssed this ideology,

> "Women now form a new social group, separate and to a degree homogeneous. Already they have evolved a group opinion and a group ideal. . . . Society will soon be compelled to make a serious survey of the opinions and ideals of women. As far as these have found collective expression, it is evident that they differ very radically from accepted opinions and ideals of men. . . . It is inevitable that this should be so. Back of the differences lie centuries of different habits, different duties, different ambitions, different rewards.[33]

League members used the term *sisterhood* to convey the idea that class was less important than gender for understanding women's status. The primary social dichotomy was a sex distinction rooted in differences between men and women. Women, league members believed, shared distinct emotional qualities: they were more gentle and moral than men, more sensitive and responsive to human needs. They were, in short, instinctively maternal. "Some of us who are not really mothers in the narrow sense express the mother instinct in the sense of social motherhood," Leonora O'Reilly stated.[34]

This ideal of sisterhood was not very helpful in the early efforts to recruit women workers. Members' first attempts reflected their inexperience. They began by holding Sunday teas. These "sociables" were designed to "stir up enthusiasm among the girls" by "drinking tea and discussing unionism." Entertainment was a feature of each tea, and guests were treated to music, dancing, and refreshments. Women from a variety of trades were invited to each party to give them a chance to discuss common problems and experiences. The gracious league socials must have been awkward affairs. The few young women workers who attended were stiff and shy in the presence of solicitous league ladies.

Discomfort cut both ways. Despite the allies' belief in sisterhood, they often found it difficult to relate to working women. "Some of the girls were simply splendid," Mary Dreier wrote

Margaret Robins about a league picnic. "There were four how-ever who seemed to me the limit—giggly girls whose sole interest in life was boys and how to attract them, and they did not hesitate to address any young fellow that passed them. . . . I don't know how to manage that sort of a girl, I don't understand the type—I can get on very well with the tomboy ones,—of which there were a few also—the other kind seem sort of oversexed and unwholesome, and I don't like them."[35]

Teas, picnics, dances, and parties were always part of the league's program. But members soon realized that teas were not a very effective recruiting method. Late in 1905, the WTUL began to supplement its sociables with more aggressive tactics. Helen Marot and Leonora O'Reilly introduced daily street meetings. Every day at noon and in the early evening, league speakers set up a platform, unfurled their banner, and "preached the gospel of trade unionism at and near the factory door." New York league members were proud of their street rallies. In part, their pride stemmed from the fact that they had discovered an effective and forceful way to reach working women. But allies were also pleased with themselves for shedding the conventions of proper femininity. At the time that the league decided to hold street meetings, Mary Dreier recalled proudly, not even suffragists dared use such a tactic.[36]

Gradually, the WTUL attracted several dozen working women. Several were skilled craftswomen and members of AFL unions in their own trades. Women from the bookbinders' female local and the goldleaf layers' union were always in attendance. Seven representatives from these two women's bookbinders' unions served on the league's executive board from 1905 through 1909. A representative from the Commercial Telegraphers' Union, Hilda Svenson, joined the WTUL during an unsuccessful strike in 1907 and remained an executive board member and an organizer for the league until 1920, when she married. A representative from the Boot and Shoe Makers' Union attended regularly. Other than the bookbinders, however, the New York league had little success attracting female craft unionists to the organization. The cigar makers did not send a woman representative to the league until 1911, and women in the International Typographical Union were reported as disinterested in the league's work.[37] Rarely did the New York local, ITU No. 6, send representatives. In addition, the craft union representatives who did attend league meetings always remained aloof from the day-to-day work. "They are

queer for they . . . never take us into their confidences or ask
our advice," Mary Dreier said of the women bookbinders in the
league. "It is very disappointing. . . . They are not exactly in the
square with us, never regarded us as friends really."[38]

Most of the women workers on the league's executive board
and on committees came from the men's and women's garment
trades. Young Jewish women from the ILGWU shirtwaist makers' local as well as the male officers of that union maintained a
close working relationship. Women from United Garment
Workers' locals of overalls makers, buttonhole finishers, and
vestmakers made up another large contingent. Capmakers,
milliners, hat trimmers, white-goods workers, and neckwear
makers served on the executive board from time to time. Unlike
the representatives from the craft unions, these women garment workers were, in the main, Jewish immigrants. Although
most of the working women attracted to the league were
industrial laborers, a few service workers joined from time to
time. Over the first few years, a waitress, a laundry worker, and
several retail clerks and clerical workers sat on the executive
board.

Very little personal data can be found on these WTUL members.[39] Most apparently did not stay longer than a year or two.
Although many sat on the executive board, few took active,
vocal roles. Many apparently lost interest and drifted away;
others appear to have left the labor movement altogether when
they married. It is clear, however, that the working-class league
members were hardly a monolithic group. Jewish and Gentile,
skilled and unskilled, socialist and conservative working
women found their way to the WTUL in its early years. These
divisions were typified by two working women who joined the
league in its first years and remained to play major roles, Rose
Schneiderman and Melinda Scott.

Rose Schneiderman, a capmaker, joined the league early in
1905. She was a WTUL leader until the organization disbanded
fifty years later. In many respects, the background Schneiderman brought to the WTUL as a twenty-three-year-old Jewish
immigrant typified the experiences of young East Side women
in the early twentieth century. Schneiderman was born in a
small Polish village to Orthodox Jewish parents, both of whom
worked in the needle trades. Her father was a tailor, her mother
a custom seamstress. When Rose was eight, the family emigrated to New York and settled on Ludlow Street, a crowded
tenement neighborhood on the lower East Side. Two years
later, Rose's father died, leaving the family destitute. For several

years the children were shuttled between orphanages and relatives while the family depended upon charity and the meager sums Rose's mother could earn by taking in boarders and home sewing. A shy, serious girl forced early into an adult role, Rose left school to go to work when she was thirteen. Her earnings of two dollars for a sixty-four-hour week as a department store cash girl were essential to her family's subsistence. In 1898, discouraged by retail clerks' low wages, Schneiderman took a job as a cap-lining maker, although her mother objected that factory work was not "genteel." Like most young immigrant women, Rose knew nothing of trade unionism during her first years at work. In 1902, however, Rose's mother moved the family to Montreal. There, Rose befriended a family named Kellert who introduced her to trade unionism and socialism. When Rose returned to New York the next year, she began to notice disparities between her working conditions and those of the unionized men in her shop. "The men had organized already," she recalled, "and had gained some advantages, but the bosses had lost nothing, as they took it out on us."[40] In the winter of 1903, Schneiderman and two other young women capmakers organized the twelve women in their factory and asked the United Cloth Hat and Cap Makers' Union for a charter. The all-male union, a successful Jewish socialist organization, had never attempted to organize the women in the trade, but union officials told Schneiderman that if she could recruit twenty-five women they would charter a female local. Within a few days, she returned with twenty-five signed membership cards, the union was chartered, and she was elected secretary. The women's local was successful. By 1905, it had several hundred members and was strong enough to win a Saturday half-holiday.

These first years of trade union activity were exhilarating for Schneiderman, who quickly became a skilled organizer and speaker. They were years of personal transformation as well. Once a lonely, unhappy young woman, she became an eager participant in the exciting intellectual and political activities of East Side radical circles. "It was such an exciting time for me," she remembered later. "A new life opened up. All of a sudden I was not lonely anymore. It was the beginning of a period that molded all my subsequent development." Despite her mother's warning that she would not find a husband if she continued her new activities, Rose joined the Socialist party and the Manhattan Liberal Club and played an increasingly active role in her union. The capmakers elected her to their general executive board and as a delegate to the Central Federated Union. Its organizers also began to ask her to speak to women capmakers throughout New York and New Jersey, and her diminutive figure and flaming red hair became a familiar sight on union soapboxes. Once, early in 1904, Schneiderman attended a WTUL meeting, but she came away skeptical about the organization's goals and membership. "I could understand why working women . . . joined, but I could not believe that men and women who were not wage-earners themselves understood the problems that workers faced," she recalled.[41]

Schneiderman revised her unfavorable impression during an industry-wide capmakers' strike in the winter of 1905. Although it eventually ended with a union victory, the protest against employers' attempts to establish an open shop was a bitter struggle that dragged on for more than three months. During the strike, Margaret Dreier called on Schneiderman and offered the league's assistance. Impressed with Dreier's sympathetic interest and with the WTUL's ability to get favorable newspaper publicity for the strike, Schneiderman joined the league immediately after the strike was settled.

Schneiderman was the first worker and labor organizer to devote herself fully to league work. She brought invaluable skills and knowledge to the WTUL—a fact that league leaders appreciated. A few months after she joined, the New York league elected her vice-president. In 1907, Irene Lewisohn provided her with a stipend of forty-one dollars a month, which enabled her to quit factory work and devote herself to organizing for the WTUL during the day and attending the Rand School in the evenings.

Schneiderman came to the league from the turbulent world of early twentieth-century Jewish radicalism. Melinda Scott, on the other hand, who joined the league early in 1907, came from a conservative craft-union tradition. Scott was an Englishwoman who grew up in Manchester and emigrated to the United States when she was sixteen. She was a hat trimmer by trade. In the predominantly female millinery industry, hat trimming was an elite trade. Trimmers were skilled craftswomen who commanded far higher wages than other millinery workers or women industrial workers generally. Around the turn of the century, Scott organized the Newark, New Jersey, trimmers into a separate women's union. Scott's organization admitted only skilled women trimmers and maintained a self-sustaining treasury—a remarkable achievement for a women's union at that time. Although affiliated with the

United Hatters, an AFL international, the local insisted upon autonomy. It made its own policies concerning dues, grievance procedures, and strikes. As president of the Hat Trimmers' Union of Newark and as the only woman delegate to the Essex Trade Council, Scott played an increasingly important role as a women's organizer in northern New Jersey. In June 1907, Scott asked the New York WTUL for help in a strike of skilled Irish and German women cop winders at the Clark Thread Mills. Impressed with the league's willingness to help, Scott joined the league.[42]

Scott's approach to trade unionism was very different from Schneiderman's. In the tradition of AFL craft unionism, she wanted to concentrate the league's efforts on the small minority of skilled, English-speaking, native-born women who worked in New York's shops and factories. Her own experience as an organizer had been limited to this group. She was outspoken in her views on the desirability of immigration restriction and on the impossibility of organizing immigrant women successfully.

By 1907, the Women's Trade Union League of New York was well on its way to establishing a coalition composed of allies, trade unionists, and women workers. By that year, three of the league's five officers were working women, as was a majority of the executive board. The WTUL's general membership consisted of over two hundred women, about evenly divided between workers and allies.[43] But the league's success depended not only upon recruiting a numerically balanced membership, but also upon maintaining harmony and a sense of purpose. In these respects, WTUL members discovered that it was considerably easier to make verbal assertions of sisterhood than to put the ideal into practice. In contrast to the league's public affirmation of sorority, the organization's internal affairs were anything but harmonious. Beyond commitments to unionizing women workers and to the American Federation of Labor, there was little upon which league women agreed. From the beginning, members were constantly at odds with one another over league objectives and policies: could only working women serve as organizers, or was any willing individual qualified? What groups of women should the league attempt to unionize? How much money and energy should the league commit to organization, to educational activities, or, later, to the suffrage campaign? Should the league support protective legislation for women, and, if so, what measures? An extraordinary amount of personal animosity and rancor accompanied debates on league priorities. Leading members frequently submitted resignations or threatened to resign. They wrote angry notes denouncing one another or defending themselves against each others' attacks. "If we have failed in what might be our greatest usefulness to the workers," Leonora O'Reilly concluded wearily in 1914, "it is just in proportion as we have exhausted the energy of our friends and ourselves . . . in periodical tiffs and skermishes [sic]."[44]

Class and ethnic conflicts explain much of the league's factionalism, policy disputes, and difficult personal relationships.[45] Allies and workers came to the organization with different conceptions of social class, different attitudes toward work, and, of course, radically different social, educational, and cultural backgrounds. The ideal of sisterhood notwithstanding, difficulties and misunderstandings between women of different social backgrounds were inevitable. Yet class and ethnic conflict in and of itself is not an adequate explanation for the controversies that regularly shook the organization. Indeed, social relationships among league members sometimes tended to mitigate serious class conflict. More important, there were no simple class alignments on league issues. Clearly, other factors were involved.

The women who made up the WTUL were never able to reconcile their dedication to women as an oppressed minority within the work force with their commitment to the labor movement as a whole. Belief in sisterhood, league members were to discover again and again, was not always compatible with a belief in class solidarity. In other words, the league was unable to develop a satisfactory solution to the problem of women's dual exploitation: were women workers oppressed because they were workers or because they were female? In effect, many controversies were a reflection of the league's struggle to synthesize feminism and unionism—a struggle that had personal as well as ideological ramifications for WTUL members.

Although differences in members' social backgrounds did not fully account for members' disagreements, they were an important contributing factor. Most allies were seemingly unconscious of the genteel atmosphere that permeated their organization, despite its unpretentious headquarters in a series of lower East Side flats. They saw nothing incongruous about juxtaposing "interpretive dance recitals" with shop meetings or inviting women to stop by for an afternoon of "drinking tea and talking unionism." For working women, however, the league had an uncomfortably aristocratic air about it. Rose

Schneiderman, for example, recalled her amazement when she attended her first meeting and watched members dance the Virginia reel. The league's gentility sometimes undermined workers' self-confidence and made them feel awkward. Ideologically, the workers sometimes condemned the organization's Ruskinian character. "Contact with the Lady does harm in the long run," Leonora O'Reilly decided. "It gives the wrong standard."[46]

Ideally, allies were to learn about labor organizing from workers. In practice, however, allies often took the lead in day-to-day affairs, despite the constitutional safeguards designed to prevent such dominance. Allies were articulate, well-educated, financially independent women. Then, too, most allies were older than most working-class members, and their age may have given them additional authority in league activities. The allies' wealth also may have influenced relationships within the organization. The WTUL introduced women such as Rose Schneiderman to a world of affluence and material comfort they had never known existed. Allies frequently financed classes, vacations, and medical treatment for working-class members. When workers were elected as national WTUL convention delegates, allies would make up for their lost wages and meet their travel expenses. Such practices must have rankled, at least at times. As one New York working-class member reported to Rose Schneiderman about what she had seen of Margaret Dreier Robins and the Chicago league, "Now you know that I think an awful lot of Mrs. Robins—but the only fault I find with her is that she has made all the girls of the League think her way, and as a consequence they do not *use* their own mind and they do not act the way they feel but the way Mrs. R wants them to. . . . For instance she sends several girls to learn folk dancing, she pays for it. And many more things of that kind I don't particularly like."[47]

The allies' attitudes did not go uncriticized. Leonora O'Reilly was particularly vocal in expressing her dislike of college graduates who came to the labor movement with lofty ideals of feminism and sisterhood but who knew nothing about the realities of working for a living. She was determined that workers not be intimidated by allies' financial and academic advantages. O'Reilly carried on a running campaign against Laura Elliot, an ally who joined the league in 1910. Elliot offered courses in singing, elocution, and art history; she organized a chorus and took groups of women workers to museums and concerts. Despite the fact that O'Reilly herself had enjoyed a long-standing relationship with a mentor, Louise Perkins, who had guided her own quest for education, she found Elliot's activities pernicious. She harangued Elliot about her condescending attempts to uplift working women by filling them with useless and pretentious notions of "culture." Elliot was hurt and confused by O'Reilly's anger but insisted that she had a contribution to make to the league:

> You cannot push me out and you cannot make me afraid of my working girl sisters or render me self-conscious before them, I refuse to be afraid to take them to the Metropolitan Museum and *teach* them and *help* them. . . . I have no fear in putting my side of the proposition up to any working girl. I'm not afraid to tell her that I have something to bring her and I'm never afraid that she will misunderstand or resent what I way. She needs my present help just as the whole race needs her uprising.[48]

Gertrude Barnum was another ally who was shocked by the class conflict within the league. "I feel like warning you," she wrote Leonora O'Reilly shortly after O'Reilly had resigned temporarily from the WTUL, "that whether you stay out of the League or come in, I am with you—you can't get rid of me outside or in. Fortunately everyone does not abandon us 'allies' as soon as they disagree with us and we may be useful yet."[49] Barnum was hurt when members criticized her organizing abilities. In 1906, the WTUL abolished the position that Barnum had held as national organizer, and she left the league to work as a publicity agent for the International Ladies' Garment Workers' Union.

Allies, the executive board admitted in 1906, could be "trying."[50] Upper-class women sometimes made decisions that exasperated working-class members. Allies wanted to reprint portions of Dorothy Richardson's documentary-style novel, *The Long Day*, a sensationalist narrative of a working woman's experiences in New York City, despite Leonora O'Reilly's objections that the book exploited and misrepresented working women. On another occasion, allies scheduled a citywide conference of working women on Yom Kippur, despite Jewish members' protests. Only one league ally, Rheta Childe Dorr, studied Yiddish. Some allies held stereotypical conceptions of immigrant women. Jewish women were often described as "dark-eyed," "studious," and "revolutionary" in league literature. Italians were "docile," "fun-loving," "submissive," and "superstitious."[51]

Part of the difficulty underlying clashes between allies and workers can be attributed to the fact that the two groups came to the organization with different conceptions of class. Allies were not as acutely aware of class antagonism within the league as workers were and downplayed the importance of social background. Many allies were confused by the emphasis that workers put on class differences. As Laura Elliot wrote Leonora O'Reilly, "Before I was unconscious about this class and that class and this stupid difference and that stupid difference. Girls were just girls to me and now you people are putting all sorts of ideas in my head and making me timid and self-conscious."[52]

The differences between workers' and allies' definitions of class are illustrated by their attitudes toward socialism. A significant number of the league's early members belonged to the Socialist party, and others defined themselves as socialists. But although all league socialists stressed the importance of a classless society, allies frequently interpreted this to mean a lack of concern for class, rather than a rigorous class analysis of social relations. As Vida Scudder, a Boston WTUL officer, stated, "Class will never become to our minds a permanent factor in social life."[53] Many allies believed that an individual could transcend her social background by becoming self-sufficient and relating to working women without self-consciousness. As Helen Marot wrote of Carola Woerishoffer, "The entire naturalness of her attitude towards her fellow workers, her apparent unconsciousness of any differences between her and them, made it possible for her to fall at once into friendly relations. She was one of them."[54] Some allies even defined themselves as workers: they thought of themselves as self-supporting and resisted being categorized in their fathers' class. Violet Pike, who joined the league after she graduated from Vassar in 1907, was included among the workers on the executive board because she performed some clerical duties and joined the Bookkeepers, Stenographers, and Accountants' Union. Maud Younger was listed on the league's masthead as a representative of the New York Waitresses' Union.

Allies and workers also came to the league with different conceptions of work. For workers, there was no intrinsic appeal in crowded factory workrooms, in sixty-to-seventy-hour workweeks, or in monotonous and fatiguing toil. Work was drudgery to be left behind as soon as possible with amusements at the end of the workday and, eventually, with marriage. Upper-class members, however, like many early twentieth-century feminists, often regarded a paying job as automatic liberation from the confines of genteel and idle femininity.

Thus idealized, work automatically conferred meaning and value to a woman's life and put to rest the feelings of purposelessness that bothered many allies. Ida Rauh, a radical feminist and active WTUL ally, wrote a series of fictional sketches that deal with a young woman who lives in an apartment overlooking a factory. From her window, the leisured young woman can watch an operative at work. "I admired her efficiency, the skill with which she avoided the waste of a second of time. Then I turned from the window and became absorbed in a book."[55] Because allies often romanticized work and equated it with economic and emotional self-sufficiency, many never came to terms with the fact that most women were not independent laborers but part of a family economic unit in which work did not confer independent status. "Thank God working girls have a chance to be themselves because they earn their own wage and nobody owns them," a typical league article began. "I am pretty sure you are somebody, because you are self-supporting."[56]

That the New York league was always characterized by such class conflict there can be no doubt. But the organization was not sharply divided along class lines. It is possible to document experiences that mitigated serious, sustained conflict between upper-class and working-class women. There were cohesive as well as divisive factors that operated within the league and enabled it to function.

For example, the league members' personal relationships undercut class conflict. In their friendships and living arrangements, many WTUL women lived their ideal of sorority by establishing their closest emotional ties with other women. Mary Dreier, for instance, maintained very warm and affectionate relationships with Rose Schneiderman and Leonora O'Reilly. Her friendship with O'Reilly was particularly close and survived numerous political and personal differences. "You say you wonder whether I would always trust you," Dreier wrote O'Reilly after some disagreement over league policy. "There doesn't even seem to be such a word as trust necessary between thee and me. . . . I might not always understand, as you might not always understand my activities—but as to doubting your integrity of soul, or the assurance on which trust is built seems as impossible to me as walking on a sunbeam into the heart of the sun for any of us humans—a strange and beautiful mixture of personal and impersonal is my relationship to you and I love you."[57] In 1907, Dreier provided O'Reilly with a house and a life income.

Such relationships were common among league women. A number maintained permanent households with one another. Mary Dreier lived for many years with Frances Kellor; Helen Marot lived all her adult life with Caroline Pratt. Then, too, allies and workers vacationed together, concerned themselves with one another's families and finances, and generally shared day-to-day life experiences. Although many had suitors and offers of marriage, most chose to reject marriage in favor of woman-centered friendships and living arrangements.

That WTUL members should form such a friendship network is not surprising in light of the social conventions that governed women's social relationships in the pre-Freudian culture of the early twentieth century. Allies almost certainly came to the league familiar with such friendship patterns from college and settlement houses. Emotional attachments and intense relationships involving open expressions of tenderness and affection were accepted as natural.[58]

It would be difficult to overestimate the importance of this supportive friendship network in league members' lives. For many, the WTUL was a full-time commitment, a way of life. As Mary Dreier said, league women, in a spiritual sense, were born in 1903, the year the league was founded.[59] Their network provided invaluable emotional support for members' public work. Women encouraged one another in their speaking and organizing work at a time when they could find little encouragement from male trade unionists. Only an extremely mechanistic definition of social class could fail to take into account the fact that these women, regardless of class background, shared many important life experiences.

Finally, class conflict is not an adequate explanation for the disagreements within the organization for the simple reason that a member's social background did not dictate her stand on league policies. As the league began its work and developed its policies over the first decade of its existence, alignments were unclear. There is no evidence to support the view that working women saw the league as a labor union and allies saw it as a social reform organization. Rather, it is clear that other factors played a role in creating the controversies in which league members found themselves embroiled.

League members, regardless of class or ethnic background, viewed the WTUL both as a women's organization and as a labor organization. Therein lay an additional source of discord. Over the years, members had difficulty reconciling their commitment to organized labor with their commitment to the woman movement. If a woman dedicated herself to working for protective legislation or if she advocated separate unions for women workers, she opened herself to the charge of dividing the working class. If, on the other hand, she stayed away from women's issues altogether, she was guilty of ignoring women's special problems in the work force. This dilemma was real, and neither the league nor individual members were able to resolve it.

Some members felt strongly that dedication to the labor movement should override the league's feminism. In their analysis, the problems of working women were bound inextricably with the problems of working men. True, they said, women suffered discrimination in the labor movement, but such opposition was not insurmountable. Labor questions were primarily questions of class, not gender. Other women came to the WTUL with their orientation in the woman movement. Or, as happened frequently over the first decade of the organization's work, women first tried to cooperate with organized labor but eventually despaired of being able to change male unionists' attitudes. They then turned to other means such as woman suffrage or protective labor legislation to ameliorate women workers' conditions. These two viewpoints coexisted uneasily throughout the league's history.

Helen Marot epitomized the "woman as worker" position. Although an ally, she never wavered from her conviction that the WTUL should be committed to the working class and not to women as a special group. Women workers, she emphasized, should be regarded as inseparable from male workers: to think otherwise was to impede class solidaity and to denigrate women's capabilities. In her reports to the executive board and in one of her books, *American Labor Unions*, she argued that the exploitation women experienced in their jobs and the discrimination they met in the labor movement were facets of the larger issue of unskilled workers versus skilled craftsmen. Once unions recognized the importance of organizing the unskilled, they would include women as a matter of course. She was vehement in her opposition to women's minimum wage legislation, arguing that if women needed state protection, then unorganized men did, too.

Marot stood at one end of the continuum of league members' thinking about the relationship between women and the labor movement. Harriot Stanton Blatch and Rheta Childe Dorr stood at the other. Blatch and Dorr joined the league in 1905 and served on the executive board. Neither woman remained long.

Blatch left in 1907 to form her own organization, the Equality League for Self-Supporting Women. Dorr remained in the WTUL through 1909, but her involvement steadily waned. Neither Blatch nor Dorr was as important in the league as Marot, but their ideas were representative of another theme in league ideology. Their interest in women workers developed from their involvement in the woman movement rather than from a concern with industrial problems. Unions for women constituted only one aspect of a multifaceted campaign for women's rights.

For Blatch, any class-related issue was secondary to the vote. In part, her participation in the league was motivated by expediency: she realized that working women's support was vital for the success of the suffrage movement and that the WTUL offered an avenue by which to reach these women. But Blatch was also convinced that political equality was a prerequisite for any improvement in women's status. Only when women could vote would they command the respect of male trade unionists. And only with suffrage would women develop the confidence to fight for industrial equality. "Those young women need stirring up, need independence, and some fight instilled into them," Blatch wrote Samuel Gompers. "I am understanding of all that the vote would mean to them—[it] would help in the trade union work as nothing else could."[60]

Rheta Childe Dorr also placed more importance on feminism than on labor activities. In the late 1890s, Dorr divorced her husband and moved to New York to pursue a career as a reporter. Personally Dorr identified her own struggle to achieve independence and professional recognition with the efforts of women to win autonomy in the workplace. In her writings she argued that women constituted a caste, distinguished not only by biological characteristics but by emotional traits as well. In newspaper articles and in her books, *What Eight Million Women Want* and *A Woman of Fifty*, she made impassioned pleas for female solidarity. Trade unions were important for women's emancipation, but they were secondary to the struggle for personal liberation.

Marot, Blatch, and Dorr were sure of their objectives and ideological orientations, but the problem of women's dual status was not so clearcut for most league members or for the league as a whole. The ideal of sisterhood always coexisted uneasily with the ideal of class solidarity. For workers, the problems posed by the WTUL's dual commitment were particularly vexing. For them, the matter was not purely a theoretical issue, but frequently a personal dilemma as well. Leonora O'Reilly's commitment to the league, for instance, was always ambivalent, for she was faced with a conflict between her class background and her work in a women's organization. Her conflict was aggravated by her conviction that any serious attempt to organize working women had to be a feminist as well as a labor effort. She had long recognized the need for an organization to devote special attention to women and to goad the labor movement into action. She also recognized that as long as the labor movement refused to commit itself to such work, money had to come from sources outside the working class.

For all that, O'Reilly never came to terms with her ambivalence. She vacillated between urging the league to refrain from interfering in union affairs and stressing that the league should implement an autonomous policy. She stressed the importance of sisterhood. "Personally," she wrote, "I suffer torture dividing the woman's movement into the Industrial Group and all the other groups. Women real women anywhere and everywhere are what we must nourish and cherish."[61] Yet at other times O'Reilly denounced the league as an elitist organization that had no real concern for working people. Late in 1905, she resigned temporarily from the WTUL, complaining of "an overdose of allies" and emphasizing that working women would have to organize themselves.[62] By 1907, she was back in the league, but her feeling of alienation never left entirely.

The conflict between sisterhood and class solidarity and the problems involved in reconciling a commitment to feminism with dedication to trade unionism would always be difficult issues for WTUL members, allies and workers alike. In its first few years, however, the league, sustained by the ideal of sisterhood and by the supportive network its members created, was able to build a small but balanced membership and to turn its sights to its primary work of union organizing.

## CHAPTER 3

# Forming Unions, 1904–1909

> Why do YOU work *10 hours* a day when the organized
> bookbinders, overall-workers, and other organized women
> work only *8 hours?*
> The GIRLS of today are the MOTHERS of the future; if they
> are overworked the children pay the penalty.
> The speakers will welcome you at the Women's Trade Union
> League.

Such was the message the WTUL carried to working women
as its members ventured through the congested tenement districts of the lower East Side, through the alleys and narrow
streets of Greenwich Village, and "uptown" through the blocks
north of Fourteenth Street. In its organizing work from late
1904 until the shirtwaist strike late in 1909, the WTUL played a
unique role in the unionization of the city's women workers. It
attempted to serve as a link between women wage earners and
the labor movement and as a center for unorganized women
interested in unionism. It sought to channel women into stable
unions and to integrate them into the established labor movement. To these ends, the WTUL agitated among unorganized
Jewish, Italian, and native-born women in an effort to educate
them in the combined principles of feminism and unionism.
The executive board aided local unions' strikes and made concerted efforts to change male unionists' negative attitudes
toward women. Finally, as a self-styled "central body of
women" the league established women's unions of dressmakers, white-goods workers, buttonhole makers, finishers, milliners, hat trimmers, corset workers, neckwear workers, and
waistmakers. In addition to efforts in the needle trades, the
league worked occasionally with tobacco workers, textile
operatives, paper-box makers, candy and confectionary workers, retail clerks, waitresses, telegraphers, and laundresses.
Organizing during these early years was extremely difficult.
Only rarely did the WTUL establish organizations that lasted
longer than a season or two or included women from more
than one or two shops. Many strikes the league led failed, and
most of the others were fought to maintain existing conditions
and wages.
The league's difficulties were not surprising. The organization dealt with workers who were among the most difficult to

unionize. The great majority were unskilled or semiskilled laborers in seasonal, unrationalized industries and service occupations. Male and female workers in these categories changed jobs frequently, earned too little to pay substantial dues, had little identification with their work, and had virtually no leverage in negotiations with their employers. New York City's economy in the twentieth century's first decade intensified these problems. Unlike many small industrial towns and cities, New York was characterized by decentralized, unrationalized industries in which the typical workplace employed fewer than twenty workers.[1] The league also began its organizing work during a particularly difficult time: the city's economy slumped early in 1904 and did not recover until 1909. The business depression, combined with a concerted open-shop drive on the part of many of the city's manufacturers, resulted in a general decline of union membership.

The ethnic heterogeneity of the city's work force further complicated the league's work. Because the WTUL devoted most of its organizing efforts to women in the needle trades, the majority of women with whom members had contact were young Jewish immigrants or daughters of recent immigrants from the Russian pale. Italian women composed the second largest group. Growing numbers of Italian women worked as sewing machine operators and finishers in the men's and women's clothing trades and made up the majority of workers in the paper-box, confectionary, and artificial flower and feather industries.[2] Language barriers, ethnic conflict, and the lack of common cultural traditions hindered the league's work with immigrant women.

Then, too, as male trade unionists steadfastly maintained and as the WTUL reluctantly concluded, women were difficult to organize not only because they were unskilled but also because they were female. Far from exhibiting revolutionary fervor, league members complained, most women workers were too timid to organize, and even militant women were often apathetic when it came to maintaining a union. It was impossible, the WTUL discovered, to divorce a woman's social roles as daughter, sister, and future wife and mother from her economic role as worker.

Finally, league organizing efforts were made difficult by New York City's trade unionists, who rarely cooperated with organizing efforts among women and who occasionally tried to block the league's efforts. Because the Women's Trade Union League was strongly committed to cooperation with the American

Federation of Labor and tried to follow the federation's style of craft unionism in its organizing efforts with women, the labor movement's lack of support was particularly troublesome.

Despite the league's lack of success in forming many permanent organizations from 1904 through 1909, its attempts to form small unions are useful for delineating the problems involved in organizing women workers in the first years of the twentieth century and for illuminating the WTUL's attempt to create a cross-class alliance.

Initial organizing efforts late in 1904 and throughout 1905 were especially difficult because most WTUL members were ignorant of how such work was accomplished. Organizing required a viable theory of unionization and skills that members had to teach themselves. League women approached their work with only one certainty: they should follow the guidelines set down by the American Federation of Labor. Organization should be conducted on a shop-by-shop basis, strict jurisdictional boundaries should be observed, and "bread-and-butter" issues should be the basis of union demands. What was more, league members were united in the opinion that the WTUL should defer to AFL policies and decisions. From the start, the New York league assumed a subordinate stance and stressed that its role was to assist trade union officials in organizing women. Its policy, Walling stressed, was "to go entirely under the jurisdiction of and orders of the trade union."[3] But reliance on AFL policies provided little help in answering the myriad of questions that barraged the league: which women would respond to organization? how did an organizer channel sporadic discontent into a stable union? why did women in some trades seem more interested in unionization than women in others? why were eastern European Jewish immigrant women more responsive to organization than Italian or native-born women?

Identifying groups of women likely to respond to WTUL agitation was the first task. Without criteria by which to gauge women's readiness for organization, the first efforts were haphazard, dictated by individuals' interests. Maud Younger wanted to organize waitresses. Harriot Stanton Blatch and Mary Van Kleeck took a special interest in millinery workers. Mary Simkhovitch urged the league to organize Italian women in the candy and artificial-flower factories near Greenwich House. Unionists were interested in their own industries. Mary Dreier urged that the league seek out women in the "most exploited trades."[4]

Dreier's approach was adopted. The league spent 1905 and

the early months of 1906 making sporadic attempts to organize
paper-box makers, laundry workers, retail clerks, and waitresses, whom members identified as the most exploited female
wage earners. These first efforts were disastrous. An attempt to
organize paper-box makers foundered in a strike late in 1904.
League leaders, who referred to this incident as "the children's
strike," had little conception of the difficulties such an industry
presented to the union organizer. The 120 strikers in a large
Broadway box factory were young (many no older than fourteen), unskilled, and inexperienced in striking or maintaining a
union. It took a strikebreaker only a few hours to learn to fold,
collar, and paste paper boxes. Despite the WTUL's financial
support (for the workers had no strike fund) and public appeals, the strikers gained none of their demands: the manufacturers refused to recognize their union, and the 10 percent
piece-rate reduction that had precipitated the walkout remained in effect. Throughout 1905 the league maintained a
boxmakers' committee that tried to restore the union, but it
met with no success.[5]

League women were also interested in organizing laundresses because they, too, were among the most oppressed workers.
In New York City, most laundry workers toiled in sweltering
steam laundries at unskilled manual tasks. Standing for as long
as seventeen hours at a stretch, they sorted, tagged, bunched,
shook, and ironed garments and operated mangles.[6] The involvement of WTUL members in a protracted strike of collar
starchers in Troy, New York, also encouraged the league to try to
organize New York City's laundry workers. Early in 1905,
several hundred female employees of a large Troy collar and
cuff factory walked out to protest the introduction of a starch-
ing machine that did nothing to lighten their work but gave the
manufacturers a chance to reduce piece rates. Gertrude Barnum and Rheta Childe Dorr traveled to Troy to assist the
strikers. Other members collected donations and publicized
the strike, which, though it ultimately failed, inspired the New
York league to agitate among the city's laundry workers. New
York leaders were especially impressed that Troy's laundry
workers had been unionized since the 1870s.[7]

In the months after the Troy strike, WTUL members, accompanied by a male organizer from a successful San Francisco
laundry workers' union, visited more than one hundred
establishments but elicited "little or no response," despite the
appalling conditions. League members soon agreed with the
San Francisco organizer that the situation in New York was

"hopeless."[8] They began to realize that there were crucial differences between the situation in Troy and that of the thousands of women who worked in New York's hand and steam laundries. Troy's laundries were factories, essential parts of that city's major industry. Troy's women workers had grown up together, lived in close proximity to one another, and shared a common cultural background. In New York City, although the majority of laundry workers were of Irish and German backgrounds, significant numbers of Jewish and Italian women had found work in the city's small laundries. They did not share common cultural traditions and did not work in a centralized industry. The laundry committee disbanded early in 1906, concluding that its effort had been "untimely"—laundresses were "under too high pressure and too timid to accept action."[9]

Early members met with much the same response in their first efforts with waitresses and retail clerks. Allies were especially shocked that the few retail clerks they managed to interest wanted to meet secretly. The saleswomen explained that if they participated openly in unionizing efforts they would face certain discharge and blacklisting; but naive allies, who had expected the women to be militant, were disappointed and bewildered by such meekness. "It seems so strange to me that they hesitate to come into the union," Mary Dreier wrote her sister Margaret about a meeting of Macy's clerks and waitresses, "when they are working under such bad conditions."[10]

By early 1906, after more than a year of discouraging work with paper-box makers and laundresses and shortlived attempts to unionize waitresses and retail clerks, the executive board decided that oppression was not a sufficient basis for unionization. Henceforth, organizing should follow the path of least resistance. "Actual appeals for organization should be met," the board stated, "rather than attempts on the League's initiative to organize trades representing the worst conditions."[11] Accordingly, league organizers walked through factory neighborhoods looking for shop strikes. When they found women pickets, members circulated leaflets about their work and invited the strikers to WTUL headquarters.

The league's new organizing policy led its members to the lower East Side, where unrest among Jewish garment workers was easy to find. WTUL records document continuous protest in the rapidly expanding waist, neckwear, and white-goods industries during the first decade of the twentieth century.

Several factors help explain Jewish women's militancy. Unlike other immigrants, many Jewish women were familiar with urban, industrial work patterns before they emigrated to the United States. Of the nearly 600,000 Jewish immigrants who arrived in the United States between 1899 and 1910 with previous work experience, one-third had worked in the needle trades.[12] Rose Schneiderman's background was representative. She spent her earliest years in a traditional eastern European village, or shtetl. When she was six, her family moved to Khelm, an industrial city in Russian Poland, where both her parents labored as garment workers. Jewish women were also likely to be familiar with some form of trade unionism, both in eastern Europe and in New York. In the towns and cities of the Russian pale, men formed *chevrahs*, occupational benefit associations. A small but significant number of women joined the Bund, a revolutionary labor organization that attracted thousands of Jewish workers in the years around the turn of the century. After the abortive 1905 Russian revolution, many Bundists emigrated to the United States, where they assumed important roles in Jewish unions. By the early 1890s, Jewish immigrants had established numerous labor organizations in New York City. The United Hebrew Trades, which acted as a federation of Jewish unions on the lower East Side, the United Cloth Hat and Cap Makers' Union, and numerous organizations of cutters, cloakmakers, tailors, and other garment workers attested to the vigor of the Jewish labor movement. Jewish women in New York City were likely to have male relatives in the labor movement and were bound to come into contact with trade union propaganda. They came from a cultural background in which labor organization was well known and widespread. Finally, in traditional Jewish culture, the qualities of assertiveness, toughness, and practicality were valued in a woman. Although formally assigned a subordinate social status, in actuality, women were accustomed not only to having a central economic role, but also to making decisions.[13]

It was not surprising, then, that many Jewish women did not hesitate to express their anger at poor working conditions. Their protests were usually spontaneous. Grievances concerning wages and piece-rate reductions sparked many walkouts. "The women in the shop have been paid for a new grade of work," one typical league report read, "and no one in the shop has been able to make more than $4.00 for the week. In the same shop, girls previously made $12 to $16. Even the Italians threw the money back at the foreman, refusing to accept the rates . . . the girls will strike the next day."[14]

Oppressive working conditions also led to strikes. Contractors' practices of requiring workers to pay for needles, thread, and electricity were common grievances. In the inside shops, many walkouts were protests against strict work discipline. Jewish women in several waist and white-goods shops, for example, struck because their foremen prohibited talking. When manufacturers instituted fines for such "offenses" as lateness, laughing, singing, combing hair, eating, or washing hands, women often walked out. Harassment was another complaint. "We got man forman [who] speaks bad words and calls the girls bad names," one young woman wrote to the New York league. On one occasion, more than four hundred wrapper makers struck because of "grievances against the foreman." In 1906, the league recorded that a strike of several hundred women neckwear workers was precipitated by a subcontractor who slapped a girl because "she had not stitched her work properly." White-goods workers struck in 1907 to protest the "insults of a male employee whom the company refused to discharge." In another instance, women called an "orphan strike" in response to their employer's insistence that his attentions were merely manifestations of "fatherly affection." If his attentions were fatherly, the women told the league, then they demanded to be treated as orphans.[15]

The WTUL's support of spontaneous strikes was an important independent stand. Because the city's unions were concerned with consolidating and stabilizing their memberships and treasuries, most refused to assist such strikes. The United Garment Workers, for example, labeled such activities "wanton strikes" and "looked somewhat askance upon recruits who appear under such circumstances."[16] The ILGWU was more tolerant but was often unable or unwilling to give women strikers aid. The years 1904 through 1908 marked an extremely difficult time for the young union. Neither the locals in the women's trades nor the international office had the funds to finance strikes. In fact, during these years the international's treasury was usually empty. Then, too, a powerful conservative faction within the ILGWU leadership inveighed against the frequency of spontaneous strikes and recommended that the union refuse assistance. The ILGWU was pleased to turn the work of agitating among women over to the Women's Trade Union League. In 1906, John Dyche, the ILGWU's general secretary and a WTUL member, asked the league to make a special effort to organize waistmakers. He suggested that the WTUL recruit a woman organizer and, because the ILGWU had no money, that the league also pay her salary. Negotiations broke down because the league could not find a Yiddish-speaking woman organizer.[17]

Because labor unions were often indifferent or unable to help, women on strike turned to the league for help. By mid-1906, groups of women strikers appeared frequently before the executive board to ask the league's assistance. The WTUL placed only one condition on its aid: the women had to declare their loyalty to the American Federation of Labor.

Such requests set the league's organizing process in motion. Winning the strike was the first task, and every element of the WTUL coalition played a role. By 1906, the league had developed a core of capable organizers and strike leaders that included both workers and allies. Leonora O'Reilly, Rose Schneiderman, and Melinda Scott, and Josephine Casey, a militant and peripatetic ILGWU organizer who worked occasionally for the league, were the leading organizers. Hilda Svenson, the WTUL's representative from the Commercial Telegraphers' Union, also frequently coordinated strike efforts. Among the allies, Helen Marot, Gertrude Barnum, Bertha Poole Weyl, and Mary Dreier learned to be effective organizers, speakers, and negotiators.

Active allies walked the picket lines, paid calls on strikebreakers, and occasionally took positions as strikebreakers themselves to agitate inside the shop. Others organized consumer boycotts, street meetings, publicity campaigns, and fund-raising benefits. The league appealed to its wealthy sympathizers to give their working-class sisters financial help and to inform their church groups and women's clubs about the strikers' working conditions and grievances. Wealthy allies posted bail for arrested strikers, and league attorneys provided counsel.

The WTUL also helped organize walkouts. Under league supervision, the strikers elected officers and picket captains and formulated a clear set of demands. If a union existed in the trade, the league usually suggested that women demand union-scale prices and hours. In addition, league representatives, acting in the capacity of union business agents, accompanied the strike leaders to their negotiations.

After the settlement, league organizers stayed with the union to help establish a permanent organization. Using the shop as the basic unit, WTUL members attempted to fashion a stable union along craft lines. If the strikers were garment finishers, for example, the union's membership would consist entirely of finishers. WTUL organizers taught leaders how to hold meetings, drilled them in the intricacies of parliamentary procedure, and helped them establish dues, membership, grievance, and election policies.

League women attempted to build the union's membership by recruiting women in neighboring shops. Street meetings were one way to recruit new members. "Imagine two Italian speakers, two Yiddish, and two English," Mary Dreier wrote Margaret Robins about a Rivington Street rally. "We got 58 names of girls who seem willing to join."[18] Josephine Casey described her membership campaign for a textile union of silk-ribbon-machine operators. She reported that she was "Working with the women individually by meeting them outside the factory at noon, securing addresses, and going to their homes talking to them and securing the addresses of other women."[19] This shop-by-shop approach made for slow organizing. In a month's time, Casey succeeded in recruiting only fifteen members for the silk-ribbon makers.

Once the league established an organization, it instructed the women in trade union principles. Because the WTUL saw union principles as being synonymous with those of the AFL, league members impressed upon female workers that militant unionism and strikes should be eschewed in favor of practical, orderly methods. Members warned women of the dangers of the IWW. They emphasized the importance of the AFL union label and stressed the greater strength that the women would have under the wing of a male organization. Gertrude Barnum's stories for women workers illustrate the WTUL's early trade union philosophy. Barnum's stories include a number of stock characters. The "pale Russian Jewish girl" who is usually "explaining a Marxian socialist tract" is one common character. The silly young woman who reads "dream books" and sentimental novels is another. Heroines are practical American-born workers who understand the futility of both novels and Marxist tracts. When a problem arises in the shop, the native-born woman answers the Jewish radical and the sentimental novel reader with good business acumen. "What can we do? . . . Well, you ask the cutters. They didn't get their ten hours and scale of prices by writing literature. . . . They got it by being skilled cutters that were needed . . . and then laying down the hours and the prices they would stand for. It's up to us to put up the kind of sewing they can't find from every immigrant that lands at Governor's Island and then get the cutters to stand by us. We can get a contract, that's what." In another story, the didactic Anglo-Saxon heroine admonishes her sister workers to "Stop being helpless. . . . Cut out appealing with your soft blue eyes and talk United States with your tongue fair and square. . . . Business men are alright but you gotta talk business to 'em."[20]

The WTUL stressed that in order to be successful unionists, women needed training in self-assertion. To counter traditional feminine passivity, league members insisted that women elect officers, chair meetings, and make decisions without assistance from male co-workers or relatives. Helen Marot described the successful operation of this process in a union of garment finishers. The women, she said, "handled their own meetings and the strike themselves — only getting advice and cooperation from others. This is in marked comparison to the advice of the men who had come to help them. They had started the idea among the girls that they must have a [male] leader. It was interesting to see how the girls took up the idea of being their own leader."[21]

Once the league deemed a shop organization stable, its leaders suggested that the organization affiliate with an AFL union. The league acted as a go-between in the affiliation process, communicating with the AFL union and urging its officers to grant the women's organization a charter and assistance. WTUL leaders suggested that AFL unions incorporate women in parallel fashion, so as not to violate the autonomy of crafts. A local of female buttonhole workers, for example, could exist side by side with a male local of cutters; a local of cigar strippers with a local of cigar makers. Although the WTUL professed a preference for unions with both female and male members, this insistence on craft autonomy meant that in practice virtually all the unions the league helped establish were segregated by sex.

After a shop organization affiliated with a national union, the WTUL's work was officially completed. The New York league did not consider its efforts successful, however, unless the new local received sufficient assistance from the international. The league expected the union to help finance an organizing campaign, to lend its authority in settling shop disputes, and to give women equal benefits. The league also expected new members to assert themselves in union affairs. In short, its work ended with the full integration of women into the established labor movement.

Two individuals, Rose Schneiderman and Melinda Scott, eventually emerged as the WTUL's most effective strike leaders and negotiators. In the years before the 1909 shirtwaist strike, both women enjoyed reputations as successful organizers—Schneiderman with Jewis unions on the East Side, Scott with native-born hat trimmers and dressmakers.

After joining the league in 1905, Schneiderman devoted most of her time to Jewish women in East Side clothing factories. In 1908 she was appointed the WTUL's East Side, or Jewish, organizer. Fluent in Yiddish, increasingly confident in her abilities as an organizer and speaker, Schneiderman soon became well known on the East Side.

Schneiderman organized the WTUL's white-goods union, one of the few organizations that survived the progression from spontaneous strike to established organization. White-goods workers made women's underwear and lingerie. Although the white-goods workers came under the ILGWU's jurisdiction, the union showed little inclination to organize the trade's ten thousand women. The processes involved in making women's underwear were simple, mechanized tucking and seam stitching. Because the work could be learned quickly, white-goods shops were often the first places an inexperienced worker looked for a job. Young women—their average age, according to a league survey, was nineteen—made up nearly 95 percent of the trade's work force.[22] Unwilling to risk the money and effort, the ILGWU left organizing white-goods workers to the Women's Trade Union League.

In April 1907, women in one white-goods shop struck to protest a work speedup and appealed to the league for assistance. With Schneiderman's help, the strikers won a piece-rate increase. Although the manufacturer refused to recognize the WTUL-sponsored union, it grew rapidly, claiming three hundred members by the end of the year.[23] The league was pleased with the new union. Marot reported that the Jewish women who made up the membership were "carrying on business by themselves. Up until recently, they have had a member of the Hebrew Trades presiding; now they have one of their own girls elected as president and presiding."[24]

The 1908 depression nearly destroyed the union. At one point only the officers remained. A series of shop strikes in the summer of 1908 enabled Schneiderman to rebuild the union, and early in 1909 the union affiliated with the ILGWU. Although the international would not promise an organizer or financial help until the women could show "their power to organize themselves,"[25] the league was pleased and, to celebrate, sponsored a large ball for the new ILGWU Local No. 62.

During the same years that Schneiderman was working with

women on the lower East Side, Melinda Scott was gaining a
reputation as a superb organizer among native-born, English-
speaking women in the "uptown" branches of the clothing
trades. Through a process similar to that Schneiderman followed with the white-goods workers, Scott organized a local of
dressmakers that affiliated with the ILGWU in 1909. Her
proudest achievement was the organization of New York's hat
trimmers, who were unorganized until 1909. Scott successfully
unionized the women during a protracted strike of New York
hatters and trimmers that lasted nearly nine months. In June
1909, she negotiated a settlement, and the trimmers affiliated
with the United Hatters. "The hatters are winning and we are
radiant," Mary Dreier wrote to her sister. Melinda Scott, she
went on, "is a wonder."[26] In celebration, the WTUL sponsored a
formal ball for two thousand hat trimmers and allies. Under
Scott's presidency, the union flourished. By the end of 1909,
more than 80 percent of the city's hat trimmers worked in union
shops. Scott also proved to be an especially shrewd and adept
business agent, "good at keeping off reductions and gaining
piece rate increases."[27]

Schneiderman's efforts with the white-goods workers and
Scott's with the dressmakers and hat trimmers were unusually
successful. Before the shirtwaist strike late in 1909, the New
York league could point to few tangible organizing achieve-
ments. Obstacles faced the WTUL at every stage of its organizing work.

The first problem league organizers reported was the difficulty of interesting women in organization. WTUL members
learned that although unrest and protest were widespread on
the East Side, even militant Jewish women were frequently
indifferent to unionization. They were willing to strike, but
their enthusiasm waned when faced with the work of maintaining an organization. Even more discouraging, most women
with whom the WTUL came into contact were fearful about
joining unions. "Timid," "passive," "afraid," and "intimidated"
were adjectives league organizers used again and again to
describe women's response to their appeals. "The men have
formed an organization and have a charter," a typical report
read. "The women started out all right, but after some interference from the forelady stopped coming to meetings. . . . They
seem to be afraid."[28]

Members soon gained insight into women's resistance. Most
workers, they emphasized, were young girls who had been
denied the joys of childhood and forced prematurely into an

adult role—they were bound to be "frivolous and light-minded."[29] Women's status as temporary and transient workers also made them difficult to organize. According to a league survey, most female industrial workers held two to five different positions during a year.[30] Young women also regarded themselves as temporary workers because they left the labor force when they married. Despite the fact that the average female wage earner spent six or seven years at work, she saw this period as an interlude between childhood and her adult status as wife and mother. Finally, the league maintained that unorganized women were often submissive and timid in the workplace and apathetic in their unions because they had internalized traditional female roles. Women had not overcome what Gertrude Barnum described as the "ever-lasting superstition that women are only the sisters, daughters, and sweethearts of men."[31] A woman who learned to be a dutiful and submissive daughter at home, league members emphasized, could hardly be a militant unionist at work.

To counter women's reluctance, the league developed a program of preparatory work designed to make contact with unorganized women. English-language classes were one aspect of this program. The league's text, *New World Lessons for Old World People*, was a series of essays dealing with the problems young women workers faced in America. Subjects included working conditions, factory laws, homework, fire safety, and ethnic conflict. Each essay stressed the advantages of unions. In an early lesson, the story's heroine works in an unorganized shop:

> I go to work at eight o'clock.
> I work until six o'clock.
> I have only one half hour for lunch.
> I work overtime in the busy season.
> I do not get extra pay for overtime work.
> I earn eight dollars a week in the busy season.
> I earn three or four dollars a week in the slow season.
> I have no work at all for three months.
> I pay for my needles and thread.
> I pay for my electric power.
> My trade is a bad trade.

In the next lesson, entitled "A Trade with a Union," the conditions are much better:

> I met a friend yesterday.
> She works at a good trade.
> She goes home at five o'clock.

> She goes home at twelve o'clock on Saturday.
> She has one hour for lunch every day.
> Sometimes she works overtime in the busy season.
> She gets extra pay for overtime.
> She belongs to the Union in her trade.

Other lessons deal with employers' practice of hiring non-English-speaking women for lower wages. In "The Story of Yetta," for example, the heroine goes to a factory and agrees to work for five dollars a week, although the American-born women in the shop are earning nine dollars.

> Yetta thought $5.00 was a lot of money. . . . A year went by. There were no more Americans in the shop. They would not work for $5.00 a week. Yetta began to learn English. She learned many other things. It costs a lot of money to live in America. Food costs more money. Clothes cost more money. . . . One day the boss brought a strange girl to work. She did not speak Yetta's language. . . . She got only $4.00 a week. Yetta felt afraid.[32]

The league also sponsored lectures and classes on "Women in Industry" and "Women in Society." Relying on the gynecocentric theories of contemporary sociologists Lester Frank Ward and W. I. Thomas and feminist Charlotte Perkins Gilman, who occasionally spoke to WTUL audiences herself, league lecturers stressed that women had always been important workers, that in "primitive cultures" woman's social and economic importance was far greater than that of man. While man wandered in search of food, woman was the "inventor, the discoverer, the teacher, the leader."[33] In preindustrial Europe and America, league lecturers explained, women were often skilled craftsmen. The lectures ended with an analysis of woman's role in industrial society. Far from being an aberration, women's work outside the home was an organic continuation of their productive role throughout human history.

League speakers also dealt with marriage, stressing that if women were to gain a sense of themselves as workers, their conceptions of marriage would have to change. The WTUL emphasized that women's experience as workers would have great impact on their future well-being as wives and mothers. Good ventilation, seats at work, reasonable hours, regular breaks—all conditions that only a union could enforce—were essential to women's health. Fatigue and the physical and nervous strain that resulted from poor working conditions would result in difficult childbearing and general poor health later in life. To reinforce these points, the WTUL formed a Good Health

League. For ten cents a month, the organization provided the services of a woman physician and sponsored frequent lectures on women's health. These "popular health talks" included lectures on personal hygiene, sex hygiene, and the relationship between industrial conditions and women's health. The WTUL was akin to other reform organizations, most notably the Consumers' League and the American Association for Labor Legislation, in this emphasis on the special health hazards that industry presented to women and on the impact of industrial conditions on maternity. Their arguments were similar to those made in the Brandeis brief and in the Supreme Court's 1908 ruling in *Muller v. Oregon*. Unlike other reformers, however, the WTUL insisted during its early years that unionization rather than legislation was the solution to these problems.

The time a woman spent as a trade unionist would help her in other ways as well. She could teach her children trade union ideals and understand her husband's activities. "The world is beginning to change its opinion of marriage and 'the home,' to demand character there," Harriot Stanton Blatch declared at a street meeting. "It is in the labor union that the working woman can get the training that will make her . . . a decent, self-respecting wife and mother."[34] To emphasize the fact that the labor movement could be an important part of a working-class woman's life after she married, the league formed an auxiliary committee of trade unionists' wives. League members also told working women that traditional expectations of marriage were romantic and unrealistic. Marriage did not liberate women from drudgery; it merely substituted one form of exploitation for another. "If you think you will be a grand lady after you leave the factory and are married to the workingman," Rose Schneiderman told working women at street rallies, "you are sadly mistaken, for you will have to work yourself to death."[35]

The league's preparatory work represented members' attempts to come to terms with the totality of working women's situation, at home as well as at work. Their lectures, classes, leaflets, and speeches indicate that members recognized that a young woman's role at work was closely related to her role at home. But league members—allies and workers alike—underestimated the tenacity of the patriarchal cultural traditions that surrounded woman's role. In a very real sense, life for an Italian or Jewish girl did not begin until marriage, and a girl's childhood and adolescence were merely preparation for her roles as wife and mother.[36]

Leaflets and speeches urging women to change their attitudes toward marriage could not have had much impact. An
Italian woman, for instance, learned very early that she lived in
a patriarchal society and that she belonged to her father and
her brothers, just as later she would belong to her husband.
"*Mia moglia è mia proprieta*," a southern Italian saying ran.[37]
The Italian woman learned that males were more important
and powerful than she and that familial decisions and authority fell to them. A good part of a girl's socialization consisted of internalizing traditional standards of submission and
obedience.[38] Joining a union presupposed an independence
from the influence of her family and Italian mores that very few
women could be expected to possess. It meant relinquishing the
protection of family males. Finally, joining a union required
that a woman think of herself as an independent wage earner,
and few Italian women thought of themselves in that light.
Despite the stress that league members put on Jewish women's
militance and despite the general impression that radical socialist thinking permeated East Side life and culture in the early
twentieth century, the fact remains that the backgrounds of
young Jewish women were nearly as conservative as those of
Italian women. An Orthodox Jewish girl, whether she grew up
in a shtetl, an eastern European city, or New York, also learned
that her place was at home and that her most important roles
were as wife and mother. Like Italian women, Jewish women in
the United States did not work outside the home after they
married. Although probably given more personal autonomy
than Italians, young Jewish women also led home-centered
lives. It was a rare young woman who joined the Bund or other
radical political movement in the countries of the late
nineteenth-century Russian pale.[39]

Most WTUL members were ill equipped to deal with the
special problems immigrant women posed for labor organizers. In their efforts to unionize women, members were
sometimes impatient with women's docility. Sometimes they
betrayed a thinly veiled irritation with women's submissive-
ness. Mary Dreier said of Italian women, for example, "They
have no collective vision. They follow willingly and devotedly a
leader whom they trust."[40] Helen Marot spoke of Jewish
women's "childlike dependence" and of their habit of relying
upon men to make their decisions for them.[41] WTUL members
prided themselves on their independence and strength. What
they interpreted as submission and docility disappointed them.

Then, too, almost all league members—workers and allies

alike—rejected marriage for themselves. They might well have been unable to understand the importance marriage assumed in other women's lives, both at home and at work. The expectation of marriage was an important facet of young women's work culture. Talk of romance, beaux, and their future role as wives helped young working women to weather the monotony of their working hours. Quite possibly, women's expectations of marriage, coupled with their strong perception of work as temporary, help explain the seeming paradox that bewildered WTUL organizers commented upon time and again—that women could be angry and yet be apathetic when it came to organizing or striking. Perhaps for these women work was simply too transitory, and thus they saw no need to make the kind of personal investment that joining a union required.[42]

Language barriers exacerbated the league's difficulties. Speakers and organizers were often forced to rely on translators for even the most basic communication. During one strike of jute-mill workers, for instance, there were "times when we needed two interpreters to get information from the workers—the Lithuanians, who could speak Polish and therefore had to be interpreted and then the Polish back to English."[43] Very few league members knew Yiddish. Before 1909, only Rose Schneiderman spoke it fluently. Italian presented almost as great a problem. Some allies spoke the language, but they did not know the southern Italian dialects.

When the league did manage to interest women in organizing, it faced new difficulties. WTUL organizers discovered how powerless women were when they attempted to negotiate strike settlements. The organization's records suggest that it was unusual for the league to win a written contract. Oral agreements concerning wages, hours, and working conditions were more common. In addition, victories were frequently holding actions rather than improvements. If women struck to protest a wage cut, for example, usually the best the league could do was to compel the manufacturer to reinstate previous wage or piece rates. Manufacturers often agreed to improve sanitary conditions—to provide separate toilets for women and men, clean drinking water, and so on—but even in this area the best the league could win was minimum compliance with state laws. Union recognition was another demand that the WTUL could win only infrequently. In strikes of unskilled women, the league came to regard such a demand as "premature."[44] It was rare for a manufacturer to recognize the league-sponsored union as a permanent bargaining agent.

Few records of WTUL bargaining conferences are extant, but one report illustrates the weak settlements the league was able to make. In the first bargaining session, a manufacturer agreed to reinstate the strikers, abolish the fining system, and give the women time to wash before they left in the evening. In the second conference he flatly refused to reinstate the previous piece rates. "We discussed the whole situation," the strike committee reported, "and felt that it was the best we could do for an unorganized group in an unskilled trade . . . we put the whole matter before the strikers which was a 15% reduction instead of 35% which they accepted."[45]

The WTUL's organizing work was complicated further by the seasonal nature of much of the city's industry. The needle trades' busy season began in late September and peaked in April. Summer was the slack season. In some trades more than 60 percent of the work force was laid off. Worker unrest was correlated with seasonal fluctuations: most strikes took place in the late fall and early spring when jobs were plentiful, piece rates for new styles were set, and speedups and long hours were common. The league coordinated its organizing campaigns with the busy seasons. But the league organized on a shop-by-shop basis—a method unsuited to seasonal fluctuations and to the small size of most of New York's industrial establishments. The WTUL would painstakingly build a union during the busy season only to see it decline or collapse during the summer. Women lost interest, found work in other shops, or became discouraged when the union could not maintain good conditions or wages.[46]

The last stage of the league's organizing process, affiliation with an AFL union, also posed difficulties. When the league called upon unions for concrete assistance, the unions seldom complied. Jurisdictional disputes, rank-and-file hostility toward women, and the AFL's craft structure undermined the league's efforts. The indifference with which New York City's unions met league efforts was especially significant because the WTUL was so dependent on official labor movement policies in its early years. The league did not offer alternatives to traditional AFL-style unionism, but rather worked to integrate women into the existing structure. Early league members wanted to convince male unionists that they were not feminists intent upon elevating the interests of women above the solidarity of the working class. "We don't want people to think that . . . we think women can at all stand alone in organization or that they should be organized separate [sic] from the men where they work," one working-class member told the press.[47] Had the federation or its affiliates repaid the league with a commensurate amount of support, or had AFL unions manifested new concern for organizing women, the league's reliance on their policies would have been profitable. As it was, however, the WTUL's dependence on the federation and its identification with its goals, principles, and policies hampered its organizing work, stifled its creativity, and weakened its feminist commitment.

In its first years, the WTUL was optimistic about receiving local labor support and accepted unionists' suspicions as understandable.[48] Although a WTUL member often considered herself independent of her father's or husband's class, she understood that unionists were not likely to do so. "In the early days," one ally recalled, "many unionists . . . feared that it [the WTUL] would undertake to control or dominate the women's unions."[49]

The WTUL interpreted unionists' presence on its executive board as evidence of official encouragement and support. By the spring of 1904, every New York City union with women members was represented on the board: the International Ladies' Garment Workers' Union; the United Garment Workers; the Cigar Makers' International Union; the International Typographical Union; the Brotherhood of Bookbinders; the International Brotherhood of Electrical Workers; the Shirt, Waist, and Laundry Workers' International Union; and the United Hebrew Trades. Yet, as late as 1909, despite persistent proselytizing, only fourteen labor organizations—twelve unions and two wives' auxiliaries—had affiliated with the league. Most affiliates were weak organizations, such as the paper-box makers' union, whose trades included a majority of women and who commanded little influence in the labor movement. Only the International Ladies' Garment Workers' Union, itself an unstable organization in the first decade of the twentieth century, took a consistent interest in the league. Occasionally, small female locals of craft unions affiliated with the league. Women's locals of the cigar makers and the Typographical Union were represented on the executive board. Generally, however, the powerful craft unions remained aloof.

Because it considered itself a central body of women, one of the league's goals was to gain representation in the Central Federated Union of New York City and the Bronx and in the Brooklyn Central Labor Union. Although local leagues in Chicago, Kansas City, and St. Louis quickly won representation in their cities' central bodies, those groups in New York proved reluctant to offer the WTUL representation. Year after year, the CFU turned the league down on the grounds that it was an outside organization. "We tried to explain to them that we were not an outside body but belonged on the inside—[it] didn't seem to have much effect," Mary Dreier complained to her sister Margaret.[50] Finally, after extended appeals, the central bodies and the State Workingmen's Federation admitted two league delegates with voice and vote. The league also sent a fraternal delegate to the United Hebrew Trades. Enormously pleased, Mary Dreier reported that the CFU meetings were "very nice" and that she liked the president—"a jolly bartender with a lovely sense of humor"—very much.[51] But the New York league does not seem to have established any influence within the CFU or to have been consulted regularly about its activities. Instead, central bodies' acceptance of the league was always tenuous. In 1916, for instance, the CFU temporarily disfranchised the WTUL representatives.[52]

The league's dependence on AFL policies was most obvious in its insistence on craft organization. Despite their recognition that unskilled women had little bargaining power, WTUL members tried to form miniature "craft" unions. Craft organization was unsuited to the realities of most women's work and was an ineffective way to organize them. Unskilled workers in small craft unions were isolated and powerless. Even when the small unions affiliated with AFL internationals, this problem was still acute, for affiliation did not guarantee the support of skilled male workers' locals. It made little difference whether or not a union of buttonhole workers could claim affiliation with the ILGWU or the UGW if the skilled tailors and cutters who worked alongside the buttonhole workers did not include them in their contracts.

The league's work with the United Garment Workers illustrates these difficulties. In 1905, the WTUL formed a women's union of buttonhole workers and finishers that affiliated with the UGW. Local 102 began with about twenty-five members and never had a membership much over seventy-five. The WTUL was pleased with Local 102 and its possibilities for success. "In the fall I wondered if it would ever be possible to make that Local of young girls, untrained women, speaking different languages comprehend and carry out the purposes of their meetings," Helen Marot reported. "At this meeting the shop chairman made her report and the difficulties which arose were thoroughly thrashed out and settled impartially. It seemed to me thinking over the difficulties of starting a union of such workers that it would be nothing short of criminal to let it lapse."[53]

Yet it did lapse, for the United Garment Workers had no interest in sustaining or encouraging its growth. The union's label policy was one factor that seriously hindered the women's organization. The UGW issued the label to New York tailoring and vestmaking establishments without requiring that the women who worked in these shops be organized. The WTUL repeatedly requested that the union withdraw the label from factories that employed unorganized buttonhole workers and finishers, but the union, despite promises to the contrary, refused.

Rank-and-file hostility compounded the small union's difficulties. Throughout 1906 and 1907, representatives from male tailors' and vestmakers' locals promised the league that they would work to organize the women and incorporate them into their unions once the women's local was "strong." No such action was taken. Instead, men called strikes without consulting the local and without including its members in their settlements.[54]

What assistance the local received came from the league. When the UGW refused to withdraw its label from open shops, the league threatened to expose the union's dishonest label policy to the AFL and the public. When the UGW refused to hire an organizer, the league hired Clara Silver, a buttonhole maker, to organize for Local 102. Silver eventually found the difficulties overwhelming and resigned, and the UGW refused to hire a replacement. When, ultimately, another young woman was authorized to act as an organizer, the league paid her salary and assisted her in the day-to-day work.[55]

The summer of 1907 marked Local 102's last efforts. Members joined male vestmakers and tailors in two strikes. The vestmakers included the buttonhole makers in their settlement, but neither they nor the tailors helped build the local's membership. Thus, women in many shops had no knowledge of the union. The UGW leaders "showed little inclination to do anything," Helen Marot told the league, "but acknowledged the hopefulness of the situation. They offered plans of action which did not involve them and which were obviously worthless to the Local." In August, Marot confronted men from the Brotherhood of Tailors and the United Garment Workers' vestmakers' local about their refusal to organize the women. In a stormy meeting, the men admitted they thought that "the organization of the women would hurt the men" and denounced the women's local.[56]

Similarly, women's locals in the ILGWU had to work harder and longer to gain the union's assistance than did the men's locals. The white-goods workers, for example, had to survive on their own resources from 1909, when Local 62 was chartered, until 1912, before the international deemed the organization sufficiently stable to warrant hiring a male organizer, appointing a male president, and granting the union financial assistance.

Sometimes a union would refuse to broaden its jurisdiction to include unorganized women. This was a problem in the league's attempts to organize steam-laundry workers. A union called the Shirt, Waist, and Laundry Workers' International Union existed, and its president served on the WTUL's executive board. However, the union refused to organize women in steam laundries because it limited its jurisdiction to workers in factory laundries.[57]

Some AFL unions refused to admit women altogether. Early in the summer of 1909, for example, a cigar packers' strike provided an opportunity to organize the city's several hundred women packers. Mary Dreier and Helen Marot met with the two cigar packers' locals to urge them to include women. The men were firm in their opposition. The women, they maintained, "could only do poor sort of work . . . because women had no colour discrimination."[58] Marot concluded that they found "the same attitudes we find so often in New York locals—an attitude of resentment to women entering the trade and a want of confidence in their ability to organize." After several hours of argument, one of the two locals agreed to "form a committee" to consider the question of admitting women. There the matter ended. "Have heard nothing from them," the secretary reported several months later.[59]

The AFL position on union dues also posed difficulties. League unions had low dues, usually ten cents a week. However, many of the AFL unions charged dues and initiation fees that were impossibly expensive for a woman who earned a weekly wage of six or seven dollars. Even the ILGWU, which had low dues by federation standards, pressured locals in the women's trades to raise their dues and initiation fees. When the WTUL's white-goods workers' union affiliated with the ILGWU, for instance, the international insisted that it raise its weekly dues from ten to fifteen cents. League members supported the AFL policy of setting high dues and apparently expected women to pay whatever an AFL union required. They were justifiably critical of unions that charged women lower dues than men, for such a policy was coupled with fewer benefits for the women and resulted in innate inequality for female members. It was common practice, for instance, for women's strike benefits to be about 50 percent of men's. But high dues were one aspect of trade unionism that may have alienated women.[60]

Other aspects of male trade unions made integrating women into the AFL difficult. Such a seemingly simple matter as a meeting place was often a stumbling block. Male unions traditionally met in such exclusively masculine establishments as saloons, where they could combine union business with socializing. Women, however, were understandably reluctant to enter saloons or to meet late at night. Female workers sometimes expressed a preference for segregated organizations for these reasons. One spokeswoman for a UGW local recalled that her union had included men originally but that members were happier with a separate organization. "The reason why the women had to draw out from the men was because the men wanted to come late to the meetings and stay late while the women wanted to go early and come home early." This woman was expressing the notion that sex-segregated unions could follow the contours of a working woman's day and could take into account the probability that she had domestic responsibilities as well as outside work. On other occasions, women complained to the league that men monopolized their meetings or that they were afraid to express themselves in meetings with men.[61]

Despite these difficulties and discouragements, however, league members were intensely idealistic about the labor movement in their first years of work. They were elated whenever one of their shop unions affiliated with an AFL union. When the dressmakers affiliated with the ILGWU, for instance, Mary Dreier reported that they were "so proud . . . so happy to belong to a great organization—it gives them a sense of dignity not had before."[62] Overt discrimination and indifference did not immediately shake the league's faith in the labor movement or weaken its conviction that its rightful place was as a subordinate of the AFL. Nor did organized labor's disinterest encourage the league to take independent action. Instead, rebuffs seemed to strengthen the WTUL's resolve to win AFL approval. Members believed that constant effort, sincerity, and agitation would ultimately win women a place in the labor movement.

When league leaders were in doubt about a decision, they

consulted federation leaders to make sure their policies were acceptable. In 1907, for example, the league found itself in the middle of a jurisdictional dispute between the Progressive Rolled Cigarette Makers, an independent union with a predominantly female membership, and the Tobacco Workers, an AFL international. When the cigarette makers applied for WTUL affiliation, league leaders questioned them about their status as an independent union. The cigarette makers explained that they had wanted to affiliate with the cigar makers, but the cigar makers' union had rejected them because their piece-rate scale was too low. They did not want to affiliate with the tobacco workers because the ITW refused to grant their union a charter and would accept members only as individuals. High dues and initiation fees made this alternative untenable. The executive board told the union that it could not affiliate until the league had determined "whether or not they were antagonistic to the American Federation of Labor."[63] Samuel Gompers told the WTUL that the AFL considered the organization a dual union, an unofficial competitive organization not recognized by the federation. As a result of Gompers's ruling, the small union apparently was denied permission to affiliate with the league.[64]

This incident illustrates both the league's subservience to the AFL in its first years and the difficulties small women's unions faced at the turn of the century. By insisting that independent unions affiliate with the AFL, the league was sometimes asking women to act against their own interests. The cigarette makers had good reasons to avoid affiliating with the tobacco workers, reasons many small unions could have given. High dues and initiation fees and curtailment of local autonomy limited the advantages of affiliation. Internationals' discrimination against women provided an additional reason for women's organizations to avoid affiliation.

Why, if AFL unionism was so unsatisfactory, did the WTUL persist in its loyalty to AFL principles and policies? First, WTUL leaders seemed trapped by a desire to appear as respectable trade unionists in the eyes of federation leaders. Their acute awareness of their status as outsiders and their fear of being considered dual unionists or feminists who lacked working-class consciousness possibly prevented them from taking action. Only by its integrity and hard work, Helen Marot emphasized, had the league "secured the confidence of the official movement." Because the league was composed "of two groups of people, unionists and sympathizers [it] is in danger of creating a feeling that the latter look for strength to forces other than labor."[65] To have advocated separate women's unions or to have criticized the labor movement would have confirmed labor leaders' suspicions that the WTUL was merely a group of wealthy and meddlesome philanthropists.

WTUL members' idealism about labor unions may have been a factor also. "I wonder if it is true that I am the first of my class to be a fully accredited delegate in a federation of labor in this country," Margaret Dreier Robins wrote her sister Mary." It is my closest touch with the great human story and I am so happy about it that I could sit down and cry for the joy of it."[66] Like Margaret Dreier Robins, most league leaders came to the organization without previous work in or knowledge of the labor movement. Quite possibly, they did not have enough experience to find fault with the AFL or to envision alternatives to it.

Equally important in explaining the league's insistence on following AFL policies was the fact that there were no satisfactory alternatives the WTUL could have implemented. Theoretical alternatives to AFL craft unionism included independent women's unions, federal unions, and a separate female labor federation. In the early twentieth century, however, none was realistic.

The most obvious alternative to an integrationist policy would have been the formation of independent women's unions. Separate organizations might have offered women more possibilities for leadership roles and might have facilitated the WTUL ideal of feminist unionism in ways AFL unions did not. Certainly the league knew of and worked with successful women's unions. Organized women in the bookbinding and hat-trimming trades, for instance, belonged to sex-segregated locals. But the league rejected this alternative on ideological and economic grounds. To have pursued such a course would have been tantamount to dual unionism, and league leaders realized that there was no better way to alienate organized labor. Then, too, in its first years the league's dominant ideology was that class was more important than gender in determining women's treatment at work. Women such as Harriot Stanton Blatch who emphasized feminism over class consciousness were in a definite minority. A consideration of working women's economic situation was probably more important in explaining why the WTUL had no choice but to reject separate independent unions for women. Women bookbinders and hat trimmers were considerably more skilled and better paid than the average female industrial worker. Because women were unable to pay substantial dues, most women's unions were usually too poor to survive more than a season or two, let alone offer their members benefits or finance a strike. Because women were usually temporary, transient workers, turnover was rapid, making it difficult to build a stable membership. Because women were unskilled, such unions could not expect to meet with success in bargaining.

One possible solution to the problems of independent women's unions might have been a federation of female workers. Occasionally, league members talked about creating such a federation. The executive board discussed and rejected this alternative as early as 1906, and the idea came up frequently in league correspondence and meetings.[67] Rose Schneiderman advocated such a federation at the national WTUL convention in 1909. She explained that a federation could be open to all female workers who could not recruit a sufficient number of individuals in their own trades to form a viable organization. A federation could avoid the difficulties common to women's unions: its membership and treasury could be large enough to ensure stability. Schneiderman also suggested that a federation could offer benefits of particular interest to women. Because customary union benefits were rarely attractive to women who were not permanent workers, she proposed offering a marriage benefit in place of the standard union death benefit.[68] Schneiderman borrowed her ideas from the successful National Federation of Women Workers, which the British Women's Trade Union League had organized in 1906. The English federation was self-sustaining and open to any female worker.[69] The federation concept was also reminiscent of the Knights of Labor, which organized across occupational lines.

The New York league did not act to implement Schneiderman's proposal. Nor did the WTUL organize federal unions—a form of organization that women who organized independently sometimes adopted. A federal union included women from several unrelated trades. The AFL approved such a structure if none of the trades involved was covered by an affiliate's jurisdiction.

Instead, the league tried to mediate between women's needs and AFL policies in less radical ways. They stressed the importance of special benefits and attractions for women and urged unions to initiate such policies as marriage benefits. More important, they were aware of women's discomfort in the male atmosphere of trade-union meetings. One of the league's major goals was to buy a large house in a working-class district to serve as a center for women unionists from all trades. As Mary Dreier explained, "If we could get a building where all women unionists had quarters and meetings, [it would] give them a sense of solidarity they lack now. The girls have to meet in all sorts of horrid, really disgustingly dirty halls sometimes, and it would be a splendid thing if they had a decent meeting place—new unions would immediately get a sense of becoming part of a great movement."[70] In the spring of 1909, the league bought a large townhouse on East Twenty-Second Street, in the heart of the "uptown" clothing district. The league's new headquarters did serve as a kind of center for the city's women unionists and also, some years later, as the home of several of the city's woman suffrage organizations.

In its first years, however, the league did not explore alternatives for women's unions. In the early twentieth century, the AFL represented the only model for successful unionism, despite its severe limitations for female industrial workers. For the league, it was *the* labor movement, and the WTUL saw no alternative but to carry on its organizing campaigns within the AFL's framework.

Despite discouragements throughout these first years, the league continued to believe in its ability to organize large numbers of working women, integrate them into the labor movement, and teach them to be outspoken, militant unionists. As Helen Marot wrote Leonora O'Reilly in 1907, "We are looking forward to a revolution in New York among working women."[71] Two years later, the league would think that its hopes for such a revolution had been realized.

## CHAPTER 4

# Revolution in the Garment Trades, 1909–1913

"I have listened to all the speeches," a young girl cried in Yiddish to thousands of shirtwaist makers assembled in Cooper Union. "I am one who thinks and feels from the things they describe. I, too, have worked and suffered. I am tired of talking. I move that we go on general strike!" The waistmakers broke into applause as they carried Clara Lemlich's motion. By afternoon of the next day, 24 November 1909, more than twenty thousand waistmakers had walked out of five hundred Manhattan and Brooklyn shops.[1]

The shirtwaist strike heralded a revolution in the women's clothing industry and in the history of women's unionism. From late 1909 through 1913, nearly one hundred thousand New York City garment workers participated in a series of general strikes. Cloakmakers, white-goods workers, children's dressmakers, and wrapper and kimono workers struck for standardized conditions, higher wages, and union recognition. The strikes laid the foundation for widespread unionization of New York's garment workers. Women's Trade Union League members were elated by the shirtwaist strike, for it was spectacular proof that five years of work on the East Side had produced results: women could strike and could be committed unionists.

The waistmakers' strike was the climax to a year of unrest in the waist trade. Throughout 1909, walkouts in the large waist factories around Washington Square were common. It is not surprising that waistmakers were discontented, for in some ways that industry combined the worst of the sweatshop and the modern factory. The trade was mechanized and dominated by large inside shops. Workers were subjected to strict work discipline: fines for lateness and sewing errors were common. At the same time, large manufacturers relied upon a subcontracting system[2] that was reminiscent of the sweatshop, and workers had to purchase their own needles and thread. Such practices were particularly onerous in light of declining wages, for piece rates had fallen steadily since the 1907–1908 depression, despite the fact that the industry was prosperous by 1909. An experienced sewing machine operator could earn twelve or thirteen dollars a week early in 1908; late in 1909 she was lucky to make nine or ten.[3]

During the summer of 1909 women came to the WTUL for help in disputes with three of the largest waist companies. In July, sewing machine operators, cutters, finishers, and pressers struck the Rosen Company, demanding a 20 percent pay increase and union recognition. Within a month, the management capitulated and granted the workers' demands. News of the successful strike spread throughout the trade, and workers began to flock to ILGWU Local No. 25, the waistmakers' union. In early September, workers in the Leiserson shop walked out. A few weeks later, the Triangle Shirtwaist Company, in an attempt to break the union, locked out its workers and fired those who belonged to Local 25. The remaining workers struck in protest. These strikes were unusual, since garment workers rarely struck during the summer slack season, when unemployment was high and work scarce. Then, too, the strike cut across occupational lines. In an extraordinary display of unity, cutters, pressers, operators, and finishers walked out together. Even some subcontractors took part.

As the Leiserson and Triangle strikes dragged on into late fall, violence on the picket lines became increasingly commonplace. Manufacturers hired thugs who insulted and beat young women pickets, and police made frequent arrests. As the violence intensified, the waistmakers' union turned to the WTUL for help. League members joined strikers on the picket lines, formed picket observation teams, and tried to prevent arrests. The assaults and arrests continued unabated, however. Several hundred women, including Mary Dreier and other league pickets, were arrested during the fall.

The publicity given the strikes generated interest in the union. Before August 1909, Local 25 had fewer than one hundred members. By October its membership surpassed one thousand. Encouraged by this upsurge in interest, Local 25's leaders began to consider a general strike. The Russian Jewish socialists who headed the local shared their deliberations with the WTUL, since any effort would need the league's financial backing. The two organizations rented Cooper Union for the night of 23 November to present the proposal to the rank and file.

As late as the evening of the Cooper Union meeting, neither the union nor the WTUL was sure about what action to take. On the speakers' platform, Mary Dreier, Meyer London, Samuel Gompers, and representatives from Local 25 equivocated and urged caution. It remained for Clara Lemlich, a young striker from the Leiserson shop, to articulate the sentiments of the thousands of waistmakers who jammed the auditorium and overflowed into the streets outside. As the cheering that greeted her proposal for an immediate general strike subsided, the chairman of the meeting cried, "Do you mean faith? Will you take the old Jewish oath?" and the waistmakers intoned, "If I turn traitor to the cause I now pledge, may this hand wither from the arm I now raise."[4]

The next morning, waistmakers in shop after shop walked out. One young woman remembered the event as it happened in her factory:

> I did not know how many workers in my shop had taken the oath at that meeting. I could not tell how many would go on strike in our factory the next day. When we came back the next morning to the factory, though, no one went to the dressing-room. We all sat at the machines with our hats and coats beside us, ready to leave. . . . And there was whispering and talking softly all around the room among the machines: "Shall we wait like this?" "There is a general strike" "Who will get up first?" . . . Well, so we stayed whispering and no one knowing what the other would do, not making up our minds for two hours. Then I started to get up. And at just the same minute all—we all got up together, in a second. No one after the other, no one before. And when I saw it—that time—oh, it excites me so yet I can hardly talk about it. . . . We hardly knew where to go—what to do next. But one of the American girls who knew how to telephone, called up the Women's Trade Union League and they told us to come to a big hall a few blocks away. After we were there, we wrote out on paper what terms we wanted: not any night work, except as it would be arranged for some special need for it in the trade; and shorter hours, and to have wages arbitrated by a committee to arbitrate the price for everyone fairly; and to have better treatment from the bosses.[5]

The union and the WTUL had underestimated the extent of discontent among shirtwaist makers, and they were stunned by the turnout. At most they had expected four or five thousand Jewish workers to strike. Instead, close to thirty thousand waistmakers walked out. Although four-fifths of the strikers were Jewish, several thousand Italian and native-born American women participated as well.[6]

For eleven weeks, waistmakers fought for a fifty-two-hour week, piece-rate increases and an equitable, standard means for determining wage and piece rates, the abolition of subcontracting, and the elimination of charges and fines. The waistmakers also demanded union recognition and a union shop. Although most small manufacturers and contractors settled with the union and granted workers improved conditions and higher wages, the large manufacturers never settled with Local 25. Despite its failure to win a union shop, however, the shirtwaist strike was a turning point in the history of women's unionism: it was the first major women's strike. The uprising was also unique in the history of American labor to the extent that it captured the sympathy and support of women from every class background.

The strike's first days were chaotic. Neither the ILGWU nor the league was prepared for the administrative difficulties the uprising posed. The union negotiated contracts on a shop-by-shop basis: workers in each shop determined wages and piece rates, and employers settled individually with the union. By 27 November, more than one hundred manufacturers had agreed to their workers' demands and ten thousand waistmakers were back at work. Because many small manufacturers settled quickly, the WTUL and Local 25 were optimistic that the strike would be short. But the employers who settled in the first few days were small contractors who could not afford a protracted stoppage in the middle of the trade's busy season. The major battle was fought with the owners of the large inside shops. These employers formed the Manufacturers' Association, which included nearly a third of the city's waist manufacturers. By the first week of December, the strike was stalemated. Although small-shop owners continued to settle with the union and to reinstate their workers with union conditions, the large manufacturers hired strikebreakers and resisted a settlement.

Throughout December, despite the unusually bitter cold, strikers continued to picket and to negotiate. By 20 December, the strike had spread to Philadelphia. But as time went on and neither strikers nor manufacturers weakened, violence escalated. Day after day, women were assaulted on the picket lines as police stood by. Police arrested more than seven hundred strikers for talking to strikebreakers, for loitering, and for disorderly conduct. By mid-December, magistrates were sentencing convicted women to the Blackwell's Island workhouse.

Police brutality and judicial discrimination horrified WTUL members. From the beginning of the strike the league circulated copies of a handbill entitled "Rules for Pickets" that detailed pickets' legal rights and cautioned them to maintain order and decorum. The WTUL also recruited seventy-five volunteer pickets and watchers who acted as court witnesses. League members assembled a legal staff and posted bail for arrested strikers. To protest the harsh treatment that the women were receiving at the hands of the police, the WTUL also organized marches and rallies. Early in December some ten thousand strikers, many carrying banners reading "Peaceful picketing is the right of every woman," marched to City Hall, where they petitioned Mayor George McClellan to have the police commissioner keep his men under closer surveillance.

Throughout December the WTUL used the strike to educate the public about working women's conditions and their need for unions. Members made special efforts to enlist women's support by speaking to club women, college students, and suffragists. They described the callousness of police magistrates who sentenced young women to several weeks of hard labor in the workhouse for offenses as minor as yelling *scab* at strikebreakers. Under league auspices, young strikers spoke at clubs and women's colleges about their working conditions. League members couched their appeals to upper-class women in the language of sisterhood. They stressed that women should demonstrate their solidarity with the strikers by joining their working-class sisters on picket lines and by boycotting non-union waists. "Now is the time for women in New York, Philadelphia, and in fact everywhere American shirtwaists are worn, to rise in their might and demonstrate that with them bargain-hunting can be subordinated to principle and that they have said goodbye to the products of the sweatshop. . . . Friends, let us stop talking about sisterhood, and MAKE SISTERHOOD A FACT!"[7] The league's publicity and fund-raising efforts elicited unprecedented support from leisure-class women. The WTUL received more than twenty thousand dollars from club women, and scores of Vassar, Bryn Mawr, Barnard, and Wellesley students served as volunteer pickets.

Anne Morgan, J. P. Morgan's daughter, was one stirred by league members' descriptions of East Side working and living conditions. Mary Dreier persuaded her to appear on a waistmakers' picket line and to underwrite the WTUL's publicity work. Immediately, she was elected to the executive board. Alva Belmont, widow of financier Oliver Belmont and president of a militant city suffrage organization, the Political Equality League, also took part in the strike and was named to the WTUL's executive board. As a suffragist, Belmont regarded the strike as a women's struggle rather than as a labor uprising and worked to link the suffrage cause with the strike. At a highly publicized appearance at the Jefferson Market Courthouse, she stressed women's need for the ballot. "During those six hours I spent in that police court I saw enough to convince me and all who were with me beyond the smallest doubt of the absolute necessity of woman suffrage . . . and the direct influence of women over judges, jury, and policemen."[8] Belmont arranged weekly suffragist motorcades through East Side neighborhoods and sponsored a mass "women's rally" at the Hippodrome Theatre with leading suffragists and trade unionists as speakers.

The participation of prominent suffragists and society women divided the WTUL's membership. For some members, inviting Anne Morgan and Alva Belmont to sit on the executive board was consistent with the league's commitment to a cross-class alliance, and they argued that the strike was a magnificent demonstration of sisterhood. Helen Marot, who usually took a hard line on workers' self-determination, commented that if upper-class women had been moved to participate in the strike from "sensational or personal motives, they were disarmed when they came into contact with the strikers." The strike, she said, broke down all class barriers.[9] Then, too, practical considerations played a role. Local 25 had only four dollars in its treasury when the strike began, and the waistmakers received little financial support from the labor movement. The league counted on wealthy women's sense of sisterhood to finance the strike. In addition, Morgan's and Belmont's presence on picket lines and in the night court made the strike front-page news not only in East Side papers but in the *New York Times* as well.

Others disagreed. Leonora O'Reilly was one of those distressed by society women's participation in league activities during the strike, stating that members no longer felt free to voice their own opinions but felt bound to agree with women who donated money.[10] Socialist members were especially vocal in criticizing the league's alliance with wealthy suffragists as "dangerous and futile." They also complained that their daily picketing, fund-raising, and organizing efforts were ignored while Belmont's and Morgan's token efforts were highly touted. "There has perhaps never been a more humiliating position in the history of the labor movement than that occupied by Socialist women in the shirtwaist makers strike," Theresa Malkiel declared. "So long as they did the work of the black man 'Friday' they were tolerated and permitted to go on; but no sooner did they attempt to do anything that would count officially than they were put in the background."[11]

The "magnificent demonstration of sisterhood" lasted through most of December. But events in the strike soon caused outsiders' interest to wane. In mid-December, after most nonassociation shops had settled with Local 25, the Manufacturers' Association agreed to negotiate. In a contract presented to the strikers, the association agreed to a fifty-two-hour week, piece-rate increases, the abolition of fines, and the improvement of sanitary conditions. The association, however, refused to recognize the union.

The strikers rejected this open-shop settlement. Their decision to continue the strike alienated many supporters. The Consumers' League, many suffragists and settlement workers, and upper-class women who had based their support of the strike on a romantic conception of sisterhood abruptly lost interest. Anne Morgan, for example, resigned from the league as quickly as she had joined, denouncing it as "a socialist organization."[12]

Throughout January and February the strike was deadlocked on the issue of union recognition. Although some Manufacturing Association members settled independently, the most powerful companies refused to grant the union's demands. In mid-February, Local 25 declared the strike ended. More than 150 large firms had not settled.

Despite the strike's less than satisfactory end, it was the New York league's finest hour. It was spectacular proof that women were capable of expressing discontent forcefully and collectively. What was more, women could organize as well as strike. The waistmakers' union was the largest ILGWU local, with nearly twenty thousand members, 80 percent of whom were women.[13] The league's strike activities also helped attract more working women to the organization. The composition of league committees reflected the increase of workers. In the years before 1909, trade committees were headed by allies; by 1910, all were chaired by working women. Although allies still outnumbered working-class members, more than two hundred workers belonged to the WTUL. Finally, the shirtwaist strike seemed to herald the New York league's acceptance by the labor movement. Local 25 solicited the WTUL's assistance and advice in formulating strategy and settlements. As a guarantee of future cooperation, the union elected Rose Schneiderman to its executive board. When Leonora O'Reilly attended the New York State Federation of Labor convention in the summer of 1910, she noted that the delegates greeted her warmly and were very interested in the league's work.

This new acceptance and a $10,000 gift from Carola Woerishoffer to establish a permanent league strike council gave the league confidence. The executive board set definite guidelines for WTUL policy during future strikes. Any union that wanted the league's assistance was to permit two WTUL representatives on its strike committee. The new guidelines marked a departure from the league's customary policy of unquestioningly acceding to unions' requests for help. The executive board made it clear that the WTUL intended to take a more active role in labor affairs and demand a more vocal role in policies that affected women. As Helen Marot stated, the New York league would no longer be "the kind sister" in the trade union world.[14]

The future seemed bright early in 1910. Within months, however, WTUL members were disillusioned with the labor movement and disappointed with the progress of unionization among the city's women workers. The organization's relationship with the ILGWU, in particular, rapidly deteriorated. When the shirtwaist strike ended, the ILGWU and the league could point to definite gains. Women who had worked sixty or more hours a week now had a guaranteed workweek of fifty-two hours. Piece rates had increased by 20 percent. Workers no longer had to pay for power or materials. Some manufacturers had agreed to abolish subcontracting. But the waistmakers' contracts were weak. Because manufacturers made individual settlements and because each shop determined its own piece-rate scales, conditions and grievance procedures were not standardized. Women were soon coming to the league to report violations, and shop strikes again became common.

The waistmakers' difficulties contrasted sharply with the success of the cloakmakers' strike in the summer of 1910. Unlike Local 25's leaders, the cloakmakers' officers planned their strike carefully, had adequate funds, and enjoyed the international's full support. After a ten-week walkout, the cloakmakers and the Cloak Manufacturers' Association negotiated a comprehensive settlement, the Protocol of Peace. The protocol, which was to become a model for garment-union settlements, was a uniform agreement for the entire cloak industry. It provided for improved conditions, standardized wage and piece rates, and a "preferential shop" clause that required manufacturers to hire union members in preference to unorganized workers. The protocol also established an industry-wide grievance procedure and a permanent enforcement committee, the Joint Board of Sanitary Control. The settlement had important implications for unskilled women, for the agreement covered wages and conditions for every worker in the trade, from skilled tailors to finishers.[15]

The league played a peripheral role in the cloakmakers'

strike, in part because women made up only a small percentage of workers in that trade, but also because the union, considerably stronger than the waistmakers union, had less need for the league's assistance. Members, however, were excited about the settlement.

The comparison between the cloakmakers and the waistmakers was especially acute in the last months of 1910, when the waistmakers began to negotiate new shop agreements. Too weak to renew its contracts alone, Local 25 asked representatives from the WTUL, the *Jewish Daily Forward*, the Central Federated Union, and the United Hebrew Trades to help. The waistmakers had lost ground in the year following the strike. Almost half of the manufacturers who had settled with the union in 1909 had gone out of business or moved out of the city. Of the 200 shops that remained, the union could only renew agreements with 164. Most Manufacturers' Association shops remained unorganized. Union membership had dropped from nearly 20,000 to about 7,000.[16]

One of the largest nonunion firms was the Triangle Shirtwaist Company, located in an overcrowded loft building near Washington Square. On a late March afternoon in 1911, a few months after Local 25 renegotiated its contracts, a cigarette dropped into a remnant drawer ignited one of the large workrooms. Piles of shirtwaists and floors strewn with remnants fed the flames as the fire spread rapidly to the wooden staircase and to workrooms on other floors. Some workers on the top floor managed to hoist themselves through the skylight and climb across the roof to an adjoining building. Others reached the elevator or the narrow stairs before fire consumed the hallways. Many workers on the top floors had no choice but to jump to the Washington Place pavement. Girl after girl flung herself from the high workroom windows to the sidewalk eight or nine stories below, despite the uselessness of the fire department's nets and the crowd's shouts not to jump. What the horrified spectators did not know was that there was no other escape from some of the workrooms: the doors were locked from the outside. By early evening, 146 Triangle workers were dead.[17]

The Triangle fire demoralized the New York league, for the tragedy dramatized how little progress had been made in improving working women's conditions. Rose Schneiderman's impassioned speech at the Metropolitan Opera House a few days after the fire best expressed the outrage of the league and the city's workers. "This is not the first time girls have been burned alive in the city," she told the audience of mourners.

"Every week I must learn of the untimely death of one of my sister workers. Every year thousands of us are maimed. The life of men and women is so cheap and property is so sacred."[18]

Events in the months after the fire only deepened the league's frustration. A few days after the fire the Triangle Shirtwaist Company was open for business as usual, having quickly transferred its operations to another location. Several months later, a jury acquitted Max Harris and Isaac Blanck, the manufacturers, of manslaughter charges, despite testimony from more than one hundred witnesses about the crowded conditions and locked workroom doors.[19]

In the spring of 1911, after the fire and the disappointing contracts, the waistmakers' union began to agitate for a second general strike to recoup its losses and win a protocol agreement. The WTUL strongly opposed this plan for in the time since the 1909 uprising league leaders had become disillusioned with the tactic. While conceding that a strike was effective in mobilizing large numbers of women, members had doubts that any real gains followed. Then, too, league members thought that Local 25's leaders were incompetent. "It is becoming clear to the League," Helen Marot wrote in 1911, "that it is a betrayal of the faith and fine spirit of the girls to encourage them to organize into trade unions if their union is to be dominated by men without business sense or executive ability and by men competent [sic] to talk but not to act."[20] Part of the league's disillusionment with the union's leaders stemmed from the men's refusal to abide by the orderly, businesslike methods of the AFL. The leaders of the waistmakers' union were radical socialists, far more idealistic than AFL functionaries and constantly at odds with a more conservative "bread-and-butter" faction within the ILGWU. The league aligned itself with the conservatives, led by John Dyche, because that group was committed to AFL-style organization. Local 25's problems, Marot stressed, were due to its leaders' "inability to grasp the fact that their employers who are business men must be fought not with fine phrases or idealistic sentiments but with business methods."[21] What was more, the Russian Jewish socialists who managed Local 25 and the other ILGWU locals in the women's trades thought little of women's ability to participate in union activities—a fact that angered WTUL women. "These men get me so mad," Mary Dreier wrote, "they treat us like two cents."[22] Over 80 percent of the waistmakers' rank and file was female, but men were the unchallenged leaders. No women held positions of power within the union hierarchy. This "want of confidence in the women," according to Marot, also contributed to the union's weakness.[23] The general strike tactic reinforced and perpetuated women's inferiority, for although women were in the forefront, they had no opportunities to learn about organizing or managing a union. In light of this situation, the league began to reexamine its policies. Members argued that it meant little to organize large numbers of women if they had no more power in their unions than they did in their shops.

Throughout the spring and summer of 1911, as agitation for a second general strike increased, members disagreed over how to deal with Local 25. One faction, led by Helen Marot and Mary Dreier, wanted the league to urge rank-and-file union members to vote for the conservative wing of the union's leadership in the upcoming elections. Other WTUL leaders were appalled by this plan. "They are concerned we are butting in," Mary Dreier wrote Margaret Robins,

> but the union [is] about to go to pieces. . . . Leonora, Rose, even Linda cry out in holy horror that the League is usurping authority and seem to think it is wiser to let the whole thing go to smash rather than go one step beyond the prescribed distance. . . . [It] seems so terrible when there are 7,000 girls that we should hold back in going to the limit to help them even if it would mean that the labor men on the East Side particularly would resent our interference.[24]

When the executive board rejected this proposal, Marot took matters into her own hands. In a letter to the *Jewish Daily Forward* she detailed the inadequacies of Local 25's radical socialist leaders, warned members against a second general strike, and urged them to vote for the conservative faction in the coming election. A "misgoverned, badly managed union," she concluded, "is worse than no union."[25] The executive board of the WTUL censured Marot, stating that public criticism of a union was not in keeping with the league's role. But the damage was done, and when the radical officers were elected, the rift between the waistmakers' union and the league widened.

Although many members did not like Marot's tactics, they agreed with her about the inadvisability of a general strike. When Local 25 called a second strike in October 1911, the league refused its endorsement. The organization provided legal assistance, and members served as volunteer pickets; but members did not provide substantial aid, even though they realized that their refusal to support a union was a drastic departure from customary policies. "Up to the present time," Marot wrote, "the League has always cooperated with the unions to the full in accordance with the plans the union has mapped out." She recommended, however, that the WTUL break relations with East Side unions. "It is the stand which we must continue in regard to the methods followed by the East Side unions. . . . As the Jewish working women are greater numerically than any other nationality it will be necessary for us if we are to make them understand our refusal to accept their methods to show them what our methods are . . . [and] show absolute results in organization."[26] Following Marot's advice, the WTUL launched a concerted shop-by-shop organizing campaign among American-born workers in the uptown waist shops.

During the same months the league was trying to avert a second waistmakers' strike, small unions in other women's trades began to agitate for general strikes as a way to organize many workers and win standardized agreements. Wrapper and kimono workers (ILGWU Local No. 41), children's dressmakers (ILGWU Local No. 50), and white-goods workers (ILGWU Local No. 62) made repeated requests to the international for permission to call general strikes. The international, unwilling to risk large sums of money on trades composed predominantly of unskilled women, and preoccupied with the struggle to maintain the cloakmakers' protocol, refused to endorse general strikes or to pay for organizers.[27]

The white-goods union turned to the WTUL for support after the international rejected its requests. As the league's East Side organizer, Rose Schneiderman spent much of her time with the local. Throughout 1911 and 1912, she petitioned the league to fund an organizer and support a general strike. The union, she pointed out, had about two hundred members and had won improved conditions. But these gains were precarious: the isolated union shops could not even win written contracts. In such an industry, Schneiderman argued, only a general strike could help the union obtain the members and the treasury it needed to enforce union-scale wages and conditions. She also stressed that the women themselves, impressed by the general strikes in the waist and cloak trades and frightened by the Triangle fire, were agitating for a general strike.[28]

The league paid Schneiderman to devote herself exclusively to organizing white-goods workers but refused to endorse a general strike. Rather, she was told to conduct a shop-by-shop drive. That way, women could be instructed in trade-union principles and have the opportunity to participate in union affairs. As Helen Marot declared, "the business of the League

. . . [is] to bring women into places of responsibility in the organization of the trade." In a general strike, men dominated and women had "no place and power and . . . mostly no voice."[29]

Late in 1912, the international authorized a general strike in the white-goods industry and appointed male officers and a male organizer for Local 62. The league supported this strike call grudgingly. "The New York League has held off this strike for over a year," one executive board member wrote to the national WTUL headquarters, "but now feel that it is inevitable."[30] On 6 January 1913, about seven thousand white-goods workers—approximately half the work force—answered the strike call. In the five weeks the walkout lasted, Local 62 and the WTUL succeeded in enrolling nearly five thousand women into the union. But the white-goods uprising did not touch the public conscience in the same way that the shirtwaist strike had done. The league concluded that it could not summon much enthusiasm from its general membership. It donated only one thousand dollars to the strike fund and raised only six thousand in contributions—far below the response that greeted the waistmakers' cause.[31] Throughout the strike, WTUL members complained that the union constantly interfered with their work. The league held itself aloof from Local 62's leaders. In the waistmakers' strike, WTUL members had been proud to serve as secretaries to union officers. By 1913, they had become more independent.

When the strike ended in February 1913, the white-goods workers had won their own protocol. The contract specified a fifty-hour workweek, the abolition of payment for power and thread, a 10 percent piece-rate increase, and an industry-wide minimum wage of five dollars a week. More important, the white-goods workers won a preferential shop.

The general strike era ended with the 1913 uprising of the white-goods workers. When the Women's Trade Union League looked back over the period from late 1909 to early 1913, its members could see that trade unionism had made definite and impressive gains. Workers in the waist industry—80 percent of whom were women—won a modified protocol agreement in 1913, as did wrapper and kimono makers and children's dressmakers. When compared to the situation of women in the clothing trades before the general strikes, these improvements in the women's trades were dramatic. The increase in female union membership was also extraordinary. In September 1909, about 3,000 women belonged to garment unions. A year later,

16,716 women were members. By September 1913, New York State trade union returns listed 63,872 women as members of New York City needle trades' unions.[32]

But the league could not ignore the fact that improvements and dramatic membership gains were limited to the garment industry. In September 1913, nearly 72,000 women belonged to the city's labor unions. More than 63,000 belonged to unions in garments and textiles. Of the 9,000 others, more than 2,000 belonged to tobacco unions—a figure that had remained stable since the turn of the century. Nearly 3,000 were members of printing and bookbinding unions, also a stable figure. Three thousand women belonged to musicians' and theatrical unions. The remaining women were scattered in small, isolated organizations in marginal industries such as paper-box making and in service occupations.[33] Thus, the state of organization in the city's marginal industries remained much the same as it had been ten years earlier. The experiences of WTUL women with unskilled artificial-flower-and-feather workers, boxmakers, human-hair workers, leather-goods workers, candy makers, and laundresses during these years deepened their growing disenchantment with unionization as the best way to ameliorate women's working conditions. Women's strikes in these industries failed between 1910 and 1913, and working conditions remained unchanged.

The 1912 laundry workers' strike was an especially discouraging experience for the WTUL. On 2 January 1912, three organizations of workers in steam and hand laundries called a general strike. Six hundred workers, 450 of whom were women, walked out of eighteen establishments. Although nearly 4,000 people worked in these laundries and although additional hundreds of establishments were unaffected by the strike, the walkout was spectacular in comparison to previous activity among laundry workers. The strikers, influenced by the success of the general strikes in the garment trades, demanded a fifty-four-hour week, a wage scale that guaranteed all workers at least six dollars a week, safety guards on machinery, and union recognition.[34]

The WTUL enthusiastically supported this strike. Members collected enough money from sympathizers and unions to pay a few dollars a week in strike benefits and gave the strike wide publicity. In addition, the State Board of Mediation and Arbitration held four days of open hearings on the reasons for the walkout. The board concluded that intolerable conditions and low wages had brought about the strike and ended its report by recommending that employers grant workers' demands and recognize the union. Despite these efforts, the strike failed. When it ended on 31 January 1912, only six establishments recognized the union and agreed to pay higher wages. The other laundries simply replaced the unskilled women.[35]

During the same years that WTUL relations with the ILGWU were deteriorating, other developments prompted members to reevaluate their organization's relationship with the American Federation of Labor. Gradually, league leaders' idealism and naiveté about the AFL gave way to the realization that their organization's identification with the federation saddled them with methods and an ideology that were inappropriate for unskilled immigrant women.

In part, the disenchantment of league members resulted from their failure to win the approval and support of male union leaders. Despite the league's efforts to please the AFL, individuals important in the federation and its affiliates often attacked the league for being a socialist organization or a group of philanthropic dilettantes. Samuel Gompers, for example, stated that because so many league leaders were upper-class outsiders, they were more susceptible to socialist ideas.[36] When Melinda Scott went to Philadelphia to help start a local league there, the president of that city's central labor union stated that the league was "a suffrage organization, a socialist organization, and that in some instances . . . had organized unions who were seceded to the boni-fide [sic] trade unions.[37] Occasionally federation organizers warned women to stay away from the league, calling it a "political organization."[38]

The most sustained attack on the New York league occurred early in 1910 and was led by Eva McDonald Valesh, an *American Federationist* editor and a friend of Gompers. Valesh came to New York to assist the WTUL during the 1909 shirtwaist strike. League leaders, knowing that Valesh was respected in federation circles, immediately granted her membership. When the waistmakers voted against the open-shop settlement late in December 1909, Valesh criticized the league for supporting the strikers' decision and claimed that the WTUL was "full of socialism, masked by its perfunctory interest in the strikers."[39] Gompers wrote Mary Dreier that he "deplored" Valesh's attack, but he made no public move to contradict her.

Such attacks, combined with the AFL's continuing indifference to the needs of working women, help explain league

members' change in attitude toward the AFL. Among themselves, league members lamented the insensitivity of AFL
leaders. "It is just as well I have no illusions regarding the men,"
Margaret Robins confided to her sister Mary.[40] Melinda Scott
expressed herself more bluntly. The federation, she told Leonora O'Reilly, "is a bag of wind."[41] By the end of the period of
general strikes from 1909 through 1913, members were criticizing the labor movement openly. Melinda Scott, for instance,
rebutted labor leaders' criticism of the league. She acknowledged that many WTUL women were suffragists but declared
that it was male unionists' attitudes that "made suffragists out
of thinking women. . . . One of the things that made some of us
attached to the Women's Trade Union League was because of
the fact that we had to fight every inch of the ground we had
gone for recognition."[42]

Two monumental labor struggles—the 1910 strike of men's
clothing workers in Chicago and the 1912 uprising of textile
operatives in Lawrence, Massachusetts—were particularly important for opening league members' eyes to AFL limitations.
Although the New York branch was not directly involved in
either struggle, the way in which the strikes were conducted
and the controversies they generated in the Chicago, Boston,
and national leagues affected the New York WTUL as well.

The Chicago garment workers' strike began late in September 1910 when several thousand young women walked off their
jobs to protest inhumane treatment and wage cuts. By early
October, more than forty thousand workers—the great majority of them Jewish, Italian, and Slavic immigrants—had joined
the strikers. Although the United Garment Workers, which
assumed leadership of the strike in late September, called the
walkout against all nonunion shops, the uprising was princi-
pally directed against the firm of Hart, Schaffner, and Marx.
That firm, with forty-eight factories and nearly ten thousand
employees, had established a near monopoly of the Chicago
trade. By mid-January, thanks in good measure to the interces-
sion of city government officials and social reform organizations and the work of Margaret Dreier Robins and the Chicago
league, the firm of Hart, Schaffner, and Marx was ready to
negotiate. The company entered into an agreement with its
workers that recognized their right to unionize and that
established a grievance procedure and an arbitration board.
Other nonunion employers, however, refused to follow the
Hart, Schaffner, and Marx example, and the strike dragged on

through the month of January. By February, the United Garment Workers' Union, unwilling to commit itself further to a strike of unskilled immigrant workers, suddenly announced that the strike was at an end. Tens of thousands of strikers were forced to go back to open shops; many lost their jobs.

The Chicago Women's Trade Union League had played a central role in conducting the strike and was pleased by the Hart, Schaffner, and Marx agreement. The league was strongly critical of the UGW's handling of the struggle, however. The UGW officers were trying to break the strike, Margaret Dreier Robins complained to Mary Dreier in the early days of the uprising. The callous and unilateral fashion in which the UGW ended the strike, without consulting the Chicago WTUL, the Chicago Federation of Labor, or the strikers themselves, appalled WTUL members, who publicly criticized the union's decision.[43]

Even before the Chicago strike, the New York league had become thoroughly exasperated with the UGW. The union's hostility toward the buttonhole makers and finishers, its repeated refusals to organize women, and its dishonest label policy still rankled. "The Garment Workers you know are against us," Mary Dreier wrote to her sister Margaret, "and have been every time we organized a union and turned it over to them, they have let it slump and go to pieces, this has been their regular policy."[44] After the league criticized the UGW's handling of the Chicago strike, relations between the two organizations deteriorated further. In New York, local UGW leaders refused to deal with the WTUL. One woman finisher reported to the executive board that the union had offered her a position as an organizer only on the condition that she not work with the league.[45]

In the winter of 1912–1913, relations were strained even further. During a large strike of New York tailors, UGW leaders behaved in a way very similar to the way they had behaved during the Chicago uprising three years earlier. When the strikers rejected a proposed settlement, UGW president Benjamin Larger unilaterally accepted an arbitration proposal and called the strike to a halt. Although the WTUL, occupied with the general strikes in the women's garment trades, played no role in the tailors' strike, league leaders sympathized with the position of the immigrant workers. Long aware of UGW corruption and of the union's hostility to urban immigrant workers, the WTUL threw its support behind the group of unionists who had broken away from the UGW to form the Amalgamated Clothing

Workers of America, despite the AFL's ruling that the Amalgamated was a dual union.

The 1912 textile strike in Lawrence, Massachusetts, was equally important for forcing league members to confront AFL limitations. Because the Industrial Workers of the World assumed leadership early in the strike, the president of AFL's United Textile Workers, John Golden, counseled the Boston league to stay out of Lawrence. The WTUL complied. Within two weeks after the strike began, however, Boston league members realized that it was a "magnificent uprising of oppressed, unskilled foreign workers. Our strike committee had many members who did not endorse IWW principles but were enthusiastic [about the] strikers."[46] In response to the Boston league's petitions, Golden permitted the league to open a relief center. Members collected funds and distributed food and clothing while the United Textile Workers tried to bring about a quick settlement. Once Golden had negotiated a settlement that was accepted by a small minority of skilled men newly organized into UTW craft unions, he declared the strike over and ordered the league to refuse relief to anyone who remained out. Although most members did not agree with Golden's tactics, the league officially withdrew.

The WTUL's acquiescence in the heavyhanded manner by which the UTW leadership tried to coerce Lawrence strikers into accepting an unsatisfactory settlement created a major controversy within the organization. The Boston league's president, Sue Ainslie Clark, summarized the conflict:

> Certain members of the Boston League believe that its course was the only one open to it since it was affiliated with AFL and aimed to propagate the principles of craft unionism endorsed by that organization. Certain others believe that we might have cooperated with the Strike Committee from the first, as individuals, though they realize the restraints imposed by the AFL affiliation. Still others think that our part has been a disgraceful one in this great struggle. Others regard the success of the Lawrence strike, through IWW methods, as an object lesson by which the League—and the AFL—must profit in order to play a vital part in the rapidly moving evolution of the labor movement today.[47]

Clark went on to state her own opinion. "To me, many of those in power in the American labor movement today seem to be selfish, reactionary, and remote from the struggle for bread and liberty of the unskilled workers. Are we, the Women's Trade Union League, to ally ourselves with the 'stand-patters' of the

Labor Movement or are we to hold ourselves ready to aid the insurgents—those who are freely fighting the fight of the exploited, the oppressed, and the weak among the workers?"[48]

New York members were outraged by the UTW's actions, declaring that Golden and the UTW were "scabbing on the workers."[49] Many members perceived the contradictions inherent in the Lawrence situation and were able to make the transition between the Lawrence strike and the organization of women workers generally. Their hostility to the IWW ebbed, and they talked increasingly of the possibilities industrial unionism held for women.

Helen Marot was one who saw the futility of supporting AFL methods while trying to organize large numbers of women who did not fit into craft designations. Even before the Lawrence strike, she recognized the crucial importance of developing new ways to reach unskilled workers and the superiority of industrial organization for that purpose. She was enormously enthusiastic about the 1910 cloakmakers' settlement, for she recognized the powerful implications of agreeing upon a blanket contract for all workers in a trade. By 1912, Marot was articulating a theory of unionization that emphasized organizing the unskilled along industrial lines. A visit to Lawrence during the strike dispelled her fears of industrial organization, and she urged the league to concentrate its energies on finding new ways to reach unskilled workers, stating, "The organization of the unskilled worker has become an all-important question in the labor movement."[50]

In the wake of growing disillusionment with organized labor throughout the general strike period, leading league members modified their policy of requiring independent unions to affiliate with AFL organizations. In contrast to the way in which the WTUL had handled the Progressive Rolled Cigarette Makers' Union seven years before, when the league refused to support an organization Gompers considered a dual union, a serious controversy developed over the question of a department store workers' union's affiliation with an AFL international. Elizabeth Dutcher and Laura Elliot, both allies, had worked with the union since 1911. They told the women in 1913 that the time had come to affiliate with the Retail Clerks' Protective Association, warning that no more funds would be coming from the league unless they did so. The union's president emphatically rejected the WTUL's ultimatum, insisting that his organization did not want organizers from the AFL or from the retail clerks' union. When the majority of the department store workers voted to remain independent, Dutcher and Elliot severed the league's connections with the small union. A month later, after several acrimonious executive board meetings, Rose Schneiderman and Melinda Scott told the women that the league did not want the organization to affiliate with the international if its members declined to do so. Understandably, however, the affair left a residue of bitterness. One of the women union officers told the league that she had learned one thing from her experience with the WTUL: leisure-class women could not organize working women. She hoped that the outcome of the matter "would be the realization on the part of workingwomen that they must organize each other."[51]

Despite their increasing disillusionment with the possibility of changing the labor movement's attitudes and policies toward women, WTUL members still did not formulate alternatives to the existing AFL structure. They did not seriously entertain ideas about breaking away from the AFL and creating new types of unions for women. WTUL leaders continued to reject the alternative of independent women's unions for the same realistic reasons they had earlier: such segregated organizations could not maintain an adequate economic base. Occasionally members revived the idea of forming a federation of women workers. In 1917, the national WTUL appointed a committee to study the feasibility of such a plan. The committee, whose members included Rose Schneiderman, Melinda Scott, and Margaret Dreier Robins, decided that a federation would duplicate the work of the WTUL. Rather than establish a separate federation, the committee recommended that local leagues work harder to make membership easy for all working women and that they serve as centers for "educational, legislative, and social activities for trade union women." Finally, the committee suggested that when women wanted to organize "where there is no organization in the trade and not a sufficient number of members to form a strong union or where the youth of the girl workers makes a strong union difficult in the beginning or where the existing organization is a men's organization that excludes women," then the women should be organized as individual WTUL members; they also suggested "that through such membership trade committees be organized until their strength permits of the organization of a trade union."[52] The national WTUL convention accepted this proposal, although it introduced no new strategies.

Nor did the WTUL organize federal unions, although a plan for WTUL-chartered independent federal unions surfaced later

in the league's history. In 1921, the national Women's Trade
Union League petitioned the AFL to charter federal unions for
women who were excluded from federation affiliates. The
league called for a plan "whereby unorganized, unskilled, and
scattered groups of women may be federated or otherwise
united for mutual support under the American Federation of
Labor and . . . if no such plan is possible under the American
Federation of Labor . . . that the AFL agree that charters in such
cases be issued by the National Women's Trade Union
League."[53] This plan was a dramatic departure for the WTUL.
It was unusual for the league to suggest that the AFL modify its
policies or structure. Even more striking was the suggestion
that independent unions be chartered by the league.

This plan resulted from the New York league's efforts to
organize New York City copyholders, or proofreaders' assis-
tants. The league formed a copyholders' union late in 1919 and
urged the one hundred members to apply to the International
Typographical Union for a charter. Despite the fact that
copyholders worked side by side with union printers and proofreaders in union label shops, the ITU refused to grant a charter
because the women were unskilled. The women, still under the
league's guidance, then applied directly to the AFL for a federal
union charter. The federation replied that "nothing could be
done until the ITU relinquished its jurisdiction." Within a year
the union dissolved.[54]

The federation refused to endorse the WTUL plan for federal
unions, and the WTUL, still caught in the trap of supporting the
AFL, acquiesced in the decision. Despite their disappointment
with the labor movement, the league could never disentangle
itself sufficiently from the AFL to strike out on its own. In
matters of union structure and organizing, federation policies
remained paramount. As Raymond Robins summarized the
league's position to Mary Dreier, "The American Federation of
Labor with all its shortcomings—and few people know these
better than ourselves—is none the less the true representative
body of organized labor in this country. . . . As a matter of
expediency you must cooperate with the policy of the American
Federation of Labor."[55]

Instead of pursuing an independent path, the Women's Trade
Union League continued in its efforts to persuade male trade
unionists to organize women and to integrate women into
existing craft unions. Helen Marot, for instance, recommended
that the league petition the national craft unions for money to
help WTUL organizing drives. "The organization of the un-

skilled is imperative," she stated, "and the financing of the organization of the unskilled must be borne in part by the organization of the skilled."[56] Others hoped that individual AFL leaders other than Gompers could be persuaded to take a major interest in organizing women. WTUL members identified John Mitchell, president of the United Mine Workers, as sensitive to the problems of unskilled workers and committed to industrial organization. In addition, league leaders found Mitchell sympathetic to working women. According to Margaret Dreier Robins, Mitchell was "the one man who understands the industrial struggle of our day and understands and sympathizes with the unskilled worker. He, therefore, has the vision of what our woman's movement needs and the handicaps we are under."[57]

Thus, despite the league's earnest and continual efforts to integrate women into the labor movement, both women and the WTUL remained outsiders. Throughout the years 1910 through 1913, increasing numbers of league women in New York and elsewhere realized that the integrationist policy was unsuccessful and that strict adherence to AFL principles and methods made their work impossibly difficult. As one Boston league leader expressed this realization, "I don't see how a League linked strictly to a disintegrating AFL can become real."[58] Nevertheless, WTUL women were unable to divorce themselves from the AFL and to formulate organizational alternatives. Instead, their dealings with the labor movement in New York City and on the national level gradually caused many members to lose faith in the efficacy of labor organization altogether.

## CHAPTER 5

# Sisterhood and Class Conflict

Just as WTUL members became disillusioned with the labor movement during the general strike era, so, too, did they become discouraged with their own organizing efforts. When they began their work in 1904, league members were convinced that they could reach large numbers of the city's working women and help them unionize. A decade later, the WTUL's organizing campaign had fallen into disarray. Many members had come to believe that most women, particularly Italian and Jewish immigrants, could never unionize successfully. Members' growing conviction of the futility of their organizing efforts and their inability to overcome ethnic and class barriers both within the WTUL and with the city's workers also help explain the league's ultimate disillusionment with unionization and its concurrent shift to suffrage and protective legislation.

The league's organizing difficulties began during the 1909 shirtwaist strike. Until that event, WTUL organizers treated women of all ethnic backgrounds in basically the same ways. But the 1909 uprising was an overwhelmingly Jewish strike. Fewer than three thousand of the strikers were Italian and native-born American women, and many of them went back to work before settlements were reached.[1] The poor showing among these women convinced league leaders that organizing efforts had to be directed specifically to these groups and that new ways of reaching them had to be devised.

The league identified Italian women as most resistant to organization. Members were convinced that employers hired Italian women to lower wage rates, weaken existing unions, and foment what they called "race antagonism" between Italians and Jews. WTUL efforts to form small shop unions sometimes foundered because organizers could not induce Italians to join. "They can do nothing until they get the Italian workers in," a typical league report read. "The Italians do the work for less money, not knowing that they get less money, for they take work home at night when the other girls have refused," a Jewish human-hair worker reported in 1908. "They now have an Italian man in the union who gets a number of girls to promise to come to the meetings and they mean it when they promise, but when the meeting night comes some old superstition or some old tradition that girls ought to be at home at night keeps the Italian girls away."[2]

In their efforts to organize Italian women, league members faced serious obstacles. Few knew the language or had ties with the Italian community. No Italian women belonged to the organization. Realizing these problems, the WTUL began its organizing campaign by assisting the Russell Sage Foundation to conduct an investigation of the working conditions and family roles of Italian women. The project was headed by Louise Odencrantz, a league member and a social investigator for the Russell Sage Foundation. Investigators interviewed 1,095 Italian women wage earners who lived and worked in lower Manhattan and recorded the living conditions of 544 Italian families.[3]

The league learned that like most women workers, Italians were generally young unmarried daughters who lived in their parents' home and turned their wages over to the head of the household. Eighty-six percent of the women interviewed turned their earnings over to their fathers or brothers. A small minority—eighty-three women—turned over part of their wages and kept the remainder for necessities such as lunches, clothes, and carfare. Only thirteen kept the entire sum, and only one was allowed to spend the money as she pleased. Italian women's wages were essential to their families' survival. Sixty-two percent of all persons in the families investigated contributed to family income. In three-fourths of the families, at least two women worked.[4]

In several ways, Italian women's work patterns and family roles in New York City were similar to those in southern Italy. Women did not regard themselves as autonomous wage earners but rather as part of a family economic unit. Then, too, Italian families continued to regard women, particularly daughters, as property. As the New York State Factory Investigating Commission noted, "The family very frequently looks upon the daughter as a piece of productive property which should be invested to the best advantage until the time comes when it must be lost through marriage."[5]

Although the Italian family survived in its traditional patriarchal form in the New World, the conditions of industrial work made a definite impact upon the young Italian women who went to work in New York City factories. Odencrantz found, for instance, that the name of her industry and her job were usually the first English words an Italian woman learned. "A woman will shrug her shoulders helplessly when you ask her where she lives or how long she has been in this country," Odencrantz reported. "Her attempt to answer you with 'feenisher', 'press', 'west', 'dress', or 'cloding' suggests that her work forms her strongest link with the New World."[6]

Italian women frequently voiced the same sorts of grievances expressed by Jewish and native-born American women. Northern Italian women who came to the United States with industrial experience as lace seamstresses, embroidery workers, or dressmakers compared New York factory work unfavorably with their previous jobs. The subdivision of work processes and work speedups were especially obnoxious. The women complained, "You have to do only one part of the waist, sleeves, closing-in, or hemming, and you have to work fast at that one thing." Speed stripped work of any intrinsic satisfaction. "They only do cheap work in this country," one woman lamented. "Everything must be done in a hurry. In Italy it would take six months to do a pillow and here it must be done in three or four hours. Cheap work!"[7]

Such complaints encouraged WTUL organizers, for they suggested that Italian women were discontented in their work. But the New York league also found Italian women discouragingly submissive and tractable. Italian women, Mary Dreier concluded, "are the oppressed of the race, absolutely under the dominance of the men of their family, and heavily shackled by old customs and traditions. They are very much afraid of trade unions."[8] The WTUL's program centered on changing women's role in Italian culture, both by working with the women themselves and by trying to educate Italian men about the role of women in the United States. In trying to educate Italian men to accept a new, modern view of women's role and in trying to raise Italian women's consciousness, however, league members severely underestimated the tenacity of Italian cultural mores.

To interest Italians in organizing, the executive board hired Arturo Caroti, a northern Italian socialist. Caroti was a freelance writer and lecturer, an organizer for the United Textile Workers, and the manager of the Silk Workers' Union's cooperative store in Paterson, New Jersey. He told the league that if it were to be successful in organizing Italian women, members would have to learn the psychology of Italian men. The only way women would join unions, he maintained, was by convincing their fathers and brothers of the wisdom of the idea. Under league auspices, Caroti spoke to local Italian unions and social clubs, organized briefly for the waistmakers, and wrote for the Italian daily the *Bolletino della Sera*.

To interest Italian women, the league formed Italian benefit clubs. The WTUL modeled these clubs after men's benefit

societies, reasoning that if women had opportunities to so-
cialize with one another as men did, trade union organization
would follow. Club meetings combined socializing with read-
ings of socialist poetry and with lectures on industrial conditions, hygiene, and trade unionism. Women who joined were
entitled to a marriage benefit, which they could collect when
they left work to marry, sick-leave payments, and free health
care. The WTUL formed several clubs in Greenwich Village and
in Italian neighborhoods on the upper East Side. They attracted
about two hundred members.

The clubs were controversial. WTUL members disagreed
over whether they should offer marriage or strike benefits.
Those in favor of the former argued that strike benefits would
alienate Italian women. Others, however, criticized marriage
benefits as inappropriate for a labor organization and con-
tended that the clubs themselves were a more suitable project
for a settlement house than for the league. The trade union
position eventually triumphed. In 1912, the executive board
instructed the Italian committee to make more direct efforts to
interest Italian women in unionism. The committee reported
some time later that it was doing all it could "to make the girls
take a serious interest in their trades—they had put it to them
pretty stiffly and the result was unquestioningly a falling off of
interest."[9]

In keeping with the emphasis on actual unionization, the
WTUL formed a second organization, the Italian Girls' Industrial League. This group was composed of about thirty-five
Italian women who were already union members and whom
the league identified as good candidates for leadership roles.
The industrial league, however, was discontinued in less than a
year.

By early 1913, the New York league concluded that its efforts
to reach Italian women had failed. The chairwoman of the
Italian committee reported, "While the subject of trade unionism in the abstract had been discussed the members of the club
were genial but they had not responded when it came time to
join various unions."[10] After the 1913 white-goods workers'
strike, again marked by poor Italian participation, the WTUL
abruptly terminated its special organizing efforts and concluded that Italian women were incapable of organization.[11]

The league also became disenchanted with Jewish women
during the same time period and concluded that they, too, had
little sustained interest in unionization. This position was very
different from league leaders' earlier opinions. Throughout

their first years of work, WTUL members regarded Jewish
women as the most organizable of the city's female work force.
They praised Jewish women's militancy and their interest in
economic conditions. One league ally concluded, "The Jewish
girl . . . often displays an eager zest for discussion of labor
problems. . . . she will probably plunge at once into a discussion of her trade—its advantages and disadvantages, wages,
hours of work, and instances of shabby treatment in the shops
or of unsanitary conditions in the workrooms."[12] The shirtwaist strike was proof of Jewish women's readiness for unionization. However, as the waistmakers' union steadily lost its
membership in the years after the strike, as few women
emerged to challenge the male leadership of that union, and as
Rose Schneiderman encountered severe difficulties in recruiting
Jewish women for other organizations, league members began
to revise their original assessment of Jewish women's capabilities as unionists. They noted that most Jewish women seemed
to take little interest in their unions once they were established.
Like other young working women, they regarded their time in
the work force as a temporary hiatus between childhood and
marriage.

The league's relationships with the Jewish community and
labor movement, however, were very different from its relationship with New York's Italian immigrants. The league had
always had ties with the ILGWU and the United Hebrew
Trades. Then, too, several dozen Jewish working women from
ILGWU Locals No. 25 and 62 joined the WTUL during the
general strike period. Finally, the league had two fine East Side
organizers, Rose Schneiderman and Pauline Newman.

Newman, a waistmaker, joined the New York league during
the 1909 shirtwaist strike. Although only eighteen at the time,
she came to the WTUL with years of experience in the garment
industry. Just months after her arrival in New York from
Lithuania in 1901, she went to work as a thread trimmer in the
Triangle Shirtwaist factory. Newman came into her own as a
capable speaker and organizer during the shirtwaist strike.
Afterward, she divided her time among the league, the ILGWU,
and the Socialist party. For the league she worked as an organizer and speaker in East Side neighborhoods and, in 1915,
helped establish a WTUL branch in Philadelphia. For the union,
she worked as a sanitary inspector and as an organizer
throughout the northeast and midwest. A fiery soapbox orator,
she worked as a Socialist party speaker as well.

Both Schneiderman and Newman were exceptionally skillful

organizers. Unlike other league organizers, they knew Yiddish and could understand and empathize with the conflicting pressures on young Jewish women unionists. They understood, as WTUL allies did not, the pressure for marriage and the cultural mores that dictated that proper Jewish girls stayed at home. Thus, they could make appeals to Jewish women based on shared identity, language, and culture. Both women agreed with the executive board's assessment that Jewish women were hard to organize. "Now you and I know that the East Side element is the hardest to work with," Newman wrote Schneiderman, "that is, hardest to keep . . . within the organization."[13]

In the years from 1910 through 1912, Schneiderman, the official East Side organizer, concentrated on consolidating the gains won in the general strikes and on building new unions of human-hair workers, corsetmakers, and umbrella makers. But her progress was slow, and the executive board became impatient. The league's increasingly strained relations with the ILGWU also made Schneiderman's work difficult.

In light of these problems, league leaders became unwilling to devote major efforts to East Side women. While Schneiderman struggled to establish stable unions, others began to advocate organizing native-born American women. Before the 1909 shirtwaist strike, the WTUL had little enthusiasm for organizing native-born women, for they seemed nearly as reluctant to unionize as Italians. After the strike, however, league organizers decided that native-born women were alienated from trade unions because union leaders and most of the rank and file were Jewish immigrants. Women who joined ILGWU locals, for instance, brought complaints to the league about union meetings conducted entirely in Yiddish. "The girls," Mary Dreier reported, "are bitter toward the union and also to the Jews, whom they say have not treated them fairly. Yet the girls are good stuff—we are all pining to get ahold of the American girls."[14] As a solution to ethnic discord, the WTUL proposed organizing native-born women into English-speaking locals and appointed Melinda Scott as the "American" organizer.

Scott's ideas about the labor movement and union organizing differed radically from those of Newman and Schneiderman. Politically conservative, a supporter of immigration restriction, and a defender of pure and simple unionism, Scott possessed little sympathy for lower East Side women or Jewish socialist unions. Her attitudes created long-lasting enmity between her and the league's Jewish members. The antipathy of other workers bewildered and distressed Scott. "I have felt lately . . . that there was something under the surface, some undercurrent that I do not understand," she confided to Leonora O'Reilly.[15]

Early in 1910, the waistmakers' union, ILGWU Local No. 25, gave the league permission to organize an English-speaking branch in the uptown waist and dress shops in which most native-born women worked. Later that year, the Neckwear Makers' Union asked the league's help in organizing American-born workers in the uptown branches of that trade. Melinda Scott successfully organized the two new locals. She proved to be a strong negotiator as well, winning wage increases, the abolition of fines, and the end of the contracting system in seven uptown neckwear shops. But Scott undercut the Jewish labor movement, for she advised the women not to affiliate with the Neckwear Makers' Union, a Jewish organization, but with the United Textile Workers instead.[16]

Buoyed by these successes, Scott and Helen Marot argued that the league should devote itself entirely to organizing American-born women. They based their argument on Scott's progress in uptown waist, dress, and neckwear shops, on the strained relations between the league and the ILGWU, and on the difficulties Rose Schneiderman was encountering on the East Side. "I think the League is ready to take the position that the future success of organization among Italian and Jewish women depends upon the organization of American women," Marot told the executive board late in 1911. "In every trade where Miss Schneiderman has been organizing she finds that it is the bigger shops and the better-paid workers that control the situation and that the work in these shops is done almost entirely by American girls."[17] Marot and Scott won Mary Dreier's support for their position. Early in 1912, the executive board decided that the WTUL should drop its East Side work and concentrate upon unionizing native-born women. The league, then, withdrew from sustained contact with Jewish working women at the same time that its relations with Jewish unions were deteriorating.

The league's Jewish workers were enraged by this decision. Although both Schneiderman and Newman agreed with Marot that Jewish women were hard to organize and although both were disenchanted with the Jewish labor movement, they did not want the league to abandon its East Side work. Schneiderman resigned as East Side organizer. Pauline Newman consoled her friend. "I can just understand how you feel about your position, Rose! For people do not take into consideration the fact that paving the way is harder work and work that must be done whether you get results or not. . . . As to Melinda being more successful than you are, well, H.M. and M.D. [Helen Marot and Mary Dreier] will have to learn the psychology of the East Side girl and the up-town girl in order to know who is responcible [sic] for the success or failure."[18]

These ethnic and class tensions within the league peaked during a bitterly contested presidential contest in 1914. When Mary Dreier resigned because of poor health, the two major contenders for the WTUL presidency were Rose Schneiderman and Melinda Scott. Although both were workers, support for the two candidates divided along class and ethnic lines: allies backed Scott, while working women, particularly the younger Jewish immigrants who had joined the league during the general strikes, voted for Schneiderman. When Scott won by four votes, Pauline Newman concluded that the league was divided into two camps, the "social workers" and the "trade unionists." She assured Schneiderman,

> your vote, with the exception of three or four was a real trade Union vote. On the other hand, the vote for Linda was purely a vote of the social workers. People who have not been near the League for four or five years, came to vote. Imagine Frances Kellor and Mrs. Simcovitch [sic] and Ida Rau [sic]. . . they have not been near the League for ever so long, but they could not get the girls from the Unions to vote against you. . . . So you see, that nothing was left undone by them to line up a vote for Linda on the ground that you were a socialist, a Jewes [sic] and one interested in suffrage.[19]

The conflict over organizing priorities, the abandonment of the East Side, and the bitterness that accompanied the 1914 election provide the clearest illustrations of league members' difficulties in transcending the barriers of ethnicity and class.

Political differences also divided league women. Many of the garment workers who joined the WTUL during the general strike period were socialists. By 1913, the socialists composed a vocal faction within the organization. Although the league had always included a significant number of socialist members within its ranks, the new women from ILGWU locals seemed more militant and more united as a bloc. Much to the distress of more conservative members such as Mary Dreier and Melinda Scott, the socialists, voting together, commited the league to marching in the 1913 May Day parade. Alarmed by the new trend, Dreier turned to Margaret and Raymond Robins for help. They advised her to take a firm stand against using the WTUL as a socialist forum and to rally support for

Melinda Scott as a responsible trade unionist. Scott, Robins argued, "is working all the time to organize working women for their industrial freedom. Most of the others are working for a socialist millennium."[20]

These tensions affected working-class members most, for they brought to the surface the women's confusion and ambivalence about their role in the league. The numbers amd influence of working women had increased dramatically over the years. By 1914, every WTUL officer was a worker: Melinda Scott was president, Schneiderman and a young unionist from the bookbinders were vice-presidents. Eight out of the eleven executive board members were working women. The total membership of nearly five hundred women was evenly balanced between workers and allies.[21] Nevertheless, many workers still felt that the league was fundamentally an upper-class organization. Leonora O'Reilly, for instance, vacillated between maintaining her commitment to the organization and abandoning it altogether. The league, she told Mary Dreier after the 1914 election, "ought to die, the sooner, the better."[22]

For Jewish members, ambivalence and alienation were especially intense. Rose Schneiderman and Pauline Newman were torn between working in the WTUL and devoting themselves to the Jewish labor movement. On the one hand, they identified with the East Side community in which they had grown up and with which they still had many ties. On the other, they considered themselves feminists, concerned with women's issues, such as suffrage, with which Jewish labor unions were not concerned. The league, despite its shortcomings, offered the companionship of women who shared many of the same concerns and experiences. In the overwhelmingly male world of early twentieth-century unions, such a female network was of incalculable value for personal support. Then, too, the league gave women more opportunities for leadership and responsibility and far more experience as organizers and negotiators than unions did.

Both Schneiderman and Newman left the league temporarily to work as ILGWU organizers. But to organize for a male-dominated trade union, both women discovered, was an isolated, lonely experience. If the league was not sufficiently interested in the unionization of East Side women and did not appreciate the efforts and abilities of its immigrant organizers, the Jewish unions discriminated against women and ignored the special problems of women altogether.

From 1915 through 1917, Rose Schneiderman organized

waistmakers, cloakmakers, and corsetmakers throughout the Midwest and New England. She was continually thwarted in her efforts by union officers' sexist attitudes. For instance, while in Cleveland trying to rekindle women cloakmakers' interest in the union, she was shunned by the male ILGWU organizer. In Boston, late in 1915, Schneiderman successfully laid the groundwork for a general strike of the city's shirtwaist makers. The day before the strike was to begin, the international sent male organizers to manage the walkout and negotiate a settlement. Furious, Schneiderman drafted a letter of resignation, stating that the atmosphere of "rudeness and distrust" had made her work impossible.[23] Although she decided against leaving, her action revealed her profound disaffection with the male labor movement. Once her appointment as an organizer came to an end, she returned permanently to the league.

Pauline Newman's experiences were similar. In the years after she joined the WTUL in 1909, she also worked for the ILGWU in New England and the Midwest and led women's strikes of Philadelphia waistmakers and Kalamazoo corsetmakers. She, like Schneiderman, found that male union officials did not appreciate her organizing or her leadership abilities. Several times she quit, angered when she was expected to work for less pay than other organizers received.[24]

Unionists' sexist attitudes were not the only difficulties with which a woman organizer had to contend. Early twentieth-century social proprieties made their work difficult as well. Traveling alone posed problems, for suitable accommodations for single women were hard to come by. Male union officials exacerbated this problem by expecting women organizers to observe conventional mores. John Mitchell, for instance, although one of the most sympathetic AFL leaders when it came to women's concerns, distinctly disapproved of women organizers traveling by themselves and boarding in public accommodations. According to Margaret Robins, he had "some old fashioned notions expressing themselves in his dislike of seeing a woman 'travel on the road' and so forth."[25]

Time on the road also meant loneliness. Home was often a succession of dreary boarding houses. Schneiderman and Newman missed the companionship the league provided and found that they could not depend upon men for support in the same way. Only in Chicago and Philadelphia, both of which had WTUL branches, were the two women able to find friendship and interest in their work.

The tension and ambivalence that working-class women

experienced took a heavy toll. Although Schneiderman and Newman remained in the WTUL until it closed its doors in 1955, other talented women left, discouraged and disillusioned. Many of the young garment workers, such as Clara Lemlich, who had joined the league after the 1909 waistmakers' strike lost interest in the organization. Leonora O'Reilly resigned in 1915, stating that her usefulness to the WTUL had ended and that workers must organize themselves.[26] By the time she left the WTUL, O'Reilly had become disillusioned with the labor movement altogether. "Now don't drop dead, but this is my last labor convention," she wrote Mary Dreier after attending the 1915 New York Federation of Labor convention, at which delegates had criticized the league. "Trade unions are necessary. They must be worked for in season and out. Women must be organized better than men are organized. The powers that be in the labor movement in New York State do not and will not recognize an outside body's right to help with the work. Worse than that, they attribute their own shortcomings to the outside body's disinterestedness."[27] Although Dreier tried to dissuade her, arguing that if all women had let men deter them from their goals "there never would have been a chance of our ever learning to read and write,"[28] O'Reilly was determined to resign. In increasingly poor health due to a chronic heart condition, O'Reilly went on to other interests. Like most WTUL members, she worked hard for woman suffrage. She also joined the women's peace movement in the years before World War I and represented the national Women's Trade Union League at the 1915 Women's International Peace Conference at The Hague. In the last years before she died in 1927, O'Reilly dedicated herself to the cause of Irish independence. She never resumed active work with the labor movement.[29]

Melinda Scott left the WTUL in 1917. Long discouraged by the atmosphere of suspicion and distrust that surrounded her work in the league, she had begun to talk of resigning as president the year before. An appointment to the National War Labor Board shortly after the United States entered World War I provided the opportunity for leaving. Unlike O'Reilly, Scott remained active in the labor movement as an organizer for the United Textile Workers.

Thus, by the end of the general strike era, WTUL members had lost their original optimism about organizing the city's working women and integrating them into the labor movement. They had also learned that creating an egalitarian cross-class alliance was far more difficult than they had originally anticipated. By 1914, league members were thoroughly confused about the direction their organization should take. Increasingly, however, they looked to feminist rather than unionist solutions for improving women's position in the labor force.

## CHAPTER 6

# The Suffrage Campaign

In the summer of 1916, Mary Dreier wrote a long and painful letter to her close friend Leonora O'Reilly. Summarizing the changes in her thinking about the Women's Trade Union League and working women's position in the labor movement, she ended by stating, "The enfranchisement of all women is the paramount issue for me . . . [and] the only way to obtain it is to go after it, irrespective of all else. . . . The attitude of the labor men to the working women has changed me from being an ardent supporter of labor to a somewhat rabid supporter of women and to feel that the enfranchisement of women and especially my working-class sisters is the supreme issue."[1] Dreier's letter expressed many league members' thoughts in the years following the general strikes. Originally the New York WTUL had subordinated feminism to the interests of labor solidarity, its members convinced that enfranchisement was irrelevant to women's industrial conditions. But as members grew disillusioned with the labor movement, suffrage became a major issue. As Melinda Scott summarized the shift in her own sentiments, "I am a suffragist, but I had been first a trade unionist."[2] By 1913, as the general strike era came to an end, suffrage was a major priority for many league women. By 1915, the year of the first New York suffrage referendum, allies and working-class members alike devoted nearly all their energy and much of their money to winning the vote. Although the WTUL continued to organize, its unionizing efforts steadily lost ground to new political and legislative objectives.

In short, the Women's Trade Union League of New York was a different organization in the years after 1913. Its new commitments to suffrage and to women's protective labor legislation indicate that two basic changes had taken place. First, as a social reform organization, the New York league relied increasingly on legislative measures instead of on direct organizing work. As issues, protective legislation and woman suffrage naturally went hand in hand. In part, the WTUL's increasing emphasis on the vote resulted from members' first experiences as lobbyists for the women's fifty-four-hour bill. As members entered the political arena and became familiar with the workings of the legislature, Tammany, and special interest groups, they realized that enfranchisement was an essential prerequi-

site for effecting social change. "I did some lobbying work last
year for the 54-hour bill," Rose Schneiderman told a suffrage
rally,

> and I can tell you how courteous our Senators and Assem-
> blymen are when a disenfranchised citizen tries to convince
> them of the necessity of shorter hours for working women. . . .
> During the hearing at Albany our learned Senators listened to
> the opposition very carefully; . . . But when the Committee,
> who spoke for the working women came to plead for the bill,
> there was only one Senator left in the room. . . . Mind you, we
> were pleading for a shorter work week for working women.
> We had evidence to show that physical exhaustion leads to
> moral exhaustion and the physical and moral exhaustion of
> women will lead to the deterioration of the human species.
> What did these men care? We were voteless working
> women—no matter what we felt or thought could not come
> back at them.[3]

Second, the league's commitments to suffrage and protective
legislation suggest that members had begun to cast their lot
with women's organizations and feminist issues rather than
with the male-dominated labor movement. In other words, in
their continual efforts to reconcile the needs of women workers
as part of the working class with their needs as an oppressed
minority within the work force and within American society as
a whole, league members increasingly leaned toward emphasizing the latter. WTUL women also increasingly viewed
their difficulties with organized labor as a fundamental conflict
between men and women rather than as a conflict between
workers and a predominantly upper-class organization.

This shift from a labor to a feminist perspective was neither
abrupt nor unchallenged. On suffrage and on protective legislation, as on every substantive issue, league members found
themselves in disagreement. One WTUL leader, Helen Marot,
resigned over the change from a labor to a feminist perspective,
and others disagreed among themselves about the league's new
orientation. By 1914, however, the shift had clearly taken place.
For the rest of its history, despite a membership increasingly
working class in character, the New York league remained
primarily concerned with women's social legislation and only
secondarily concerned with union organizing.

Suffrage was an old issue for league members. Although the
national WTUL did not officially endorse votes for women until
1907, the New York officers were attending suffrage meetings
as early as 1905 and urging others to do likewise.[4] Allies seem to

have come to the organization already committed to woman suffrage, and workers, although probably less familiar with the issue, appear to have adopted a favorable position readily. Many league women belonged to suffrage organizations, and at least one prominent member, Harriot Stanton Blatch, was known nationally for her suffrage work. Leonora O'Reilly and Gertrude Barnum addressed conventions of the National American Woman Suffrage Association (NAWSA). Rose Schneiderman, representing the capmakers' union, Mary Duffy, of the overalls workers' union, and Clara Silver, of the buttonhole makers' union—all league organizers—testified occasionally at the New York State Assembly hearings on woman suffrage in the years before 1910. Mary Dreier, Bertha Weyl, Mary Beard, and Ida Rauh, all allies, were also enthusiastic suffragists in the early years.

But these activities were individual and sporadic. For most WTUL women, the vote was a peripheral issue with little relevance to working women's situation. Throughout its first years, league members were aware that to work too enthusiastically for the ballot might have undermined their credibility with male trade unionists. Early in the 1909 waistmakers' strike, for instance, despite the highly publicized participation of suffragists who identified themselves with the WTUL, some members avoided associating the league with the suffrage movement. "This is a strike," ally Violet Pike emphasized to reporters, "not a political movement. . . . There may be suffragettes among the strikers, and I believe there are, but this is a trade union movement pure and simple."[5]

The WTUL was largely indifferent to woman suffrage in its early years because most members did not see a direct link between the ballot and the realities confronting working women. The vote would not shorten working hours, raise wages, or keep factories safe from fire. "Woman suffrage is beginning at the other end," a friend wrote Leonora O'Reilly. "What the women need is *economic* emancipation. . . . And they can't get it without organization, and so you have begun at the root."[6] League members who participated in the suffrage campaign before 1915 emphasized this point. When NAWSA hired Rose Schneiderman as a suffrage organizer for the 1912 Ohio referendum campaign, she made it clear that she was a socialist and a trade unionist whose first allegiance was to the labor movement. The ballot, she told NAWSA's president, Anna Howard Shaw, "was a tool in the hands of working women with which, through legislation, they could correct the terrible conditions existing in industry."[7]

The character of the early twentieth-century suffrage movement reinforced members' opinion that the vote was largely irrelevant for working women, however desirable suffrage may have been in the abstract. The wealthy matrons who dominated the city's suffrage organizations did not try to appeal to working women. Suffragist propaganda frequently included anti-immigrant references. In fact, one common suffragist argument in the industrial northeast was that native-born women were humiliated by being denied the franchise when ignorant foreign men could vote soon after their arrival.[8] Furthermore, the NAWSA, the major American suffrage organization, refused to endorse the labor movement. Even at the high point of women's unionism, the 1909 shirtwaist strike, NAWSA remained neutral, declaring that it "neither stands for labor organization nor against it."[9]

Despite the fact that individual WTUL members belonged to various city suffrage organizations, there was little interaction between the league as an organization and local suffrage societies. When suffragists occasionally attended WTUL social functions, they were regarded as outsiders. Even Mary Dreier, who was an early suffrage advocate and who had many social and personal ties with upper-class suffrage leaders, was critical of some "ardent suffragists" who attended an early league tea. "I think they think about nothing else," she observed. "Yesterday evening at the office the suffragist ladies were commented upon, and the others present said they were dried up old things who had no interest in anything but that. In fact they did sit together and did not seem to converse with anyone else but themselves."[10] Working-class members were especially uncomfortable with wealthy suffragists. "I feel as if I have butted in where I was not wanted," a working-class member wrote Leonora O'Reilly about her experiences at a New York City Woman Suffrage party conference, "not a word of labor spoken at this convention so far."[11]

WTUL members began to reevaluate their attitudes toward the suffrage movement around 1910. In part, their deepening interest in the vote can be attributed to the changing nature of the suffrage campaign, both in New York City and in the nation. By 1910, the fight for the ballot commmanded more attention than it had for a generation. What had been a stagnating cause was emerging as a visible and extraordinarily well-organized movement. Suffrage clubs and societies proliferated rapidly in New York City and recruited large memberships. The push to put suffrage referenda on state ballots was gaining momentum, and the new strategy to fight for a federal constitutional amendment lent hope to suffrage leaders. A young and increasingly influential faction within the movement introduced new tactics such as mass rallies, marches, pageants, and street meetings, which, while hardly militant, were considerably more dramatic than the parlor lectures that had previously been suffragists' primary tactic. Most important, suffrage leaders such as NAWSA's president, Anna Howard Shaw, and local suffrage leaders such as the president of the Women's Political Union, Harriot Stanton Blatch, the president of the New York Political Equality League, Alva Belmont, and New York City Woman Suffrage party leaders Harriet Burton Laidlaw and Mary Garret Hay believed their movement's success depended on their ability to convert the city's immigrant workers to the cause. The movement, they stressed, needed workers' signatures on petitions, working women's arguments against antisuffragists, and working men's votes on the state referendum.

The participation of local suffragists in the 1909 shirtwaist strike reflected their new interest in reaching working women and their willingness to cooperate with the WTUL. Although suffragists maintained that the vote was more valuable to women than trade unionism and analyzed any oppression in terms of political disfranchisement, they played a significant role in bringing the strike before the public.[12] What was more, suffrage leaders who spent time on picket lines and in court professed to have learned a great deal about the exploitation of their working sisters. After Alva Belmont spent a night at the Jefferson Market Courthouse, she declared that what she had seen that evening was proof of women's need for political power. "A hundred-fold it was impressed upon me in the cases of the women of the streets who were brought before the judge, that every woman who sits complacently amidst the comforts of her home and says, 'I have all the rights I want' should spend one night in the Jefferson Market Court. She would then know that there are other women who have no rights which man or law or society recognize."[13]

The defeat of an Ohio suffrage referendum in 1912 heightened suffragists' interest in winning the labor vote. The Ohio campaign was the suffragists' first major effort in a large industrial state and, as such, was a testing ground for the issue's reception in the industrial northeast. Several central labor bodies in large urban areas came out against the issue. In the aftermath of the election, suffrage leaders concluded that the loss of the labor vote was the major reason for the defeat. "We have got a chance of winning this state if we can get some of these—well, damned—wet labor people to quit knifing us," one Ohio suffrage leader wrote to Margaret Dreier Robins, appealing for her assistance in a second referendum campaign in 1914. "You know how the municipal federations blackballed us last time. . . . Dayton and Cincinnati and I am told Cleveland have refused to endorse us *this* time."[14]

The English suffrage movement, particularly the militant Pankhurst faction, also influenced the league's interest in the vote. Mary Dreier had close personal ties with the Pankhursts: her sisters Katharine and Dorothea spent much time in England, where they knew Emmeline and Cristabel Pankhurst well and were active supporters of the Pankhursts' organization, the Women's Social and Political Union. In addition, Margaret Dreier Robins's sister-in-law, Elizabeth Robins, was a leading WSPU activist. Thanks to these ties, the WTUL was one of Mrs. Pankhurst's hosts during her American tours in 1909 and 1913, and members met her personally. "I have met Mrs. Pankhurst," Mary Dreier wrote to her sister Katharine. "She is such a very remarkable woman. . . . I am more impressed than I can tell you with the sense I have after I have seen her, of the reality of a real civil war in England and of her leadership. I think it is a wonderful spectacle."[15] League members turned out en masse to hear Emmeline Pankhurst speak and described her as "inspiring." Although the WTUL, like the American suffrage movement generally, never adopted militant tactics, its members were clearly influenced and impressed by the English movement.[16]

During the general strike era, then, suffrage emerged as a major goal for the WTUL, although it was still far from predominant. The organization began to work with the suffrage movement, and several individual leaders began to devote a good deal of time to the campaign. Most notably, Rose Schneiderman and Leonora O'Reilly turned from labor organizing to suffrage agitation. In 1912, O'Reilly helped the WTUL form the Wage Earners' Suffrage League. In the same year, shortly after her resignation as East Side organizer, Schneiderman took a leave of absence from the league to work for the NAWSA in the Ohio referendum campaign.

Members continued to differ among themselves, however,

about the issue's importance. One of the arguments opponents marshaled against Schneiderman in the 1914 presidential contest was that she was too interested in suffrage to be an effective WTUL president. O'Reilly noted, "Some of our folk . . . think I have lost my sense of proportion because of my present activity for V[otes] for W[omen]."[17]

An important change in leadership also reflected some members' unhappiness with the WTUL's shift in priorities. Helen Marot resigned as the league's secretary in 1913. Her action was not surprising: friends had been aware of her frustration with the league's new emphasis on suffrage and protective legislation at the expense of organizing. She had always been outspoken in her disapproval of most protective legislation, and although she was a suffragist she disagreed with the league's increasing stress on the vote. She explained her resignation as secretary by saying that to her thinking the work of the league should be done by women wage earners themselves.[18] Although Marot remained a WTUL member, she never resumed an active career in the labor movement. She summarized her experiences and her ideas on the importance of industrial unionism and the undesirability of protective legislation in her book, *American Labor Unions: By a Member*, published in 1915. For several years immediately following her resignation, Marot worked as an editor for *The Masses*. The remainder of her life she spent in retirement on Cape Cod with her companion Caroline Pratt.

Maud O'Farrell Swartz eventually replaced Marot as the league's secretary. Swartz had emigrated to the United States from Ireland at the turn of the century and worked as a proofreader in a foreign language printing firm. In 1912, she joined the New York City Woman Suffrage party. Significantly, it was her involvement in the suffrage movement that led her to the league. Because she spoke Italian fluently, she conducted suffrage meetings in Italian neighborhoods. Rose Schneiderman heard her speak to immigrant audiences and invited her to join the WTUL. Although a worker, Swartz came to the WTUL without experience in trade unionism. Only after the WTUL accepted her for membership did she join Local 6 of the International Typographical Union. At the same time, she began to take a serious interest in unionism and studied at the national WTUL's school for organizers in Chicago. It was in 1916, when she returned to New York City from Chicago, that she was elected secretary.[19]

That the New York league was more concerned with political

and legislative issues than with labor organizing was borne out by its choice of Swartz as secretary. Under Marot, the secretary's office had been the center for the league's organizing efforts. Swartz, however, was more concerned with coordinating legislative and suffrage work. A politically astute and effective lobbyist, she spent much time in Albany working to convince reluctant legislators of the importance of women's protective legislation. In addition, she brought new concerns to the WTUL, among them agitation for the passage and enforcement of good compensation laws. To these ends, Swartz established and single-handedly ran the successful Women's Compensation Bureau under WTUL auspices. Swartz was not primarily a union organizer, but her skills and interests were compatible with the WTUL's new priorities.

By 1915, disagreements over league priorities and the primacy of legislation and suffrage seem to have ended. WTUL members devoted almost all their time to the state referendum campaign. The league's major organizers—Rose Schneiderman, Pauline Newman, Melinda Scott, and Leonora O'Reilly—turned their attention to full-time suffrage agitation. The WTUL hired Margaret Hinchey, a laundry worker who had helped conduct the 1912 laundry workers' strike, and Clara Lemlich, famous for her role in the waistmakers' strike, as special suffrage organizers. Allies were also active in the suffrage campaign. Mary Dreier, Ida Rauh, and Mary Beard coordinated the league's suffrage efforts with those of the New York City Woman's Suffrage party (WSP), an NAWSA affiliate, and made daily suffrage speeches to both middle-class and working-class audiences. After Mary Dreier resigned as WTUL president in 1914, she devoted her time to the suffrage campaign as chairwoman of the Woman Suffrage party's Industrial Section.

Suffrage was a very visible issue for New Yorkers in the fall of 1915. For months before the 2 November election, suffragists bombarded every neighborhood in the city with propaganda. Each of several dozen suffrage societies distributed leaflets and handbills and advocated its cause by such means as mime shows in store windows (called "talking windows"), "subway ladies" who rode the trains with suffrage posters on their laps, "sandwich board ladies" in midtown, and continual street meetings and rallies. The WSP scheduled daily meetings in each of the city's assembly districts and conducted a house-to-house canvass. In the last two weeks of the campaign, the unprecedented publicity effort intensified. More than one hundred meetings a night were held in the city. The campaign's climax was the magnificent parade on 23 October in which twenty-five thousand marchers, most dressed in white with yellow suffrage sashes and banners, paraded up Fifth Avenue.[20]

Throughout the campaign the WTUL acted as the official voice of working women. League members saw their organization as an intermediary between the suffrage movement and the city's workers. As such, it was charged with the dual responsibility of conveying the significance of the suffrage issue to working-class audiences and representing the needs and opinions of working women to the overwhelmingly middle-class, native-born movement.

The WTUL coordinated its suffrage work with the New York City WSP. The WSP's officers organized its membership along regular party lines, electing leaders for each assembly district and appointing captains for each ward. It systematically conducted a house-to-house canvass, organized citywide publicity, and lobbied neighborhood political leaders. The WTUL took charge of the party's Industrial Section, formed in 1914. The Industrial Section organized street meetings in working-class neighborhoods, spoke at union meetings, oversaw the translation of suffrage leaflets into Yiddish, Italian, and German, and sponsored a series of pamphlets addressed to working men and union members.

The WSP rank and file, however, included few working women, and the WTUL realized that its greatest contribution would be to broaden the movement's base by making suffrage a meaningful issue to women workers. Because working women were not comfortable in the city's suffrage organizations, the WTUL established and financed a special suffrage society, the Wage Earners' Suffrage League. The Wage Earners' Suffrage League began as the East Side Wage Earners' League, formed in 1908 to educate immigrant women about naturalization procedures. In 1912, the WTUL expanded the East Side society into a citywide suffrage organization that restricted its membership to working women. Such a policy was necessary, the WTUL emphasized, because other suffrage groups were middle class in their orientation. As Leonora O'Reilly, president of the group, explained to Margaret Dreier Robins, "We are the only people who can make the W. W. [working woman] understand her own relation to the vote and as well make the leisure-class women understand the workers' point of view—we must get a wage-earning woman to work it up and there's the rub, for really and truly the other women with the best intentions in the world rub the fur the wrong way, they really don't speak our language and so they use the W. W. and then throw them over."[21]

The league also recognized the importance of having working women serve as suffrage speakers and organizers. As Pauline Newman explained, "The 'cultured' ladies may be very sincere in their desire for the ballot, I don't doubt their sincerity, but because their views are narrow, and their knowledge of social conditions limited, they cannot do as well as some of us can. And as I come in contact with these women day after day, they are beginning to see the necessity of having a working girl tour a State rather than some professor."[22] The best WTUL suffrage organizer was Margaret Hinchey, a rugged Irish woman who had worked in a long succession of New York City steam laundries. While other league organizers had limited success in collecting signatures on suffrage petitions and convincing men to vote for the referendum, Hinchey usually made converts. A tireless campaigner, she spoke to working men in every corner of the city—in factories, in subway excavations, along each of the fifty North River piers. "Spoke outside of 3 factories at noon hour," she reported jubilantly to Leonora O'Reilly,

> and when I got through the men took of there hats and hurray votes for women. . . . In spite of it all I left a Pretty good feeling by all the fighting and drops of water falling from my forhead asking the men to think for themselves and not heed [a] few People who is looking for their own Personial Inst. . . . They received me with a kold piece of ice but when I got speaking one looked at the other in amaisement and when I was wishing them good by at last they got friendly and clapped. . . . We hat a street meeting last night when we got there were 2 people. . . . I got upon a chare and atared in hollin and in 10 minutes we had 150 people all mothers and men. Mrs. Cammons and myself laughed at the way I collected people she said I could be herd 1/2 mile away we got 14 signitures all voters I do think it paid.[23]

In addition to organizing, the league's task during the referendum campaign was to translate the libertarian abstractions that had made up the traditional nineteenth-century suffrage rationale into arguments that would appeal to working-class women and men. Like all suffragists, league women came to believe that the vote would bring about major changes in women's status. But WTUL women did not argue that women should have the vote simply as a natural right. Like other social feminists in the early twentieth century, they emphasized the differences between women and men and the special needs that women could meet only with the ballot.[24] The theme of social motherhood, so important in reformers' and suffragists' arguments for the vote, was also prominent in league suffrage ideology. "In our homes, as wives, mothers, daughters," Leonora O'Reilly declared, "we need the ballot to do justice to our work as home-keepers. Children need pure milk and pure food, good schools and playgrounds, sanitary homes and safe streets."[25] The distinguishing feature of the WTUL's suffrage rationale was its emphasis on the specific ways the vote would meet the needs of women workers: suffrage would help abolish the sweatshop, raise women's wages, and help women unionize. The vote, league suffragists emphasized, was too important to be left in the hands of leisure-class women. It is clear that changes in members' thinking about the causes of women's exploitation in the work force underlay the league's suffrage arguments. By 1915, members had reversed their ideas about the causes of women's exploitation. Now they argued that women's political powerlessness was the crucial variable for explaining the conditions under which women worked.

WTUL suffrage workers made their arguments to working women, male trade unionists and workers, workingmen's wives, and, in a general way, to the public at large. One major league argument was that the vote would make women more amenable to unionization by imbuing them with self-respect. Once they could vote, women would automatically gain the independence and confidence that WTUL organizers thought they lacked. League members did not question that self-confidence would be an important benefit of political equality. The right to vote would also gain women more respect from men. Even unionization, league suffragists stressed, was not sufficient to command decent treatment from male authorities. "If Mayor McClellan knew that we girls have a vote," Clara Lemlich asked a suffrage rally, "do you suppose he would have laughed at us when we marched to City Hall during the shirtwaist strike? Oh no. He would have been very courteous to us. And the police, they would not have been dragging us to the station house without the slightest provocation."[26]

WTUL members argued that political disfranchisement restricted women's bargaining power. Because women lacked political rights, employers could exploit them with impunity. Full citizenship in addition to unionization was necessary to ensure that men would take women's demands for better working conditions and higher wages seriously. League suffragists went so far as to argue that women's disfranchisement was the cause of their inferior position in the work force. Women were underbidders because they were a disfranchised group. "Behind suffrage," Leonora O'Reilly told a meeting of the International Brotherhood of Electrical Workers, "is the demand for equal pay for equal work."[27] Using the same argument, the executive board presented a resolution at the 1914 New York State Federation of Labor convention stating, "The disfranchised worker is always the lowest paid." Thus, WTUL suffragists tried to impress union men with the argument that voteless women would always undercut wages.

To the general public, league members worked to uncover the hypocrisy and absurdity of antisuffrage arguments by using working women as examples. In one well-attended Wage Earners' Suffrage League rally at Cooper Union, advertised as a mock debate between state senators and working women, each of the working women who spoke framed her talk around recent antisuffrage statements made by New York senators. Antisuffragist legislators, for instance, argued that the vote would rob women of their femininity and "destroy their incentive to motherhood." League members pointed out the upper-class bias of these arguments and their foolishness when applied to working women's experience. Did not working twelve hours a day rob a woman of her femininity, "charm," and "delicacy"? Did not constant standing and exhausting physical labor destroy a woman's "incentive to motherhood"? League members countered the notion held by the "antis" that women were "relieved from the burdens and responsibilities of life" by making the obvious point that hundreds of thousands of the state's women were already in the work force. They emphasized that far from having lost their "incentive to motherhood," working women were looking forward to assuming their responsibilities as mothers and wives. They needed the vote to protect their health and the health of future generations.[28]

Most frequently, league members argued that women needed the vote to ensure the passage of protective labor legislation. The WTUL, in the tradition of early twentieth-century social feminism, stressed that only women voters could see to it that legislators would pass laws protecting working women. Politicians, because of either venality or innate masculine insensitivity, would refuse to enact such laws without the agitation of enfranchised women. "To secure decent factories, we need the ballot," Leonora O'Reilly declared. "To abolish the sweated trades, the ballot is needed. To wipe out child labor the ballot is essential. . . . To secure these we go to City Hall and the State House, where votes and only votes count."[29] In arguing that only women could win protective laws, league members were assuming that women would recognize common interests and vote as a unified interest group. In addition, the league relied on the notion that women were naturally more compassionate than men. "I hold that the humanizing of industry is woman's business," Rose Schneiderman told a suffrage rally in 1913, "she must wield the ballot for this purpose."[30]

Clearly, the league's suffrage arguments show the league's shift from an emphasis on women's needs as workers to an emphasis on their special needs as women. Women workers required protection because they were female, and they needed the ballot to safeguard interests and concerns that were exclusively feminine. They were also oppressed in a way special to women, for only women could not vote. Thus, sex, not class, had become the primary distinction for the New York Women's Trade Union League. Men could be categorized together: male employers could refuse their female workers' demands for better working conditions and higher wages, male public officials could ignore their pleas for social justice, male police could assault them on picket lines, and male unionists could exclude them from the labor movement, all because women could not vote.

It is difficult to assess the league's success in interesting working women in suffrage. No membership statistics are extant for the Wage Earners' Suffrage League. We know that contingents of women workers marched with their unions and with the WTUL in the spectacular suffrage parade of 23 October, but we do not know how many. We have no evidence to give us any sense of how well rallies and meetings held for working women were attended. That suffrage never became an important issue for the great majority of the city's working women, however, seems clear. One small but revealing piece of evidence indicating this is a letter to Leonora O'Reilly from the president of one of the city's working girls' clubs. The president declined O'Reilly's offer to speak to the young women about suffrage because O'Reilly's fee of ten dollars was too high "in light of the fact that only one-fourth of our workers firmly believe in suffrage."[31]

Most league efforts in the 1915 campaign, however, were directed not to working women but to union men. Members conducted a systematic canvass of the city's unions, wrote leaflets addressed to male unionists, met frequently with union officers to discuss suffrage, and made numerous speeches to rank-and-file audiences at union meetings.

Ostensibly, suffragists should have had very little difficulty winning labor support. By 1915, most state labor organizations were already on record in favor of the reform. The New York State Federation of Labor and its predecessor, the New York Workingmen's Federation, had supported woman suffrage since 1884. The International Ladies' Garment Workers' Union had supported suffrage since its founding in 1900. Official labor support was so widespread that when the New Jersey State Federation of Labor refused its support for the 1915 referendum in that state it was conspicuous for its stand. At least one union, the United Hat Trimmers, withdrew temporarily in protest.[32]

But organized labor's public endorsement masked a strong undercurrent of rank-and-file hostility. WTUL suffrage speakers frequently found themselves the targets of heckling and ridicule when they spoke to labor audiences. When Ida Rauh addressed the New York City Central Federated Union in 1911, just a few months after that organization had endorsed woman suffrage, her speech was a disaster. According to one delegate, most of Rauh's presentation was "consumed by interruptions by men who apparently lacked all sense of justice or reason." Her efforts to persuade the men that suffrage would enable women to win better hours and wages so that they "will not be cheap labor anymore" fell on deaf ears.[33]

Male indifference and hostility seem to have been the reactions WTUL members encountered most frequently among unionists. In large measure, workingmen's hostility derived from the issue's association with temperance—an unpopular cause among urban immigrant workers. Also important in New York City was workers' conception of suffrage as an upper-class issue. Much of the opposition Ida Rauh encountered at the disastrous Central Federated Union meeting, for example, came from men demanding to know how the WTUL expected workers to support a movement that involved wealthy women such as Alva Belmont, widow of the antiunion millionaire O. H. P. Belmont. The labor and socialist press and newspapers popular with workers, such as the *Evening Journal* and the *World*, reinforced this view. Although the *Call*, the *Jewish Daily Forward*, the *New York Evening Journal*, and the *World* formally endorsed suffrage—unlike the conservative

*New York Times*—they portrayed the movement as upper class in character and minimized working people's interest in it. The idea that suffrage was a secondary issue with little relevance to working people's lives was tenacious and one that the WTUL was never able to dispel.

Despite their well-organized, unified, and lavishly financed campaign, suffragists failed in 1915. New York voters defeated the referendum by almost 200,000 votes. In New York City, suffrage lost by 89,000 votes. The defeat was part of a larger pattern in the industrial northeast. In New Jersey, where Essex County boss Ted Nugent fought the issue, suffrage suffered an overwhelming defeat in mid-October. Voters in Pennsylvania and Massachusetts also rejected the issue by large margins.

The election returns give a clearer picture of how the city's immigrant workers voted on the issue. Only two of the city's thirty-one districts went for suffrage—both by very narrow margins—but one of these, the sixth, on the lower East Side, was primarily Jewish. In the remaining districts, the margin of defeat was about the same in every district—two votes against suffrage for every vote in favor. It is clear that although immigrant workers did not strongly favor suffrage, they did not reject the measure in greater numbers than voters in native-born, middle-class districts.[34]

Neither the WTUL's efforts to influence local suffragists nor the election returns dissuaded some of the most influential of the city's suffrage leaders from blaming immigrant workers for the overwhelming defeat. Much to the league's dismay, Harriot Stanton Blatch, the president of the militant organization the Women's Political Union, was vocal in making this point. "No women in the world are so humiliated in asking for the vote as the American woman," Blatch said at a press conference a few days after the election.

> The English, the French, the German women all appeal to the men of their own nationality. The American woman appeals to men of 26 nationalities, not including the Indian. I asked for one of the most difficult places to [poll] watch for I wanted to feel this, and I wanted to feel it hard. I went down on Eldridge Street and saw the young men who had been in this country only a short time, but who were citizens and whom our own men were forcing us to ask for a vote. I am glad that they are free . . . but I call it tyranny and license for them to have power to pass upon me and upon the native-born women of America and a disgrace that the men of our country will force us to submit to it. Never again will I do it.[35]

Prominent East Side reformers, including WTUL members, were quick to deny Blatch's allegations. They pointed to the election returns as proof that immigrant workers, while not strongly in support of woman suffrage, certainly did not cause its defeat. But Blatch's statement indicates how little real impact the New York WTUL had on changing local suffrage leaders' attitudes. Although local suffragists courted workers' votes, the league's efforts to make suffrage leaders more sympathetic to workers do not seem to have met with much success. Virtually all local suffrage efforts to reach workers— the WSP's Industrial Section, the Wage Earners' Suffrage League, the canvassing of unions, and workers' rallies—were initiated and implemented by the WTUL.[36]

The WTUL's involvement with suffrage did not diminish after the 1915 defeat, despite the rejection of immigrant workers by suffrage leaders. Suffrage remained one of the WTUL's primary concerns throughout 1916 and 1917. During the same period, members spent more time in Albany lobbying for protective legislation. These new priorities hurt the WTUL's organizing efforts. WTUL members undertook far less organizing work in 1916–1917, despite an upsurge in the city's labor activity. Renewed organizing efforts in the needle trades as well as citywide strikes by transit and sanitation workers are scarcely mentioned in league records.

The league persisted in its suffrage efforts despite increasing factionalism within suffrage ranks. The impressive degree of harmony that had characterized the 1915 campaign disintegrated after the defeat. The most militant of the local organizations—Blatch's Women's Political Union—broke its temporary alliance with the Woman Suffrage party and merged with the Congressional Union for Woman Suffrage. The moderate suffrage societies remained with the NAWSA-affiliated WSP. Although both factions emphasized the primary importance of a federal amendment after the 1915 setbacks, they differed in their tactics. The Congressional Union, modeled after the English militants, stressed the importance of a small, disciplined cadre of workers who would fight for the federal suffrage amendment in a variety of forceful and often controversial ways: intensive congressional lobbying, picketing at the White House, and hunger strikes. In addition, the CU and its offspring in the suffrage states, the National Woman's party, adopted a partisan policy, also borrowed from the English militants, of supporting politicians and parties that endorsed a federal amendment and attempting to undermine those who did not.

NAWSA and its local affiliates such as the WSP remained non-partisan and stressed the importance of a broad-based movement. They pushed for a second state referendum as well as a federal amendment.

Although the WTUL continued to work with the Woman Suffrage party and to devote its efforts to winning labor support for a second state referendum, supporters of both factions could be found in the organization. As was the case with every league issue, the alliances of the members on the issue of suffrage crossed class lines. Workers as well as allies could be found among the WTUL's Congressional Union supporters, despite the CU's lack of concern for labor. Melinda Scott, for instance, campaigned for the Congressional Union.

Conflict between the two factions surfaced only once, during the 1916 presidential campaign. Despite organized labor's endorsement of Wilson, many league members supported Hughes because he, unlike Wilson, favored a federal suffrage amendment. Mary Dreier was especially vocal in her support of Hughes. Privately she conceded that his labor record was poor, but she was determined to support him publicly solely on the basis of his suffrage position. Rose Schneiderman and Melinda Scott, despite her Congressional Union affiliation, were appalled that Dreier could support a candidate with a poor labor record. As Dreier explained to her sister Margaret, "To them, Wilson is a great man and suffrage doesn't matter particularly."[37]

Although the federal suffrage amendment was not ratified until 1920, New York women won the vote in a second referendum late in 1917. Once again, the WTUL took charge of efforts to reach working men. For several months before the election, members canvassed unions in the city and upstate and found themselves received quite cordially. "It has been very amazing to me to find on the whole such a favorable sentiment for suffrage," Mary Dreier wrote to her sister Dorothea.[38] The change in voter opinion, perhaps due to women's war work, most suffrage organizations' support of the war effort, and the support of Tammany Hall, resulted in an easy victory for woman suffrage in 1917.[39] New York women had won the long fight for political equality.

Over the next twenty years of the league's existence the vote was to be primarily important as a way to further efforts for protective labor laws. Women reformers who could vote could command more influence at the state capitol than they had been able to muster before enfranchisement.

The amount of time and energy the league poured into the suffrage campaign from 1913 through 1917 and the nature of the WTUL's suffrage arguments, however, indicate that WTUL members saw the issue as more than merely a tool to work for protective laws. The years of the New York suffrage campaign marked a major transition for the WTUL, a transition that involved not only a change in the organization's priorities but also a shift in its ideology. In their continual attempts to reconcile gender and social class, WTUL members definitely adopted a feminist perspective during these years. Ten years of disappointments, cutbacks, and frustration in their organizing efforts convinced most league members to take their stand as feminists who emphasized the special needs of women workers as a separate group within the work force rather than to try to integrate women into the male-dominated labor movement.

The question remains, however, of why the WTUL emphasized suffrage rather than defying the labor movement on its own ground. The WTUL was simply not in a position early in the twentieth century to lay the groundwork for a feminist labor movement that synthesized women's needs as workers with their needs as women. The obstacles to such a course were too great: the absence of a strong industrial union tradition, the lack of adequate financial resources, the hostility of the AFL, and the ethnic and occupational differences among women workers made this course impossible. Instead, the WTUL gradually abandoned the field of labor organizing and left the work of unionizing women to uninterested men. In that sense, the league's choice of suffrage as an answer to working women's situation was a retreat, not a feminist victory.

## CHAPTER 7

# The Fight for Protective Legislation

Protective labor legislation became one of the major goals of the New York Women's Trade Union League at the same time that suffrage did: members devoted more time and money to both causes after the general strike era. WTUL members agitated for industrial safety and fire regulations, the prohibition of night work for women, an eight-hour day for women workers, and a women's minimum wage. Some laws, safety regulations, for example, were measures designed to affect all workers regardless of sex. The most important and controversial of the proposed protective measures, however, would affect women alone.

Like the emphasis on suffrage, the WTUL's emphasis on legislation signified important changes in the organization's identity. By embracing the solution of compensatory legislation, by formulating its own rationale for protective laws, and by opposing the labor movement (for organized labor disapproved of several important legislative proposals until the 1920s), the league shifted its ideological orientation away from an emphasis on women as workers to be integrated into the labor movement to one on women workers as women, with special needs, disadvantages, and weaknesses. Like the league's participation in the suffrage campaign, its members' fight for legal protection indicated their alignment with feminism[1] at the expense of their original commitment to the American Federation of Labor.

Just as the WTUL's increased concern with suffrage stemmed from members' frustration with organized labor, so, too, did its new emphasis on legislation. "We have come to the American Federation of Labor," Rose Schneiderman concluded in 1915, "and said to them, 'Come and help us organize the American working girl' . . . but nothing was done."[2] Significantly, in its fight for protective laws, the WTUL proved far more willing to oppose organized labor than it had been previously.

The shift to protective legislation also signified new attitudes toward working women. The New York league began to waver in its insistence that unionization was the only or even the primary solution to improving most women's conditions. Indeed, WTUL leaders began to suggest that many women could never be organized. As Mary Dreier wrote the league's new president, Melinda Scott, in 1914,

> What I feel very keenly is that the Women's Trade Union League
> has a real opportunity to be of service to the hard-pressed,
> unorganized, young or old working women as, for instance,
> the girls in the paper box trades, in the millinery, flower, retail
> clerks, and candy trades, and in the kimona and white goods
> industry. . . . It seems to me that in arousing public sentiment,
> first among the workers themselves, and second among the
> general public, for the minimum [wage] the League could
> proclaim to those women who know nothing about organiza-
> tion, who are so hardpressed that there seems little chance of
> organizing them, that the Women's Trade Union League is a
> friend to them in their extremity.[3]

Ten years of disappointments, battles with organized labor,
and the meager results in the trades mentioned by Dreier
weakened members' commitment to unionization.

Increased emphasis on legislation reflected league members'
growing conviction that women were a caste within the work
force. The premise behind protective laws was that women
entered the labor force with social and biological disadvantages. Women, the reformers argued, were primarily future
wives and mothers. Most would never work long enough to be
interested in unionism. Women were physically weaker than
men: their reproductive systems put them at a serious disadvantage in the labor force. These inherent disadvantages made
women more vulnerable than men to exploitation. Thus,
women could never be "equal" in industry without state assistance.

Finally, the New York league's emphasis on protective laws
indicated that members' thinking about the role of the state
was changing. Throughout the second decade of the twentieth
century, league members developed a positive conception of
the state's responsibility for effecting social change. Like other
early twentieth-century reformers, WTUL members gradually
moved away from a local orientation that emphasized direct
action and toward a state or national orientation that stressed
legislative solutions.[4]

Many feminists, both early in the twentieth century and in
the 1970s, have maintained that laws that discriminate on the
basis of sex have restricted female opportunity and perpetuated
outmoded and inaccurate conceptions of femininity. In addition, critics have questioned the motivations of those who
worked for protective legislation, often arguing that the primary impetus for such legislation came from male unionists

who believed protective legislation would keep women at a disadvantage.[5] Such criticism, although often valid from a contemporary perspective, sheds little light on why reformers worked so diligently for protective laws. Nor is such criticism accurate, for in New York, at least, organized labor neither initiated nor consistently supported protective measures for women.

To be sure, the rationale for protective legislation rested explicitly on Victorian notions of femininity: early twentieth-century reformers believed without question that women were weaker and more sensitive than men. There is no question that this rationale was more than an expedient argument designed to circumvent early twentieth-century judges' fondness for the doctrine of freedom of contract. "I can't help feeling that no woman should be allowed in the packing houses," Mary Dreier declared in 1912. "Having them stand all day working in the hideous smell. . . . It seems too terrible for words."[6] The campaign for female factory inspectors, another issue popular with league members, also illustrated the WTUL's view that women constituted a caste. League members argued that women should be inspectors because they "naturally had more insight into sanitary conditions" and could intuitively understand the strain under which women worked far better than men could.[7] However, the conditions league members experienced and witnessed in early twentieth-century industry and the difficulties they encountered with the labor movement were more important than Victorian mores in influencing the shift to legislation. Although the issue was highly controversial both inside and outside the league, allies and workers who stayed with the organization came to believe that the obstacles to unionization were too great, that unions could benefit only a small percentage of female workers, and that the conditions under which most women worked made any means of improvement acceptable.

The WTUL always casually endorsed protective legislation, much in the way it supported suffrage. In 1904, for example, the league, following AFL policy, endorsed a legislated eight-hour day for all workers. Members took part in the campaign for a federal investigation of women's and children's working conditions—a successful effort that resulted in the 1910 Senate investigation. They agitated among trade unionists to help win an appeal of a 1907 New York appellate court decision declaring the state night-work statute unconstitutional. Although they did not play an important role, members were enthusiastic about the Supreme Court's ruling in the 1908 *Muller v. Oregon* case and applauded the Brandeis brief. Nowhere in league records is criticism expressed about the rationale developed by the Consumers' League to support maximum hours laws for women—that the state's police power could be invoked to protect women because females were weaker than males and because their health, particularly as it influenced their childbearing abilities, was of vital importance to the state.

But in the organization's first decade, members were not convinced that new laws were an effective solution to the problems facing the city's working women. They knew from day-to-day experience that statutes already on the books were rarely enforced. Working-class members remembered their own experiences with factory inspection. Pauline Newman, for example, recalled that she and other children were hidden under piles of shirtwaists when the factory inspector visited the Triangle factory. Rose Schneiderman told of the responses she received when asking women why inspectors never seemed to notice violations. "He always comes around," the women reported, "but he is right alongside of the boss and we have to say we work eight hours."[8] WTUL members also knew that even when factory inspectors reported violations, they could not win convictions because women refused to testify. League members drew a clear lesson from the intimidation of unorganized women: only organization into stable unions could regulate women's hours and conditions effectively. As Mary Dreier summarized the WTUL's original legislative philosophy in 1909, "Even while we make laws, let us not forget the more important work of organization, for we know that the greatest power to enforce labor laws is trade unions, and a strong trade union can demand better conditions and shorter hours than the law will allow, and then, too, we get education and power through organization, which we do not get through law."[9] League members did not conceive of the state as a helpful agency. If anything, they viewed it as hostile to workers' interests. The state was "restrictive," "hampering," and in the hands of corrupt politicians and manufacturing interests.[10]

An external event was crucial in influencing the league's initial decision to agitate for legislation. On 27 November 1910, fire gutted a Newark, New Jersey, loft building that housed four paper-box and white-goods factories. Twenty-four young women were killed and scores of others injured. The Newark fire was a reminder that hundreds of thousands of workers toiled in crowded deathtraps. More than one hundred women worked in the Newark building, but there was only one fire escape. The workers trampled one another on the narrow staircase and jumped from windows to escape the flames.

Less than a week after the Newark fire, the WTUL formed its first legislative committee. Spurred by the realization that Newark conditions were no different from the ones they saw in New York, the committee made fire inspection its first priority and distributed a questionnaire on working conditions. Several hundred questionnaire responses and the wave of newspaper exposés that followed the Newark fire confirmed the fact that the labor movement had made little headway in improving conditions. Of the city's 11,000 manufacturing establishments, only 100 were fireproof. Most had inadequate water supplies; nearly all had wooden staircases and inaccessible fire escapes; many had no fire escapes at all. Some respondents reported that their employers kept windows and doors locked. The questionnaire responses bore graphic testimony to the dangers in New York factories. Desperation permeated many of the replies. "This factory is in Danger of girls [sic] lives," one typical response began. "I have known girls taken out fainting with the Dust of the world on their lungs and also we Drink the water from the tank of the toilet and wash with it—you investigate yourself." Most responses were unsigned, or signed "Girl Employee." Some women omitted the names and addresses of the factories they described. Others began to sign their names, thought better of it, and crossed out their signatures, explaining, "Afraid to sign name—might lose position."[11]

When Ida Rauh, who chaired the committee, submitted her first report in March 1911, she stressed that fire safety was the committee's first priority. A few weeks after Rauh circulated the committee's findings, however, the Newark fire became only a tragic prelude to the disaster of 25 March 1911 in the Triangle Shirtwaist factory. That company, members discovered, was a model establishment by city standards. It was a modern factory, not a sweatshop. The building in which the company was located had passed the city's fire and building inspections. After the fire, the league pushed for legislative action rather than for new organizing efforts. The organization urged Governor Dix to establish a permanent industrial commission. He established the New York State Factory Investigating Commission (FIC), which was empowered not only to investigate but also to propose new legislation.

The WTUL had close ties with the FIC. Mary Dreier was one of the twelve commissioners. Allies Elizabeth Watson and Violet Pike worked as FIC investigators, and Rose Schneiderman, Elizabeth Dutcher, Helen Marot, and Melinda Scott frequently testified. They persuaded women unionists to testify at hearings and sought out women in unorganized shops and stores to speak as well.

Thus, agitation for better safety laws—legislation that would affect both men and women—marked the league's first legislative efforts. Members soon began to devote attention to a women's maximum-hours law as well. When the national Women's Trade Union League called for an eight-hour workday for women at its 1909 convention, the resolution did not precipitate any controversy within the New York branch. The issue was a familiar one, for the AFL supported both a federal eight-hour-day statute for all workers and special hours legislation for women.

The New York league was not ready to fight for an eight-hour day. The organization decided instead to back the state Consumers' League in its efforts to win a women's fifty-four-hour law. The WTUL's 1911 campaign for a fifty-four-hour statute established the organization's major legislative tactics. The league recruited six working women to testify before the Assembly Committee on Industry and Labor. Testimony by women workers was intended not only to move legislators by firsthand accounts of deplorable conditions but also to impress them that female workers themselves wanted legislative protection. The WTUL also encouraged allies to testify as "women interested in the lifting up of womankind."[12]

New York league members, like other social reformers, argued that long hours damaged women's health. In this they could point to the impressive volume of medical testimony taken by the FIC. "A woman's body is unable to withstand strain, fatigue, and privations as well as a man's," Violet Pike declared. "The nervous strain resulting from monotonous work and speeding up, intensified by the piece work system, when coupled with excessive length of working hours, can only result in undermining the whole physical structure of the woman. . . . [It] can destroy the health of women and render them unfit to perform their functions as mothers."[13] League members also stressed that a direct relationship existed between long hours and low wages: wages were higher in trades in which a union enforced short hours.

The woman's lobby was not as effective as were the state manufacturers who mounted an extensive campaign against the bill. Manufacturing lobbyists maintained that the measure would be disastrous for seasonal industries such as canning. The manufacturing interests won: although the Assembly passed the bill, the Senate defeated it.

In 1912, due primarily to the concerted lobbying efforts of the New York City Consumers' League and the last minute support of Tammany boss Charlie Murphy, the legislature passed a fifty-four-hour bill, weakened by substitutions that allowed overtime work in seasonal industries. The New York WTUL introduced its proposal for a forty-eight-hour week and an eight-hour day immediately after the fifty-four-hour law was passed. The league's bill, unlike the new law, would affect all working women, not just those under twenty-one, and would limit the hours a factory could remain open. The FIC endorsed the league's bill, and an FIC commissioner, state Senator Robert Wagner, introduced it in the spring of 1913. In every legislative session before World War I it was defeated in committee. The hours law was also threatened by a 1916 bill that would have permitted upstate cannery owners to institute as much as eleven hours of overtime a week during rush seasons. Governor Whitman vetoed the bill, but much to the league's dismay, the New York State Labor Federation supported it. Throughout the spring of 1916, the league vociferously denounced the state federation for its stand.

The maximum-hours-law campaign did not take the league away from its primary work of organization. From 1911 through 1913, the WTUL's legislative committee emphasized that its primary function was to help enforce the existing laws rather than to propose new legislation. Members clearly regarded legislation as a supplement rather than a substitute to unionization. By the end of 1913, however, the campaign for protective legislation began to take more time and was increasingly oriented to laws that applied only to women. The league singled out for "urgent" attention the forty-eight-hour week, maternity pensions, a women's minimum wage, more female factory inspectors, and the prohibition of women's night work —all measures that emphasized women's special status in the labor force.

In the years before World War I, the WTUL concentrated primarily upon the eight-hour day and a minimum wage. The campaign for maximum-hours legislation was uncomplicated: arguments were based on the premise that the law was needed as a health measure. Alignments were clear: the opponents were manufacturers; the defenders, reformers. A minimum wage for women, however, was considerably more controversial. The national WTUL included a plank for a "living wage" in its first legislative platform in 1909. A "living wage," national president Margaret Dreier Robins explained, would allow workers to earn not only money sufficient for subsistence, but enough for entertainment, for relaxation, for a few of life's amenities. The New York league did not follow the national league's lead immediately: its legislative committee committed itself only to investigating the issue, and New York leaders argued among themselves about the measure. Despite the AFL's opposition, a substantial minority of WTUL allies and workers wanted a women's minimum wage law. Rose Schneiderman was the working-class member most vocal in favor of the "living wage" idea. "I am one of the 'conservative group,'" she stated in 1915, "for nowadays when you favor legislation you are tagged 'conservative.' When you want to use both feet instead of hopping along on one they say, 'You are not trade unionists anymore.'"[14] Mary Dreier was one of the first allies convinced of the desirability of a woman's minimum wage. Her experiences as an FIC commissioner convinced her that New York should establish a minimum wage commission empowered to investigate and establish wage floors for industries that employed large numbers of women and minors.

Many members disagreed, and again the differences of opinion crossed class lines. Rose Schneiderman, Pauline Newman, and Maud Swartz—all workers—were strongly in favor of such a measure. Melinda Scott, Leonora O'Reilly, and ally Helen Marot were vehemently opposed. They voiced AFL arguments that such laws would violate workers' rights to demand wage increases and that a minimum rate would become a maximum wage. In part, the opponents' disagreement was based on the AFL's position. But they were also unhappy with the minimum wage because the measure identified women as a special group. As Helen Marot stated in testimony before the FIC, "If women need state protection on the ground that they do not organize as men do, then also do the mass of unskilled, unorganized men who do not appreciate or take advantage of organization. . . . The reasons for trade unionists to oppose state interference in wage rates apply to women workers as they do to men."[15] For these WTUL leaders, minimum wage legislation was different from maximum-hours statutes. Hours laws could apply to only women because their rationale rested on biological premises. There was no physiological reason, however, for women to earn a specified wage. Throughout 1916, the New York league's leadership remained divided, and the executive board defeated proposals to endorse a minimum wage each time the issue came to a vote.[16]

After the United States entered World War I the WTUL virtually ceased its organizing efforts and concentrated on maintaining existing protective laws and extending them to cover women workers in new wartime occupations. During the war, the league completed its transformation from a labor organization to a women's social reform organization. Despite the fact that more working women joined the league during and after the war than ever had before, the league shifted to a social reform rather than a trade unionist perspective.

Wartime developments help explain this change. Within a few months after the United States's entry into the war, several thousand women took men's places in the city's work force. For the first time, employers hired women telegraph messengers, elevator operators, letter carriers, and subway guards, ticket clerks, and conductors. Throughout 1918, as more men left for service, the number of women in these previously all-male occupations increased substantially. In New York City, employment on the transit lines was particularly important. Women eagerly sought jobs as subway guards and conductors largely because the work paid substantially better wages than did jobs traditionally held by women. A woman could earn twenty to twenty-five dollars a week as a subway guard or conductor at a time when more than 60 percent of the city's female workers earned less than fourteen dollars and only 8 percent more than twenty dollars. Also, women apparently enjoyed the work, which provided more variety than traditional female industrial and service occupations.[17]

The Women's Trade Union League, however, was not pleased by these changes. Members pointed out that women messengers, elevator operators, and transit workers were not covered by the state labor laws that limited hours and prohibited night work. They exposed examples of exploitation, such as elevator operators who worked more than ninety hours a week and were paid only eight or nine dollars. League members were especially concerned about female telegram messengers, arguing that young women's morals were endangered by such work. Early in 1918, at a special WTUL conference on women's war work, the New York league resolved to work for legislation that would extend the existing limitations on hours and night work to all women—not just to those who worked in industrial and mercantile establishments—and to prohibit any woman under twenty-five from working as a messenger.[18]

A second wartime development also distressed the WTUL. No sooner had the United States entered the war than a strong movement was underway to suspend existing labor laws. In New York, the efforts to do away with protective legislation were led by two conservative Republican upstate politicians, Thaddeus Sweet, speaker of the state assembly, and Elon Brown, who argued that patriotic duty required an indefinite suspension of all laws that interfered with maximizing production. Swept up in the patriotic hysteria generated during the war, the state labor movement joined the conservative forces calling for such measures. The WTUL fought these efforts to weaken the labor laws, but in the process the organization was vehemently denounced. "Everybody has gone mad," Mary Dreier concluded shortly after the war began, "the men were all lunatic."[19]

Despite members' dismay, the league's wartime efforts were quite successful. Not only were efforts to suspend the labor laws blocked, but new legislation was passed. In the spring of 1918, the legislature passed a bill prohibiting women under twenty-one from working as telegraph messengers. A year later, the legislature passed the Lockwood Transportation Act, which extended existing protective statutes to cover female transit workers.

From women transit workers' viewpoint, the new law was a disaster. A few days after its passage, the Brooklyn Rapid Transit Company (BRT), dismissed nearly 1,500 women guards, conductors, and ticket agents and replaced them with men. The women who lost their jobs were vehement in their denunciation of the "impractical reformers" and labor unions that had backed the bill and complained that the WTUL had never consulted the workers themselves for their opinions on the proposed law. "The sooner that society women understand that they must keep their hands off the working woman, the sooner the working woman will be better off," one BRT worker stated.[20] Margaret Hinchey, who had distinguished herself as a WTUL suffrage organizer, was one working-class league member who was exceedingly bitter about the efforts of the Transportation Act and the league's support of it. "I see it is not a League for the working woman only a Political org.," she wrote Leonora O'Reilly, "so we will have to find an org that will stand by the working women that we can trust wont sell us out while our nose is to the grinding stone. . . . Rember you told me the League was our friend and would look out for our Intersents. . . . They are certainly sorry for the women up the state but no

sorrow for the women right here in New York City let us have
sorrow at home first. . . . I stand for the right of working
women to kick themselves when and where they want work 8
or 9 hours day or night just the same as men they have no club
over them why should we?"[21]

Privately, a few WTUL leaders expressed misgivings about
the unintended effects of the Transportation Act. Maud Swartz,
for one, feared that the league might be "going too far."[22]
Publicly, however, the league defended the new law and
blamed the BRT for the mass dismissals. Members pointed out
that transit companies, in anticipation of the armistice, had
begun to lay off women before the law was passed. Furthermore, employers had the option of operating within the law's
framework and could have made the necessary adjustments
without firing the women. Instead, according to the WTUL, the
BRT took advantage of the legislation to do what it had planned
to do anyway—replace women with men after the war.[23]

The disastrous aftermath of the Transportation Act marked
the last time league members debated the merits of protective
legislation. After the armistice, the organization was firmly
committed to extending existing legislation to cover all working
women and to agitating for new laws.

In good part, this shift can be explained not only by the
league's disappointments with the labor movement, but also by
the fact that by 1917 most allies and working-class members
who opposed the new orientation were gone. Helen Marot, who
resigned as secretary in 1913, did not figure in league affairs by
the time of the war. She had been the most vocal opponent of
special laws and the most ardent proponent of organization.
Leonora O'Reilly had resigned from the league in 1915. Melinda
Scott had resigned as the league's president in 1917 to work as a
United Textile Workers organizer. Maggie Hinchey, who had
done such splendid work as a WTUL suffrage organizer, had
also left the league and was vociferous in her denunciation of
protective legislation. Rose Schneiderman, who succeeded
Melinda Scott as president in 1917, Pauline Newman, Maud
Swartz, and other working-class members were firmly committed to protective laws. Thus, without much internal debate
or opposition, the New York league adopted an unquestioning
position on protective legislation, which caused it much difficulty during the war.

Significantly, during the postwar years working women controlled the league's policies to a far greater extent than they had
earlier. By the time Rose Schneiderman was elected president,

every officer was a worker. Throughout the 1920s, Schneiderman and Maud Swartz, the league's secretary, were the two most influential league leaders. Women workers also made up a larger percentage of the league's active members than they had previously. By 1924, eleven of the twelve executive board members were unionists—a pattern that persisted for the rest of the WTUL's existence.[24]

By the same token, allies were steadily less important in the day-to-day work of the league. Of the original allies who had been so important before the war, only Mary Dreier remained. The others had left for careers in government, social service, or the labor movement. The number of allies also declined because young college women no longer flocked to the organization. The WTUL continued to depend upon allies for financial support, but the women who provided most of the league's funding after World War I did not take part in policymaking. Dorothy Straight, Florence Lamont, Cornelia Pinchot, and Eleanor Roosevelt were typical of this new breed of allies whose participation was limited to planning league benefits and attending WTUL social events. Dorothy Straight, for instance, purchased a Lexington Avenue townhouse for the WTUL early in the decade. Eleanor Roosevelt, who joined the league in 1922, spent occasional Saturdays at its headquarters, publicly endorsed its work, and invited Schneiderman and Swartz to Hyde Park. These new allies, however, did not organize or lobby. Quite clearly, the WTUL was moving away from its original ideology, which held that nonworking women could be competent and dedicated labor organizers. Instead, by 1919 the officers were recommending that allies be replaced with paid workers because the former were simply not as qualified for league work.[25]

This growing concentration of working-class women in the league indicates that the shift from direct organizing work to an emphasis on legislation was not the result of upper-class domination.[26] Rather, it was due to changes in league members' thinking. Women who joined the league in its early years came with a strong belief in the effectiveness of craft unionism and with the conviction that women could be integrated into the labor movement on an equal basis with men. As the years passed, their ideas about the labor movement and their perceptions of women workers changed. Rose Schneiderman, for example, was a strong proponent of direct organization. By 1915, however, she was looking beyond organized labor to state action and to woman suffrage for more effective solutions to the problems women faced in the work force. In part, the changes in her thinking reflected her personal disappointment with the labor movement's refusal to accept women on equal terms with men or to support the league. She was especially embittered by the state labor movement in the years immediately following the war, when James Holland, president of the New York State Federation of Labor, denounced the league as a subversive organization and Schneiderman as "Red Rose" in testimony before the New York legislature's Lusk committee.[27] Then, too, Schneiderman's strong support for protective laws reflected her disillusionment with women workers. During her years as the league's president in the 1920s, she frequently alluded to women's lack of seriousness about their work and their inability to organize. "The woman's industrial life is a short one," she declared. "As a usual thing she enters industry young—when she wants to play, she wants to meet boys, and she is looking for her mate. She doesn't begin to get serious with her job until some of that playtime has passed, or until she begins to doubt whether the mate will come. It is very difficult to make an impression upon young girls until then."[28] Schneiderman, then, gradually came to the conclusion that women presented virtually insurmountable problems to the labor organizer. At no time did she say that protective laws were preferable to organization. Rather, she stressed that her own experiences and perceptions had taught her that legislation was necessary.

Schneiderman's position reflected the league's rationale for protective legislation during the 1920s. Significantly, few of the arguments the WTUL advanced in the twenties rested on biological or physiological factors. Instead, the WTUL emphasized the social and economic conditions that dictated women's inferior status in the labor force. Members stressed that women continued to work longer hours for less pay than men received. "These laws apply only to women," one league pamphlet stated, "because women's hours as a rule are longer than men's, women's wages as a rule, are lower than men's, women's economic need is therefore greater than men's."[29] Using this argument, the league could point to an impressive array of statistical evidence. By 1920, a New York woman needed a minimum of $16 a week to support herself. Yet in New York State, 88 percent of industrial women earned less. By 1923, the average weekly wage for women in the state was $16.50, half of men's average of $31.50.[30] Workweeks, particularly in unregulated occupations such as laundries, hotels, and restaurants, continued to be longer, on the average, than the fifty-four-hour maximum for factories and stores, where hours were legislated. Women continued to be temporary workers as well. The New York Consumers' League found, for instance, that of 500 female industrial workers surveyed in 1920, 46 percent had been in the jobs less than a year.[31] Under the current social and economic conditions, then, women alone could not command a position of equality in the workplace. Their socialization usually rendered them tractable workers; their unskilled temporary status excluded them from vocational training and upward mobility; their lack of skill lessened their bargaining power. Then, too, a woman's primary social roles were still as homemaker, wife, and mother. As Maud Swartz explained, "Actual conditions of life for the working woman put her in a peculiar position. She has two jobs: her home to look after, and her work in the factory or shop. It will be a long time before the conditions of men and women will be equalized in that respect. Without the laws to protect the interests of the woman in industry she would have little chance for equality."[32]

Thus, during the 1920s, the WTUL made protective legislation its primary work. Pooling its efforts with the Joint Legislative Conference, an umbrella organization composed of representatives from the state and city consumers' leagues, the Young Women's Christian Association, the American Association for Labor Legislation, and other reform groups, the league pushed for an eight-hour day and a minimum wage. From time to time members suggested other legislative proposals, such as state maternity insurance, but these had to be dropped for lack of legislative support.

The WTUL was supported in its legislative program by the state labor movement (which dropped its earlier opposition to women's minimum wage laws) and the state Democratic party. New York Democratic governors Al Smith and Franklin Roosevelt were particularly amenable to the league's legislative program.

The league's alliance with the Democrats marked a change from earlier years. Before the war, most league members considered themselves socialists or progressive Republicans. After the ratification of the Nineteenth Amendment, however, many members and the organization as a whole moved squarely into Democratic ranks. Mary Dreier's and Rose Schneiderman's political odysseys illustrate the kinds of changes league members made. Dreier became active in politics as a Progressive during the 1912 Bull Moose presidential campaign. She, along with

Margaret and Raymond Robins, was a diligent campaign worker for Theodore Roosevelt. After the Progressive defeat Mary Dreier moved into regular party ranks, supporting Charles Evans Hughes in 1916. It became clear to Dreier during the war and the postwar antiradical hysteria that the Republican party had become the party of reaction. "The Republican Party in this state is beyond the pale!" she wrote to Margaret Robins. "It has to its credit first the betrayal of representative government in the ousting of the Socialists, second the planting of a spy system through the passage of one of the Lusk bills, and third the betrayal . . . of the working women in this state. And we have no money, no organization to fight this. It is a sickening situation."[33]

When Rose Schneiderman joined the league she was a socialist. After the war, she devoted herself briefly to the new state Labor party and ran as the Labor candidate for U.S. senator in 1920. Shortly thereafter, Schneiderman became a staunch Democrat.

One reason for Schneiderman's loyalty, as well as WTUL allegiance generally, to the Democratic party was the relationship between the league and Eleanor and Franklin Roosevelt. After Eleanor Roosevelt joined the league early in the 1920s, she became good friends with Schneiderman and Maud Swartz. During frequent visits to the Roosevelt homes in New York City and Hyde Park, these league leaders talked at length to Franklin Roosevelt, educating him about labor problems and the trade union movement. During Roosevelt's term as governor, the WTUL celebrated its twenty-fifth anniversary at Hyde Park with hundreds of the city's union women in attendance. "You were the main topic of conversation all the way down the river," Schneiderman wrote Franklin Roosevelt. "The girls were saying over and over again, 'Was not the Governor great' 'What a kind face he has' and 'How democratic he is,' etc., etc. . . . As for myself—well, I wish there were a million more like you and Eleanor."[34]

Despite political support, however, the fight for protective measures was an uphill struggle. The league's legislative successes were modest. In 1920, all female industrial, mercantile, and transportation workers were covered by the fifty-four-hour law and the night-work statute, which prohibited women from working after 10 P.M. Early in the twenties, to the league's dismay, the legislature exempted transit, bindery, and printing workers from the night-work statute. New York passed a weak forty-eight-hour law in 1927. The statute was limited to women industrial workers. Minimum wage legislation took longer. Not only was such legislation more controversial than maximum-hours laws, but for most of the decade it was unconstitutional as well. The 1923 Supreme Court decision in *Adkins v. Children's Hospital*, which invalidated the Washington, D.C., minimum wage statute on the grounds that it violated a worker's freedom of contract, retarded passage of minimum wage legislation in New York. Not until the depths of the Depression, when wages and piece rates sank to turn-of-the-century levels, was agitation for a women's minimum wage law successful. In 1933, New York established a minimum wage commission for women and minors. The Supreme Court struck it down as unconstitutional in 1936. Finally, after the court reversed itself the next year in the *West Coast Hotel v. Parrish* decision, the state's minimum wage commission was permanently established.

The most successful of the league's legislative activities was its Women's Compensation Service, which Maud Swartz established in 1922. As compensation adviser, Swartz assisted several hundred women a year in prosecuting their compensation claims. She provided clear explanations and advice on the workings of the compensation law, made referrals to physicians, social services, and rehabilitation programs, and served as an advocate for individual women.

The league's legislative defeats during the twenties were due to powerful and varied opposition. The Republicans controlled the state legislature throughout most of the decade, and the party consistently opposed labor reform measures. Manufacturers and businessmen continued to fight protective measures and, in the wave of postwar reaction, often aligned themselves with right-wing organizations such as the League for Patriotic Americanism.

The most persistent and distressing opposition the WTUL faced after World War I, however, came not from the Republicans but from other women. After the passage of the Nineteenth Amendment, American feminists split over the issues of an equal rights amendment and protective legislation. In addition, two New York working women's organizations, the Women's League for Equal Opportunity, formed in 1915, and the smaller Equal Rights League, established in 1917, vigorously opposed all protective statutes that affected only women.

These organizations were composed of women who worked in traditionally male occupations, primarily in the printing trades and on transit lines. In 1919, their ranks swelled with dismissed telegraphers, streetcar conductors, guards, and ticket agents. After the war both organizations were strong enough to send lobbyists to every legislative hearing. Their primary concern was that displacement would be the inevitable result of protective laws. As one leader stated, "It will drain women out of all highly paid and highly organized trades, because the law will prevent them from doing the same work as men do."[35] Members of these organizations blamed the WTUL for their plight. "So-called 'welfare' legislation is not asked for or wanted by real working women," the Women's League for Equal Opportunity claimed. "These welfare bills are drafted by self-styled social uplifters who assert that working women do not know enough to protect themselves, aided by a few women who once worked but who are now living off the labor movement."[36]

Working women opposed to protective legislation were supported in their stand by the National Woman's party (NWP), the successor to the militant suffrage organization, the Congressional Union. Alva Belmont, once a WTUL sympathizer, funded the NWP and was its president. Economic and labor issues were peripheral to the NWP's goal of securing a federal equal rights amendment. Consistent with its emphasis on complete legal equality for women, the NWP lobbied against protective legislation. Woman's party members testified at every legislative hearing that protective statutes solidified women's inferior social and economic status by making them frail and helpless in the eyes of the law. Protective legislation, the party stressed, no matter what its proponents' ultimate goals and attitudes, was inherently discriminatory. Party leaders emphasized that they did not oppose legislation per se, but rather the fact that laws applied only to women. "We want labor progress and labor reform," Alice Paul stated. "We do not care whether it comes through labor organization or through legislation. But we want the sex bias to be taken out of laws and arguments. We want the competition to be fair."[37]

The NWP's activities were vexing to the New York league. Every time WTUL members traveled to Albany to testify in favor of new laws, they found their arguments refuted not by crass and heavy-handed cannery owners and right-wing politicians, but by the very women with whom they had fought for suffrage a few years earlier. It was particularly troublesome that some of the league's former members had gone over to the NWP. Former allies Maud Younger and Harriot Stanton Blatch were vocal NWP members and articulate opponents of protective legislation. Gertrude Barnum, although not affiliated with the NWP, denounced the WTUL for its new legislative emphasis.[38] Margaret Hinchey and Josephine Casey, once active working-class members, now lobbied for the Woman's party.

Clashes between the league and the Woman's party were frequent and acrimonious. Josephine Casey, for instance, accused the league of "not staying on the job of organizing women. . . . The trouble is girls, that you are getting old and tired, and want some easier way."[39] Conflict between the two organizations peaked in 1926 when the U.S. Women's Bureau of the Department of Labor asked representatives from each group to plan an investigation of the effects of protective legislation. The Woman's party favored public hearings with testimony from working women. The WTUL pressed for a "technical study by experts and by scientific methods." The league argued that working women would fear employers' reprisals if they testified at public hearings and that the NWP would recruit women known to be opposed to protective laws. After several weeks of argument, the WTUL resigned from the Women's Bureau committee.[40]

The New York league tried to behave as though the Woman's party were nothing more than a minor nuisance—an irritant, to be sure, but a force that the public should not take seriously. "The National Woman's Party," one New York league report stated, "is a group of theorists."[41] League members also liked to think that manufacturers dominated the Woman's party behind-the-scenes. They pointed out that NWP leaders were wealthy, that some were married to rich industrialists, and that they had never had to work for a living. The league argued that the Woman's party, despite its professed belief in trade unions, expressed a "thoroughgoing individualist, laissez-faire philosophy for women. It is impossible to take as serious or sincere, the insistence of Woman's Party spokeswomen that their purpose is to have laws now applying to women extended to men."[42] The league, in short, tried to discredit the Woman's party by arguing that its feminism was self-serving and unrealistic. Far from advancing women's status, league members argued, the party's program, particularly the proposed equal rights amendment, contributed to the continuing exploitation of working-class women. "To seek a mere level in the name of equality," the league concluded, "is as if women had sought equal suffrage by taking the vote away from men."[43]

Working women's opposition was far more disturbing. Such opposition contradicted the league's central contentions that working women wanted protective laws and that the WTUL spoke for women workers. The WTUL had two responses to this opposition. Members argued that the Equal Rights League and the Women's League for Equal Opportunity were not working-class organizations at all but were financed secretly by manufacturing and right-wing interests. They also argued that these groups represented an atypical and marginal faction of the female work force and that many of their members were business and professional women. Both WTUL responses denied any legitimacy to working women's protests against protective laws.

The WTUL had no facts to prove that manufacturing interests financed these organizations. No doubt other opponents of protective legislation were delighted by the existence of working women's organizations that ably defended their position. An alliance, however, was improbable and unnecessary.

The league's contention that these working women were atypical had more basis in fact. Members of the Women's League for Equal Opportunity and the Equal Rights League, although not professional women as the WTUL claimed, were workers most likely to be affected adversely by protective legislation. Printers led both groups. Women in the printing trades, particularly typesetters, were unusual among women workers not only because they were skilled but also because they competed directly with men for jobs. Protective legislation, especially the prohibition of night work, put them at a distinct disadvantage in finding and keeping employment. Other women who joined these organizations had lost their jobs as telegraphers and transit workers. These women, too, had been in occupations that were traditionally male and in which they competed directly with men for work.

The league correctly stressed that most women were not in such circumstances. Given the patterns of occupational segregation by sex, the overwhelming majority of women workers labored in traditionally female occupations. What little evidence exists on these workers' attitudes toward protective legislation indicates that they favored such statutes. The New York Consumers' League conducted a survey of working women's attitudes toward an eight-hour-day law in 1927. Four out of five women answered yes to the question, "Would you be in favor of a law that limited a woman's working hours to forty-eight hours a week?"[44]

The bitter debates between the supporters and opponents of protective legislation continued through the 1930s and 1940s.

During these years, however, the National Woman's party steadily declined in numbers and influence. As the prospect of an equal rights amendment dimmed and as the federal government took up a number of the most important legislative demands, such as the minimum wage, the conflict waned.

The significance of the battles over protective legislation and the equal rights amendment is great. Underlying the debate were conflicts over the definition of feminism and how best to reconcile women's dual status as females and as workers in a male-dominated society. In trying to determine how to win equality for working women, both critics and advocates of protective laws failed to discriminate between the long-term and short-term effects of such statutes. In the short run, the WTUL's experience had given its members a better grasp of the realities of early twentieth-century working women's situation. The league never argued that legislation was preferable to organization. But members had learned that mere assertions of women's equality in the work force did not bring it about. By 1913, when the New York league's primary emphasis shifted from organization to legislation, its members had been trying for nearly ten years to convince trade unionists that women should be treated equally. Their efforts, however, had met with little success. Nor could assertions of women's equality give them control over their wages and working conditions. As Mabel Leslie, a garment worker and league secretary during the 1920s, stated, "We were free to work twelve hours a day but we were not free to refuse to do it."[45] Protective laws were necessary, the league argued, not to give women preferential treatment, but rather to bring them up to a position of equality with men. As Maud Swartz put it, "The labor laws are a means toward industrial equality for women."[46] Finally, in the short run, the league was apparently correct in its insistence that few women were hindered in their vocational opportunities as the result of protective statutes. The Women's Bureau concluded in 1928 that "regulating hour laws as applied to women engaged in manufacturing processes do not handicap them."[47] In those instances in which laws did make it difficult for women to keep their jobs, such as in the printing trades, women were generally able to win exemptions.

But the Women's Trade Union League expressed no concern over the possible long-term effects of the laws for which they worked so hard. Although such statutes apparently did not impede the great majority of women in their present jobs, they did strengthen barriers to holding other kinds of jobs. Protective legislation as a concept and as a body of statutes strengthened sexual segregation and stratification patterns in the labor force, for such laws were based on the assumption that women would always be cheap, temporary, unskilled labor. In other words, legislation strengthened traditional notions of women's work and men's work. In these respects, opponents were correct that protective statutes defined patterns of discrimination against female wage earners, limited their economic opportunities, and solidified stereotypical notions of women as frail, passive, and dependent.

Significantly, both league members and their opponents considered themselves feminists. In no way was the debate over protective legislation a fight between feminists and social reformers. Rather, the conflict was between two competing versions of feminism and two widely divergent ways of improving women's status in a male-dominated society.

The NWP and other women's organizations opposed to protective laws downplayed sex differences in much the same manner as the league had done in its first years. For women to achieve equality in the workplace and in society, gender could not be a factor in determining treatment. By the 1920s, the WTUL's definition of feminism was very different. Rather than ignoring sex differences, the league stressed that feminists, if they were to be realistic, had to take women's social limitations into account. Because women could not command equal pay for equal work, because most could not move beyond unskilled or semiskilled jobs, because most had responsibilities at home as well as at work, because many were unreceptive to unionization, because, in a word, women could not compete with men, true equality would come only with state assistance. Thus, by the 1920s, in its continual attempts to reconcile class and gender, the league had moved toward emphasizing the latter. A conviction that women composed an oppressed group within the labor force had replaced the league's original conviction that women's problems in the workplace were inseparable from those of men and that those difficulties could be solved by integrating women into the labor movement. Despite the fact that the league in the 1920s was more of a working-class organization than it had been before the war, it had moved to a position of caste rather than of class consciousness.

It was unfortunate that the league's changed emphasis did not spark an exploration of feminist alternatives to AFL craft unionism or an intensified organizing campaign. Given the

WTUL's unwillingness and inability to undertake independent trade union activity and its disillusionment with the progress of unions among New York's working women, however, its shift from organization to legislation was inevitable.

# Conclusion

The Women's Trade Union League of New York remained in existence until 1955. After World War I, however, the organization bore little resemblance to the small group of workers and allies who had set out late in 1903 to unionize New York City's women workers. The story of the New York league between 1920 and 1955 is the story of an efficient but increasingly impoverished social welfare organization devoted to lobbying for women's protective legislation and dedicated to providing a pleasant social center for young working women.

The WTUL's shift in identity from a women's labor organization to a social welfare organization was well under way before World War I. Disillusionment with the labor movement, realization of the impossibility of organizing women along craft lines, and frustration with working women caused WTUL members to change their orientation. The war, however, completed the transition. Many New York members discontinued their local activities to take assignments in state and federal agencies. Mary Dreier headed the New York State Women in Industry Committee for the Council of National Defense. Melinda Scott served on the National War Labor Board. Mary Van Kleeck worked as the director of the U.S. Department of Labor's Women in Industry Service. Other members served in federal and state employment bureaus. League members' experiences during the war familiarized them with government activity and deepened their conviction that the state could be an effective agent for social change. As Frances Perkins, who joined the New York WTUL briefly during the war, declared, "The war has taught us that an industry can be changed overnight."[1] State action, in short, seemed far more effective and efficient than the slow and arduous work of organizing.

The war changed league members' outlook in other ways, too. Before World War I, the WTUL was an enormously optimistic organization. Its members were convinced that once labor leaders and the public could be made to see the ways working women were exploited, unions would integrate them into their ranks and legislatures would enact protective laws. The antiradical hysteria the war generated and the social and political repression that followed in its wake severely disillusioned league women and killed much of their early enthusiasm and

162

vitality. Throughout the war years, WTUL members described themselves as anguished and the nation as "lunatic" and "mad." "The last years have been black to me," Margaret Dreier Robins concluded in 1920.[2] Much has been written about the persistence of the progressive reform impulse after the war.[3] The continued existence of organizations such as the WTUL is often cited as evidence that progressivism lived on into the 1920s. But this argument ignores the changed nature of the Women's Trade Union League in the postwar period. Once an organization composed of idealistic volunteers who went looking for shop strikes and delivered rousing union speeches from street corners, the WTUL of the 1920s and 1930s was composed of paid staff members who spent much of their time in Albany lobbying for protective labor statutes.

New York league members did not take up their local activities on a full-time basis after the war. Rose Schneiderman was among the labor delegates to the Paris Peace Conference. She, Mary Dreier, and Leonora O'Reilly helped establish the International Congress of Working Women. As wartime agencies were converted into permanent bureaus and departments, New York league members played important roles in them. Others went on to careers in the labor movement and social service. Gertrude Barnum and Melinda Scott organized for the International Ladies' Garment Workers' Union and the United Textile Workers. Pauline Newman served for many years as the educational director of the ILGWU's Health Center. President Roosevelt appointed Rose Schneiderman to the National Recovery Administration's Labor Advisory Board in 1933. After the NRA was declared unconstitutional, she became New York's secretary of labor. Maud Swartz headed New York's Women in Industry bureau for several years in the 1930s. After New York established a minimum wage commission, nearly every leading league member sat on minimum wage boards. Clearly, the New York WTUL had been instrumental in establishing permanent agencies devoted to workers' welfare and to training women to assume leadership positions in the labor movement and in public service. No longer naive about the workings of power in the state government or the labor movement, league women had learned to make contacts, to lobby, and to use their united political influence. WTUL leaders wholeheartedly endorsed these developments. Mary Dreier, for instance, stated that the WTUL had developed "from a small insignificant organization with little voice and no power to one held in high regard and recognized by labor unions, other organizations, and the general public as the organized voice of the working woman."[4]

By contrast, the New York league's organizing efforts, originally its primary focus, languished. The league took little part in the wave of strikes that swept the New York City garment industry in 1919 and remained aloof from the ILGWU during the left–right factional disputes of the 1920s. Organizing efforts were limited to several unsuccessful attempts to form unions of copyholders, artificial-flower makers, candy and confectionary workers, and laundresses. The league's organizing efforts in these trades made its members increasingly aware of the indifference of the AFL, as in the case of the copyholders, or of the futility of traditional organizing attempts, as in the case of artificial-flower makers. Despite general improvements in women's conditions and wages over the years, conditions in the city's marginal industries remained unchanged. Child labor, industrial homework, wages that were below subsistence levels, and unsanitary conditions continued to plague such trades.

In 1925, league leaders briefly reexamined their emphasis on legislation. President Rose Schneiderman, temporarily discouraged in the battle to win improvements through legislation, determined that the league should undertake a new and vigorous unionization campaign. "Work with the unorganized presents so many difficulties that to attempt it in the face of the present situation demands real courage," she stated. "It is in this field that the League can do unique work, work which comes only under its scope."[5] The league hired Sadie Reisch, a dressmaker, as its organizer in 1926. Throughout that year she and Schneiderman attempted to establish women's unions but met with little success. The anti-union sentiment among the public and the internal weakness and factionalism of the labor movement made organizing difficult. In addition, the WTUL had far less money to spend on organizing than it had in previous years. Although allies such as Florence Lamont continued to make contributions to the league, the money was rarely given for the purpose of organizing. The league's most generous ally, Mary Dreier, had by the 1920s expended most of her fortune on the WTUL's work and could no longer meet its expenses in an unlimited way.

In 1933, the passage of the National Recovery Act encouraged the WTUL to devote itself to organization once again, despite its near-empty treasury. In 1934, the league led a successful strike of laundry workers. The new union won its demand that the

Hotel and Laundry Owners' Association join the National Recovery Administration's Regional Labor Board. For the first time, laundry workers had a minimum wage. The union, however, beset by internal divisions, failed soon after.[6]

In addition to losing its singleminded dedication to unionization, the league also lost the sense of sisterhood that had been so important before the war. To be sure, the alliance between working-class and upper-class women had always been tenuous. The WTUL was never free from factional disputes and misunderstandings, but it was founded in the faith that women could overcome social class differences and work together for a common cause. In this faith, early league members were clearly nineteenth-century women. They had grown up in a society that fostered close ties between women and that emphasized sex differences. However repressive Victorian standards of femininity may have been, they enabled women to bond on the basis of their common womanhood. By the 1920s, this faith in sisterhood was forgotten. Paid staff members carried out day-to-day tasks and the few allies who remained were relegated to the background. What was more, the WTUL no longer attracted young upper-class women. The generation of women who came of age in the 1920s did not concern themselves with the ideal of sisterhood that had so inspired their mothers' generation. Then, too, new opportunities for paid employment in government and the social professions diminished potential interest. Women who once might have moved to a settlement house or joined the WTUL now became professional social workers.

Throughout the late 1930s and 1940s, the league played an increasingly marginal role in the city's labor movement. Under the leadership of a succession of women unionists, it continued to lobby against the proposed equal rights amendment, worked for a proposed child labor amendment, and endorsed general labor reform legislation. The WTUL maintained its Lexington Avenue townhouse as a social center for the city's working women and offered classes ranging from ceramics to public speaking and the history of the labor movement. In June 1955, the New York league executive board voted to close its doors. "Trade unions today . . . are fully able not only to carry on the jobs of organizing, education, and community activities, but also of expansion." The league, the board concluded, was "no longer needed by the trade union movement."[7]

When the New York WTUL disbanded, members such as Mary Dreier and Rose Schneiderman, who had been with the organization from the beginning, could count many of their goals achieved. A forty-eight-hour week and a minimum wage had become realities for New York's working women. The worst of sweatshop conditions, child labor, industrial homework, starvation wages, and unlimited hours had been eliminated. The federal government recognized the right of workers to unionize. But the New York Women's Trade Union League had lost sight of its original goals of integrating women into the labor movement on an equal footing with men and of creating a viable alliance of upper-class and working-class women.

The New York league's early efforts to unionize women and to create an egalitarian cross-class alliance seem quixotic today. Members lacked sophistication in the methods of labor organizing and could not develop appropriate forms of organization for early twentieth-century working women. Their relationships with women workers and with one another were always difficult. Finally, they never found a satisfactory way to synthesize class and gender. Nevertheless, the history of the New York league illustrates the possibilities as well as the difficulties of a cross-class feminist alliance. Despite its problems, the WTUL introduced thousands of New York City women to trade unionism at a time when no other organization would have done so. It educated a generation of working women as organizers, speakers, and negotiators and enabled them to take part in the labor movement. Without doubt, the Women's Trade Union League went further than any other American women's organization to ameliorate working women's situation and to come to terms with the problems women of different classes and ethnic backgrounds have in relating to one another. For these efforts, the WTUL commands admiration.

# Notes

## Introduction

1. Mary Dreier, "Expansion through Agitation and Education," p. 163.

2. Statistics on union membership were kept by the New York State Department of Labor. See State of New York, Department of Labor, *Annual Reports*, 1900–1913.

3. Gertrude Barnum, "Women in the Clothing Trades," *Weekly Bulletin of the Clothing Trades*, 4 May 1906, p. 5.

4. Secretary's Report, Women's Trade Union League of New York, 12 August 1912, Women's Trade Union League of New York Papers, State Labor Library, New York, N.Y. (hereafter cited as WTUL of NY Papers).

5. For an excellent discussion of the feminist issues involved in the conflicts between integrationist and separatist positions, see Estelle Freedman, "Separatism as Strategy: Female Institution Building and American Feminism, 1870–1930."

6. Lucretia Dewey, "Women in Labor Unions," p.43.

7. The only published study of the National Women's Trade Union League is Gladys Boone, *The Women's Trade Union Leagues in Great Britain and America.* Also see Robin Jacoby, "Feminism and Class Consciousness in the British and American Women's Trade Union Leagues," and Robin Jacoby, "The Women's Trade Union League and American Feminism." The history of the National Women's Trade Union League is well documented in three manuscript collections: the National Women's Trade Union League of America Papers, Library of Congress, Washington, D.C.; the National Women's Trade Union League of America Papers, Radcliffe College, Cambridge, Mass.; the Margaret Dreier Robins Papers, University of Florida, Gainesville, Fla.

8. The histories of the local leagues are not as well documented as the history of the national, with the exception of the New York WTUL. Only the New York WTUL left a large body of records (minutes of executive board and general membership meetings, correspondence, secretary's reports, organizers' reports, and published annual reports and monthly bulletins). Much information on the Chicago league is contained in the Margaret Dreier Robins Papers. Information on the other local leagues is largely limited to published materials such as the convention reports of the National Women's Trade Union League, which contain brief reports of the activities of local leagues.

9. National Women's Trade Union League of America, *Proceedings of the Third Biennial Convention, 1911*, p. 30.

10. National Women's Trade Union League of America, *Proceedings of the Second Biennial Convention, 1909*, p. 53

11. W. Elliot Brownlee and Mary Brownlee, *Women in the American Economy, A Documentary History* (New Haven: Yale University Press, 1976), p. 3, table I.

12. For an excellent discussion of women's relation to work in late nineteenth-century America, see Daniel T. Rodgers, *The Work Ethic in Industrial America, 1850–1920*, pp. 182–209. For contemporary discussions see Charlotte Perkins Gilman, *Women and Economics: A Study of the Economic Relation between Men and Woman as a Factor of Social Evolution*, 2d ed. (New York: Harper and Row, 1966); Rheta Childe Dorr, *What Eight Million Women Want*; Theresa Schmid McMahon, "Women and Economic Evolution, or the Effects of Industrial Changes upon the Status of Women" (Ph.D. diss., University of Wisconsin, 1908).

13. Rheta Childe Dorr, *A Woman of Fifty*, pp. 55–56.

14. Rodman quoted in June Sochen, ed., *The New Feminism in Twentieth-Century America* (Lexington, Mass.: D.C. Heath, 1971), pp. 49–50.

15. Mrs. John Van Vorst and Marie Van Vorst, *The Woman Who Toils; Being the Experience of Two Ladies as Factory Girls* (New York: Doubleday, Page, 1903). For information on the activities of women's clubs, see Jane Cunningham Croly, *The History of the Women's Club Movement in America* (New York: Henry Allen, 1898).

16. Grace Dodge, ed., *Thoughts of Busy Girls: Written by a Group of Girls Who Have Little Time for Study, and Yet Find Much Time for Thinking*; Abbie Graham, *Grace H. Dodge, Merchant of Dreams*.

17. There is very little information available on the Working Women's Society. See Maud Nathan, *The Story of an Epoch-Making Movement*, chap. 1, and Alice Henry, "Life and Letters of Josephine Shaw Lowell," *Life and Labor* 4 (July 1914): 196–200. Scattered references and letters concerning the Working Women's Society are in the Leonora O'Reilly Papers, Radcliffe College, Cambridge, Mass.

18. On the Consumers' League in New York City, see Nathan, *Epoch-Making Movement*, and Maud Nathan, *Once Upon a Time and Today*. For testimony by Consumers' League members on working women's conditions, see State of New York, Assembly, *Report of the Special Committee of the Assembly . . . to Investigate the Condition of Female Labor in the City of New York*. A good recent study is Allis Rosenberg Wolfe, "Women, Consumerism, and the National Consumers League in the Progressive Era, 1900–1923," *Labor History* 16 (Summer 1975): 378–92.

19. Mary Dreier to Margaret Dreier Robins, 29 May 1912, Robins Papers.

20. National Women's Trade Union League of America, *Proceedings of the Third Biennial Convention, 1911*, p. 4.

21. For a discussion of the relationship between women's friendship networks and social reform, see Freedman, "Separatism as Strategy." Discussions of female culture and female networks in the nineteenth and early twentieth centuries include Carroll Smith-Rosenberg, "The Female World of Love and Ritual: Relations between Women in Nineteenth-Century America"; Blanche Wiesen Cook, "Female Support Networks and Political Activism: Lillian Wald, Crystal Eastman, Emma Goldman"; and Judith Schwartz, "Yellow Clover: Katharine Lee Bates and Katharine Coman."

## Chapter 1

1. American Federation of Labor, *Report of the Proceedings of the Twenty-third Annual Convention of the American Federation of Labor held at Boston, Massachusetts, November 9–23, 1903*, pp. 105, 111, 152, 212.

2. Leo Wolman, "The Extent of Labor Organization in the United States in 1910," *Quarterly Journal of Economics* 30 (May 1916): 499–500.

3. Frank Carpenter to Agnes Nestor, 15 March 1904, Agnes Nestor Papers, Chicago Historical Society, Chicago, Ill.

4. The William English Walling Papers, Wisconsin State Historical Society, Madison, Wis., provide biographical information on Walling, although the small collection contains no information on Walling's involvement with the WTUL.

5. Mary Kenney O'Sullivan, "Autobiography of Mary Kenney O'Sullivan," Schlesinger Library, Radcliffe College, Cambridge, Mass. Also see Alice Henry, *The Trade Union Woman*.

6. "The National Women's Trade Union League," 1922, National Women's Trade Union League of America Papers, Library of Congress, Washington, D.C. (hereafter cited as NWTUL Papers).

7. National Women's Trade Union League of America, *Constitution*, p. 2, NWTUL Papers. Also see Allen F. Davis, "The Women's Trade Union League: Origins and Organization."

8. U.S., Department of Commerce and Labor, Bureau of the Census, *Twelfth Census of the United States, 1900*. Vol. 19, *Occupations*, p. 640.

9. U.S., Congress, Senate, *Report on Condition of Woman and Child Wage-Earners in the United States*, "Wage-Earning Women in Stores and Factories," p. 25. Investigators reported that New York employed more women in department and

retail stores than the six other cities in the investigation combined (Chicago, Boston, Minneapolis, St. Paul, Philadelphia, St. Louis) and contained 48 percent of the total number of industrial workers from the six cities.

10. Ibid., p. 143. According to the Senate report, the average New York City female factory worker had three years of industrial experience. A minority of women in New York City were self-supporting. Their average age was twenty-five.

11. Ibid., pp. 18, 25, 144. Senate investigators pointed out that New York City had the smallest percentage of self-supporting women of all the cities investigated. U.S., Department of Commerce and Labor, Bureau of Labor, *Economic Conditions of the Jews in Russia*, by I. M. Rubinow, pp. 487–583; Samuel Joseph, *Jewish Immigration to the United States from 1881–1910*, pp. 127–31.

12. U.S., Department of Commerce and Labor, Bureau of the Census, *Census of Manufactures: 1905, New York*, Bulletin No. 59 (Washington, D.C.: U.S. Government Printing Office, 1906), pp. 74–75.

13. The *Khazar Mark*, or "pigs' market," was a gathering place on the corner of Hester and Ludlow streets for laborers wanting employment.

14. Rose Schneiderman, *All for One*, p. 43.

15. State of New York, Department of Labor, *Second Annual Report, 1902*, 2:46. For information on tenement-house legislation, see Elizabeth Faulkner Baker, *Technology and Woman's Work*, p. 93.

16. There were several exceptions to this division. Men worked as pressers, which was an unskilled occupation but required a good deal of physical strength. Women worked as skilled dressmakers, particularly in the "uptown shops" north of Fourteenth Street.

17. Louis Levine, *The Women Garment Workers: A History of the International Ladies' Garment Workers' Union*, p. 219.

18. The best discussion of the seasonal aspect of industrial employment and its effects on women's employment patterns is Louise Odencrantz, "The Irregularity of Employment of Women Factory Workers."

19. National Women's Trade Union League of America, *Proceedings of the 1908 Interstate Conference* (New York: National Women's Trade Union League, 1908), p. 28.

20. New York, Department of Labor, *Second Annual Report, 1902*, 2:2–3; Senate, *Woman and Child Wage-Earners*, "Stores and Factories," p. 145.

21. New York, Department of Labor, *Second Annual Report, 1902*, 2:64.

22. Ibid., pp. 3, 14.

23. Odencrantz, "Irregularity of Employment of Women Factory Workers," p. 201.

24. Elizabeth Faulkner Baker, *Protective Labor Legislation*, pp. 170–71.

25. Harold U. Faulkner, *The Decline of Laissez Faire, 1897–1917*, p. 534. Contemporary studies include Louise Bollard More, *Wage-Earners' Budgets* (New York: Henry Holt, 1907).

26. Senate, *Woman and Child Wage-Earners*, "Stores and Factories," pp. 149–50.

27. New York, Factory Investigating Commission, *Fourth Report of the Factory Investigating Commission, 1915*, 5:2650.

28. *New York Call*, 16 December 1909, p. 2.

29. National Women's Trade Union League, *Proceedings of the 1908 Interstate Conference*, p. 4.

30. Pauline Newman to Rose Schneiderman, 11 July 1912. In the possession of Pauline Newman.

31. U.S., Senate, *Report on Condition of Woman and Child Wage-Earners*, "History of Women in Trade Unions," pp. 182–83, 188–91.

32. "Estimate of Number of Women Under Union Jurisdiction in Greater New York," 1904, Margaret Dreier Robins Papers, University of Florida, Gainesville, Fla.

33. New York, Department of Labor, *Annual Report, 1908*, 3:34, Table 0, "Number and Membership of Labor Unions in Each City, 1897–1908"; State of

New York, Department of Labor, *Third Annual Report of the Commissioner of Labor for the Twelve Months Ended September 30, 1903* (Albany: 1904), p. 34; New York, Department of Labor, *Second Annual Report*, 2:302.

34. New York, Department of Labor, *Annual Report, 1904*, 2:4; Minutes, Meeting of the National Executive Board, Women's Trade Union League, 26 March 1905, NWTUL Papers; Senate, *Woman and Child Wage-Earners*, "History of Women," p. 183.

35. Women's Trade Union League of New York, Minutes, 21 February 1904, Women's Trade Union League of New York Papers, New York State Labor Library, New York, N.Y. (hereafter cited as WTUL of NY Papers).

36. New York, Department of Labor, *Annual Report, 1904*, 2:4.

37. State of New York, Assembly, *Report of the Special Committee of the Assembly ... to Investigate the Condition of Female Labor in the City of New York*, 1:85.

38. The best discussion of Jewish immigrants' unionization efforts in New York City is Melvyn Dubofsky, *When Workers Organize: New York City in the Progressive Era.*

39. Edith Abbott, "Employment of Women in Industries: Cigar Making, Its History and Present Tendencies."

40. Diary of Leonora O'Reilly, 29 June 1897, Leonora O'Reilly Papers, Radcliffe College, Cambridge, Mass.

41. U.S., Senate, *Report on the Condition of Woman and Child Wage-Earners*, "Women in the Men's Clothing Industry," p. 221.

42. Thomas Kessner, *The Golden Door: Italian and Jewish Immigrant Mobility in New York City, 1800–1915*, pp. 75–76.

43. Leslie Woodcock Tentler, *Women Wage Earners: Industrial Work and Family Life in the United States, 1900–1930*, pp. 27–28.

44. Senate, *Woman and Child Wage-Earners*, "History of Women," p. 145.

45. Women's Trade Union League of New York, Minutes, 21 February 1904, WTUL of NY Papers.

46. Mabel Hurd Willett, *The Employment of Women in the Clothing Trade*, p. 183. Alice Henry's books are still good sources for examining organized labor's attitudes toward women workers. See Henry, *The Trade Union Woman*, and Alice Henry, *Women and the Labor Movement*. Another good study is Theresa Wolfson, *The Woman Worker and the Trade Unions*. More recent works include Barbara Wertheimer, *We Were There: The Story of Working Women in America* (New York: Pantheon, 1977), and Alice Kessler-Harris, "Where Are the Organized Women Workers?" *Feminist Studies* 3 (Fall 1975): 92–110.

47. Rose Cohen, *Out of the Shadow*, pp. 123–24.

48. *Weekly Bulletin of the Clothing Trades*, 16 June 1905, p. 1.

49. Ibid., 26 July 1903, p. 1.

50. Willett, *Employment of Women in the Clothing Trade*, p. 172.

51. Women's Trade Union League of New York, Minutes, 21 February 1904, WTUL of NY Papers.

52. Willett, *Employment of Women in the Clothing Trade*, p. 191.

53. Secretary's Report, Women's Trade Union League of New York, 24 April 1907, WTUL of NY Papers.

54. Diary of Leonora O'Reilly, 24 June 1897, O'Reilly Papers.

55. Willett, *Employment of Women in the Clothing Trade*, pp. 183–84.

56. International Ladies' Garment Workers' Union, *Proceedings of the Convention, 1902*, p. 3.

57. Levine, *Women Garment Workers*, pp. 148–49; International Ladies' Garment Workers' Union, *Proceedings of the Convention, 1902*, p. 22.

## Chapter 2

1. "The National Women's Trade Union League," 1922, National Women's Trade Union League of America Papers, Library of Congress, Washington, D.C. (hereafter cited as NWTUL Papers).

2. Little biographical information on Margaret Daly is available. Basic information about her organizing career is contained in Carolyn Daniel McCreesh, "On the Picket Line: Militant Women Campaign to Organize Garment Workers, 1880–1917" (Ph.D. diss.), pp. 125–26.

3. Quoted in Ellen Lagemann, *A Generation of Women: Education in the Lives of Progressive Reformers*, p. 91.

4. William English Walling to Leonora O'Reilly, 17 December 1903 (O'Reilly's note on back of letter), Leonora O'Reilly Papers, Radcliffe College, Cambridge, Mass.

5. Leonora O'Reilly, "Some Mistakes of Working Women," *Far and Near* 4 (August 1894): 139.

6. "Paper Read Before the Working Women's Society of New York," n.d., O'Reilly Papers.

7. For biographical information on Leonora O'Reilly, see the biographical essay by Edward T. James, "Leonora O'Reilly," O'Reilly Papers, Microfilm Edition; and Lagemann, *A Generation of Women*, pp. 89–112.

8. Mary E. Dreier, *Margaret Dreier Robins: Her Life, Letters, and Work*, p. 8.

9. For general biographical information on Margaret Dreier Robins, see Dreier, *Margaret Dreier Robins;* Allen Davis, "Margaret Dreier Robins." Also see Edward James's biographical sketch "Margaret Dreier Robins," Margaret Dreier Robins Papers, Microfilm Edition, University of Florida, Gainesville, Fla.

10. Mary Dreier to Margaret Dreier Robins, 19 April 1906, Robins Papers.

11. Elizabeth Robins to Margaret Dreier Robins, 6 August 1910, Robins Papers.

12. Speech quoted in Dreier, *Margaret Dreier Robins*, p. viii.

13. *Weekly Bulletin of the Clothing Trades*, 24 March 1905, p. 2.

14. For general biographical information on Gertrude Barnum, see Melvyn Dubofsky, "Gertrude Barnum." Also see "Miss Barnum's Statement of Conditions at Fall River," *Charities* 13 (4 February 1905), and "The Pittsburgh Convention and Women Unionists," *Charities and the Commons* 15 (6 January 1906): 441–42.

15. Caroline Pratt, *I Learn from Children*, pp. 18–19.

16. Sol Cohen, "Helen Marot."

17. See Cohen, "Helen Marot," for general biographical information.

18. The following discussion is based on biographical data on league officers, committee chairwomen, and executive board members in the years from 1904 through 1917. No complete membership lists are extant. The twenty-seven allies who formed the core membership over these years are Gertrude Barnum, Margaret Dreier (Robins), Mary Dreier, Helen Marot, Mary Van Kleeck, Ida Rauh, Violet Pike, Elizabeth Dutcher, Elsie Cole, Maud Younger, Carola Woerishoffer, Mary Kingsbury Simkhovitch, Lillian Wald, Bertha Poole Weyl, Mary Beard, Theresa Malkiel, Louise Odencrantz, Elizabeth Watson, Caroline Pratt, Adelaide Samuels, Laura Elliot, Harriot Stanton Blatch, Rheta Childe Dorr, Alice Bean, Bertha Rembaugh, Madeline Doty, and Frances Kellor.

19. For information on Walling's later career, see Anna Strunsky Walling, *William English Walling: A Symposium* (New York, 1938).

20. Vassar College Class of 1901, *Annual Bulletin, 1908.*

21. *Weekly Bulletin of the Clothing Trades*, 24 March 1905, p. 2.

22. Mary Dreier to Margaret Dreier Robins, 22 April 1906, Robins Papers.

23. Mary Dreier to Margaret Dreier Robins, n.d. [December 1910], Robins Papers.

24. Maud Younger, "Diary of an Amateur Waitress: An Industrial Problem from the Worker's Point of View," pp. 543–52.

25. Eleanor Flexner, "Maud Younger."

26. Biographical information on Elizabeth Dutcher compiled from Vassar College Class of 1901, *Annual Bulletins, 1902–1910.*

27. Bryn Mawr College Class of 1907, *Carola Woerishoffer: Her Life and Work*, pp. 18–19. Sue Ainslie Clark and Edith Wyatt, "Women Laundry Workers in New York." This article is based on Woerishoffer's investigation and incorporates her report. For general biographical information, see Roderick W. Nash, "Carola Woerishoffer."

28. For detailed financial information, see Women's Trade Union League of New York, *Annual Report, 1906–1907; Annual Report, 1907–1908.*

29. Minutes, Meeting Called for the Purpose of Organizing a Branch of the Woman's [*sic*] Trade Union League, Held at the University Settlement, 14 February 1904, Robins Papers.

30. Mary Dreier to Margaret Dreier Robins, 15 June 1907, Robins Papers.

31. Women's Trade Union League of New York, "Work Report," 1905, NWTUL Papers.

32. William English Walling to Leonora O'Reilly, December 1903 (O'Reilly's note on back of letter), O'Reilly Papers.

33. Rheta Childe Dorr, *What Eight Million Women Want*, p. 5. The best discussion of American feminist ideology during this period is Aileen Kraditor, *The Ideas of the Woman Suffrage Movement*, chap. 3.

34. Leonora O'Reilly to Margaret Dreier Robins, 23 September 1912, Robins Papers.

35. Mary Dreier to Margaret Dreier Robins, 11 July 1909, Robins Papers.

36. Mary Dreier, "Expansion through Agitation and Education," p. 164.

37. General Meeting, Women's Trade Union League of New York, 24 March 1905, Women's Trade Union League of New York Papers, New York State Labor Library, New York, N.Y. (hereafter cited as WTUL of NY Papers).

38. Mary Dreier to Margaret Dreier Robins, January 1911, Robins Papers.

39. Because no membership lists are extant, this biographical information is compiled from listings of New York WTUL officers, committee chairwomen, and executive board members, 1904–1917, in the *Annual Reports.*

40. Rose Schneiderman, "A Cap-Maker's Story." The fullest account of Schneiderman's background and her early union activities is her autobiography, written with Lucy Goldthwaite, *All for One.*

41. Schneiderman and Goldthwaite, *All for One*, pp. 75, 77.

42. Little biographical information is available on Melinda Scott. See Women's Trade Union League of New York, *Proceedings of the 1908 Interstate Conference*, for information on Scott's union. For information on her New Jersey organizing career, see Secretary's Report, 27 June 1907, WTUL of NY Papers. For general biographical information, see "Melinda Scott," *Life and Labor* 8 (October 1918): 214.

43. For membership statistics, see Women's Trade Union League of New York, *Annual Reports, 1907–1908, 1908–1909, 1909–1910.*

44. Leonora O'Reilly to the Executive Board, Women's Trade Union League of New York, 14 January 1914, WTUL of NY Papers.

45. Historians who have dealt briefly with the WTUL have interpreted the discord within the organization as the result of class conflict between allies and working women. William Chafe, in *The American Woman: Her Changing Social, Economic, and Political Roles, 1920–1970*, argues, for example, "Reformers viewed the WTUL's primary function as educational, and believed that the interests of the workers could best be served by investigating industrial conditions, securing legislative action, and building public support for the principle of trade unionism. Female unionists, on the other hand, insisted that organizing women and strengthening existing unions represented the League's principal purpose. One group perceived the WTUL as primarily an instrument of social uplift, the other as an agency for labor organization" (p. 71).

46. Letter to Leonora O'Reilly, 1908 (O'Reilly's note on back of letter), O'Reilly Papers.

47. Pauline Newman to Rose Schneiderman, n.d., Rose Schneiderman Papers, New York University, New York, N.Y.

48. Laura Elliot to Leonora O'Reilly, March 1911, O'Reilly Papers.

49. Gertrude Barnum to Leonora O'Reilly, 14 March 1906, O'Reilly Papers; on criticism of her organizing work, see Margaret Dreier Robins to Gertrude Barnum, 29 April 1907, NWTUL Papers; on her later career, see Dubofsky, "Gertrude Barnum."

50. Minutes, Executive Board, Women's Trade Union League of New York, 25 January 1906, WTUL of NY Papers.

51. Violet Pike, *New World Lessons for Old World People*; Gertrude Barnum, "A Story with a Moral," *Weekly Bulletin of the Clothing Trades* (20 November 1908):6; Gertrude Barnum, "At the Shirtwaist Factory: A Story," *Ladies' Garment Worker* 1 (June 1910): 4.

52. Laura Elliot to Leonora O'Reilly, March 1911, O'Reilly Papers.

53. Quoted in Alice Henry, Review of "The Forerunners," *Life and Labor* 1 (May 1911):153–54.

54. Bryn Mawr College Class of 1907, *Carola Woerishoffer*, p. 17.

55. Ida Rauh, "The Wooden Spools," *New York Evening Call*, 12 August 1908, p. 5; Ida Rauh, "A Protest," *New York Evening Call*, 21 September 1908, p. 4.

56. Gertrude Barnum, "Women Workers," *Weekly Bulletin of the Clothing Trades*, 13 July 1906, p. 8. For an excellent discussion of turn-of-the-century feminist ideas about work, see Daniel Rodgers, *The Work Ethic in Industrial America, 1850–1920*, chap. 7.

57. Mary Dreier to Leonora O'Reilly, 19 June 1908, O'Reilly Papers.

58. Women's historians have begun to explore the extent and importance of female friendship networks in nineteenth and early twentieth-century America. See Carroll Smith-Rosenberg, "The Female World of Love and Ritual: Relations between Women in Nineteenth-Century America"; Blanche Wiesen Cook, "Female Support Networks and Political Activism: Lillian Wald, Crystal Eastman, Emma Goldman"; Nancy Sahli, "Smashing: Women's Relationships before the Fall," *Chrysalis* (Summer 1979): 17–28; Judith Schwartz, "Yellow Clover: Katharine Lee Bates and Katharine Coman"; and Estelle Freedman, "Separatism as Strategy: Female Institution Building and American Feminism, 1870–1930."

59. Mary Dreier to Leonora O'Reilly, 6 September 1915, O'Reilly Papers, quoted in Lagemann, *A Generation of Women*, p. 109.

60. Harriot Stanton Blatch to Samuel Gompers, 30 December 1905, American Federation of Labor Papers, State Historical Society of Wisconsin, Madison, Wis.

61. Leonora O'Reilly to Mary Hay, 29 December 1917, O'Reilly Papers.

62. Minutes, Special Meeting of the Executive Board, Women's Trade Union League of New York, 19 November 1915, and Minutes, Executive Board, 25 January 1906, WTUL of NY Papers.

# Chapter 3

1. Melvyn Dubofsky, *When Workers Organize: New York City in the Progressive Era*, p. 6.

2. U.S., Congress, Senate, *Report on Condition of Woman and Child Wage-Earners in the United States*, "Men's Ready-Made Clothing," pp. 842–49; Mary Van Kleeck, *Artificial Flower Makers*; Louise C. Odencrantz, *Italian Women in Industry: A Study of Conditions in New York City*.

3. Minutes, Meeting of the Women's Trade Union League of New York, 14 February 1904, Margaret Dreier Robins Papers, University of Florida, Gainesville, Fla.

4. Minutes, Executive Board, Women's Trade Union League of New York, January 1905, Women's Trade Union League of New York Papers, State Labor Library, New York, N.Y. (hereafter cited as WTUL of NY Papers).

5. Ibid.

6. See State of New York, Factory Investigating Commission, *Preliminary Report of the Factory Investigating Commission, 1912*, "Women Workers in Factories in New York State," by Violet Pike, 1: 279, for conditions in laundries.

7. Minutes, Executive Board, Women's Trade Union League of New York, 28 July, 25 August, 29 September 1905, WTUL of NY Papers; Ida Rauh, "The Troy Strike," Record Book, National Women's Trade Union League Papers, Library of Congress, Washington, D.C. (hereafter cited as NWTUL Papers); Rheta Childe Dorr, "The

Women Strikers of Troy"; Carole Turbin, "And We Are Nothing But Women: Irish Working Women in Troy" in *Women of America: A History*, ed. Carol Berkin and Mary Beth Norton (Boston: Houghton, Mifflin, 1979), pp. 202–22.

8. Minutes, Executive Board, Women's Trade Union League of New York, 10 February 1905, WTUL of NY Papers.

9. Ibid., 26 April 1906.

10. Mary Dreier to Margaret Dreier Robins, 27 November 1906, Robins Papers.

11. Minutes, Executive Board, Women's Trade Union League of New York, March 1906, WTUL of NY Papers.

12. Cited in Thomas Kessner, *The Golden Door: Italian and Jewish Immigrant Mobility in New York City, 1880–1915*, pp. 33–34.

13. For good discussions of Jewish women's status and role in traditional Jewish culture, see Charlotte Baum, Paula Hyman, and Sonya Michel, *The Jewish Woman in America*, pp. 3–16, 55–120. For their role in the Bund, see Henry J. Tobias, *The Jewish Bund in Russia from its Origins to 1905*, p. 44.

14. Minutes, Executive Board, Women's Trade Union League of New York, 24 August 1909, WTUL of NY Papers.

15. *Weekly Bulletin of the Clothing Trades*, 26 July 1903, p. 1; *New York Evening Journal*, 25 April 1900, p. 8; Letter to the Women's Trade Union League of New York Legislative Committee, 1911, Fire Questionnaire file, WTUL of NY Papers; *New York Evening Journal*, 4 July 1901, p. 2; "Strike of Necktie Workers," *Weekly Bulletin of the Clothing Trades*, 20 July 1906, p. 2; *New York Evening Call*, 19 August 1908, p. 1. The orphan strike has assumed legendary status in the history of ILGWU Local No. 62. No one knows when it took place. Interview with Gerel Rubien, Educational Director, ILGWU Local No. 62 and former WTUL of NY president, 5 August 1972, New York, N.Y. See also Rose Schneiderman and Lucy Goldthwaite, *All for One*, pp. 86–87.

16. Mabel Hurd Willett, *The Employment of Women in the Clothing Trade*, p. 184; "Wanton Strikes," *Weekly Bulletin of the Clothing Trades*, 27 June 1903, p. 1.

17. Minutes, Executive Board, Women's Trade Union League of New York, 22 February, 29 March 1906, WTUL of NY Papers. For information on the ILGWU during these years, see International Ladies' Garment Workers' Union, *Proceedings of the Convention, 1904*, Report of Local 12, Waistmakers' Union, p. 9; ILGWU, *Proceedings of the Convention, 1907*, "Report of the President," p. 10; ILGWU, *Proceedings of the Convention, 1910*, "Report of John Dyche, Secretary-Treasurer," pp. 26–27. For a good discussion of the conservative-radical splits in the early ILGWU see Dubofsky, *When Workers Organize*.

18. Mary Dreier to Margaret Dreier Robins, 23 July 1909, Robins Papers.

19. Minutes, Executive Board, Women's Trade Union League of New York, 23 March 1909, WTUL of NY Papers.

20. Gertrude Barnum, "A Story with a Moral," *Weekly Bulletin of the Clothing Trades*, 20 November 1908, p. 6; Gertrude Barnum, "At the Shirtwaist Factory: A Story," *Ladies' Garment Worker*, June 1910, p. 4.

21. Secretary's Report, Women's Trade Union League of New York, 26 November 1907, WTUL of NY Papers.

22. "The Stress of the Seasons." This article summarizes the findings of the New York league's investigation of the white-goods industry.

23. Secretary's Report, Women's Trade Union League of New York, 24 April, 27 November 1907, WTUL of NY Papers; Rose Schneiderman, "Report of the Organizer, 1908–1909," WTUL of NY Papers; Rose Schneiderman, "The White Goods Workers of New York: Their Struggle for Human Conditions," *Life and Labor* 3 (May 1913): 133.

24. Secretary's Report, Women's Trade Union League of New York, 27 November 1907, WTUL of NY Papers.

25. Minutes, Executive Board, Women's Trade Union League of New York, 22 December 1908, 23 March 1909, WTUL of NY Papers.

26. Mary Dreier to Margaret Dreier Robins, June 1909, Robins Papers.

27. Mary Dreier to Margaret Dreier Robins, 13 July 1909, Robins Papers.

28. Report of the Organizer, 1914, WTUL of NY Papers.

29. Theresa Malkiel, "Union Men Must Help Women to Organize," *New York Call*, 9 January 1911, p. 2.

30. Louise Odencrantz, "The Irregularity of Employment of Women Factory Workers"; Mary Van Kleeck, *A Seasonal Industry: A Study of the Millinery Trade in New York*.

31. "The Women's Trade Union League: Mass Meeting," *Weekly Bulletin of the Clothing Trades*, 11 May 1906, p. 2.

32. Quotations from Violet Pike, *New World Lessons for Old World People*.

33. Alice Henry, *Women and the Labor Movement*, pp. 24–25; Women's Trade Union League of New York, *Bulletin*, February 1911.

34. "The Women's Trade Union League: Mass Meeting," p. 2.

35. *New York Call*, 15 June 1915, p. 1; National Women's Trade Union League, *Proceedings of the Second Biennial Convention, 1909*, p. 20.

36. For discussions of the importance of marriage in traditional Jewish culture, see Baum, Hyman, and Michel, *The Jewish Woman in America*; Mark Zborowski and Elizabeth Herzog, *Life Is with People: The Culture of the Shtetl*; Lucy Robins Lang, *Tommorrow Is Beautiful*; Rose Pesotta, "Family Album," manuscript, Rose Pesotta Papers, New York Public Library, New York, N.Y. For information on Italian family structure and the persistence of patriarchal traditions in the United States, see Virginia Yans-McLaughlin, *Family and Community: Italian Immigrants in Buffalo, 1880–1930*, pp. 157–217.

37. "My wife is my property," quoted in Leonard Covello, *The Social Background of the Italo-American School Child: A Study of the Southern Italian Family Mores and Their Effect upon the School Situation in Italy and America*, p. 206.

38. Yans-McLaughlin, *Buffalo's Italians*; Covello, *The Italo-American School Child*; Phyllis Williams, *South Italian Folkways in Europe and America: A Handbook for Social Workers, Visiting Nurses, School Teachers, and Physicians*, pp. 83–83; Odencrantz, *Italian Women in Industry*.

39. Moses Rischin, "The Jewish Labor Movement in America: A Social Interpretation"; Tobias, *The Jewish Bund in Russia*, pp. 35–48, 95–104; Aaron Antonovsky, *The Early Jewish Labor Movement in the United States*, pp. 9–18, 172–73, 343.

40. National Women's Trade Union League, *Proceedings of the Third Biennial Convention, 1911*, p. 19.

41. Secretary's Report, Women's Trade Union League of New York, 25 May 1911, WTUL of NY Papers.

42. For an excellent discussion of the importance marriage played in women's work culture, see Leslie Woodcock Tentler, *Women Wage-Earners*.

43. Mary Dreier to Margaret Dreier Robins, 10 June 1910, Robins Papers.

44. Secretary's Report, Women's Trade Union League of New York, 24 April 1907, WTUL of NY Papers.

45. "Report of the Organizer," 14 January 1914, WTUL of NY Papers.

46. Odencrantz, "The Irregularity of Employment of Women Factory Workers"; "The Stress of the Seasons"; State of New York, Department of Labor, *Eighth Annual Report, 1908*, 4:16; Women's Trade Union League of New York, *Annual Report, 1906–1907*, pp. 6–8.

47. *Union Labor Advocate*, August 1907, p. 18.

48. Minutes, National Board Meeting, National Women's Trade Union League, 20 March 1904, NWTUL Papers.

49. Women's Trade Union League of New York, *Annual Report, 1909–1910*, p. 7.

50. Mary Dreier to Margaret Dreier Robins, 8 May 1909, Robins Papers.

51. Mary Dreier to Margaret Dreier Robins, 11 July 1909, Robins Papers.

52. Minutes, Executive Board, Women's Trade Union League of New York, 11 September 1916, WTUL of NY Papers.

53. Secretary's Report, Women's Trade Union League of New York, May 1907, WTUL of NY Papers.

54. Minutes, Executive Board, Women's Trade Union League of New York, 1905 [date obliterated], 28 March, 24 April, 26 September 1907, and Secretary's Report, 24 April 1907, WTUL of NY Papers.

55. Secretary's Report, 24 April, 22 August 1907, WTUL of NY Papers.

56. Ibid., 25 July, 22 August 1907.

57. Minutes, Executive Board, Women's Trade Union League of New York, 26 April 1907, WTUL of NY Papers.

58. Quoted in Alice Kessler-Harris, "Where Are the Organized Women Workers?," p. 99.

59. Secretary's Report, Women's Trade Union League of New York, 22 June, 24 August 1909, WTUL of NY Papers.

60. National Women's Trade Union League, Proceedings of the Interstate Conference, 1908, pp. 26–27.

61. Ibid., pp. 19–20; Minutes, Executive Board, Women's Trade Union League of New York, 27 September, 25 October 1906, WTUL of NY Papers.

62. Mary Dreier to Margaret Dreier Robins, 14 January 1909, Robins Papers.

63. Secretary's Report, Women's Trade Union League of New York, 24 October 1907, 26 November 1909, WTUL of NY Papers.

64. The league's decision in this matter is not mentioned in extant WTUL materials. No further mention of the union appears in league records.

65. Secretary's Report, Women's Trade Union League of New York, 22 April 1911, WTUL of NY Papers.

66. Margaret Dreier Robins to Mary Dreier, 6 May 1907, Robins Papers.

67. Minutes, Executive Board, Women's Trade Union League of New York, March 1906, WTUL of NY Papers.

68. National Women's Trade Union League, Proceedings of the Second Biennial Convention, 1909, p. 37.

69. For information on the English National Federation of Working Women, see National Women's Trade Union League, Proceedings of the Second Biennial Convention, 1909, pp. 29–33; Mary Macarthur, "Into Industry through the Front Door," Life and Labor 9 (August 1919): 199.

70. Mary Dreier to Leonora O'Reilly 14 January 1909, Robins Papers.

71. Helen Marot to Leonora O'Reilly, 27 November 1907, Leonora O'Reilly Papers, Radcliffe College, Cambridge, Mass.

## Chapter 4

1. For accounts of the Cooper Union meeting, see Ladies' Waist Makers' Union, Souvenir History of the Strike; New York Call, 24 November 1909, p. 1.

2. Subcontracting was a variation of the traditional contracting system in the garment trades. A subcontractor contracted with a manufacturer to complete a specified amount of work for an agreed-upon price and supervised a team of workers in completing the bundles of garments. Unlike the contractor, however, the subcontractor did not own a shop, but worked in the manufacturer's large inside establishment. Subcontractors, not manufacturers, were responsible for paying their workers. When a manufacturer lowered rates in a large factory such as the Triangle Shirtwaist Company, the individuals who were affected directly were the subcontractors. They passed on the decrease to their team of workers. In a sense, the subcontractor was a transition figure between the traditional contractor and the foreman. For workers in large inside shops, he frequently embodied the worst features of each. See Melech Epstein, Jewish Labor in the U.S.A., 1882–1914 (N.p.: Ktav, 1969), and Joel Seidman, The Needle Trades, for discussions of subcontracting.

3. State of New York, Department of Labor, Eighth Annual Report, 1908, "Report of the Commissioner of Labor," 3:xxxv; New York Evening Call, 31 July 1908, p. 4; Ladies' Waist Makers' Union, Souvenir History of the Strike, p. 5.

4. Ladies' Waist Makers' Union, *Souvenir History of the Strike*, p. 12.

5. Sue Ainslie Clark and Edith Wyatt, *Making Both Ends Meet* (New York: Macmillan, 1911), pp. 65–67.

6. The exact number of strikers was never determined. Estimates range from the New York State Department of Labor Bureau of Mediation and Arbitration figure of 15,000 to Local 25's estimate of 40,000. The latter figure is clearly too high, for that would have entailed the participation of every worker in the trade. By the union's own account, strikebreakers were a serious problem. Helen Marot estimated that there were 30,000 strikers, using WTUL records. According to Marot, the overwhelming majority of the strikers were Russian Jewish women. She broke down the ethnic backgrounds of the strikers as follows: 20,000 to 21,000 Russian Jewish women, 6,000 Jewish men (cutters and pressers), 2,000 Italian women, and approximately 1,000 native-born American women. Helen Marot, "A Woman's Strike: An Appreciation of the Shirtwaist Makers of New York."

7. *New York Call*, 29 December 1909, Special Strike Edition, p. 4.

8. *New York Times*, 21 December 1909, pp. 1–2.

9. Marot, "A Woman's Strike," pp. 127–28.

10. Mary Dreier to Margaret Dreier Robins, 17 February 1910, Margaret Dreier Robins Papers, University of Florida, Gainesville, Fla.

11. Theresa Malkiel, "Socialist Women and the Shirtwaist Strike," *New York Call*, 20 December 1909, p. 1, 2 January 1910, p. 14, 8 February 1910, p. 6.

12. *New York Call*, 5 January 1910, p. 1, 23 January 1910, p. 5, 30 June 1910, p. 5.

13. John Dyche, "The Strike of the Ladies' Waist Makers of New York; Its Results: An Official Statement," *Ladies' Garment Worker*, June 1910, p. 2.

14. Secretary's Report, Women's Trade Union League of New York, 26 October 1911, Women's Trade Union League of New York Papers, State Labor Library, New York, N.Y. (hereafter cited as WTUL of NY Papers).

15. The protocol of peace was the subject of prolonged and bitter disagreement within the ILGWU. A large faction of the rank and file disapproved of the agreement, particularly of the nonstrike clause and the provision for compulsory arbitration. Hyman Berman, "The Era of the Protocol" (Ph.D. diss.); John Laslett, *Labor and the Left*, chap. 4.

16. International Ladies' Garment Workers' Union, *Proceedings of the Convention, 1912*, p. 69; *New York Call*, 22 December 1910, p. 1; Secretary's Report, Women's Trade Union League of New York, 21 December 1910, WTUL of NY Papers.

17. The best account of the Triangle fire and its aftermath is Leon Stein, *The Triangle Fire*.

18. Rose Schneiderman, *All For One*, pp. 100–101.

19. Bertha Rembaugh, "The Triangle Fire: The Courts' Decision," *Life and Labor* 2 (April 1912):117–18; Stein, *The Triangle Fire*, pp. 177–203.

20. Helen Marot to *Jewish Daily Forward*, 13 May 1911, WTUL of NY Papers.

21. Ibid.

22. Mary Dreier to Margaret Dreier Robins, 23 November 1909, Robins Papers.

23. Secretary's Report, Women's Trade Union League of New York, 25 May 1911, WTUL of NY Papers.

24. Mary Dreier to Margaret Dreier Robins, 18 May 1911, Robins Papers.

25. Helen Marot to *Jewish Daily Forward*, 13 May 1911, WTUL of NY Papers.

26. Secretary's Report, Women's Trade Union League of New York, 26 October 1911, WTUL of NY Papers.

27. "The Unrest in the Garment Trades," *Ladies' Garment Worker*, December 1911, pp. 10–11; "Minutes of the General Executive Board, held March 30, 31, and April 1," *Ladies' Garment Worker*, May 1912, pp. 7–8; International Ladies' Garment Workers' Union, *Proceedings of the Convention, 1912*, pp. 78, 88–90.

28. Minutes, Strike Council, Women's Trade Union League of New York, 2 April 1911; Minutes, Executive Board, Women's Trade Union League of New York, 26 September 1912, WTUL of NY Papers.

29. Secretary's Report, Women's Trade Union League of New York, 22 August 1912, WTUL of NY Papers.

30. Women's Trade Union League of New York Executive Board to National Women's Trade Union League Executive Board, 17 January 1913, National Women's Trade Union League of America Papers, Library of Congress, Washington, D.C. (hereafter cited as NWTUL Papers).

31. Rose Schneiderman, "The White Goods Workers of New York: Their Struggle for Human Conditions," *Life and Labor* 3 (May 1913): 132; "Victory of the White Goods Workers' Union; Full Text of the Collective Agreement," *Ladies' Garment Worker*, March 1913, pp. 5–6; *New York Call*, 1 January 1913, p. 3, 8 January 1913, p. 4, 11 February 1913, pp. 1–2; Minutes, Strike Council, Women's Trade Union League of New York, 10 February 1913, Minutes, Special Meeting, Executive Board, 10 February 1913, WTUL of NY Papers; Berman, "Era of the Protocol," pp. 187–90; Minutes, Executive Board, Women's Trade Union League of New York, 27 February 1913, WTUL of NY Papers; "The White Goods Workers' Protocol."

32. For trade union membership figures in 1909, see State of New York, Department of Labor, *Ninth Annual Report, 1909*, "Report of Bureau of Labor Statistics," appendixes 2, 3; for 1910 figures, see *Tenth Annual Report, 1910*, "Report for Bureau of Labor Statistics," appendixes 2, 4. For 1913 figures, see State of New York, Department of Labor, Bureau of Statistics and Information, *Trade Union Statistics in 1913*, p. 109. All of these figures are for September of their respective years. Figures for March, which were listed for 1909 and 1910, show decreases as a result of slack seasons.

33. State of New York, Department of Labor, *Statistics of Trade Unions in 1914*, p. 21.

34. Mary Dreier, "To Wash or Not to Wash: Ay, There's the Rub; The New York Laundry Strike," *Life and Labor* 2 (March 1912); State of New York, Department of Labor, *Strikes and Lockouts in 1912 and 1913*, pp. 38–39.

35. Minutes, Executive Board, Women's Trade Union League of New York, 26 January 1912, WTUL of NY Papers; Women's Trade Union League of New York, *Bulletin*, February 1912, p. 1, March 1912, pp. 1–2.

36. Samuel Gompers, *Seventy Years of Life and Labor*, pp. 490–91.

37. Melinda Scott to Stella Franklin, 27 November 1914, NWTUL Papers.

38. Minutes, Executive Board, Women's Trade Union League of New York, 27 April 1911, 24 October, 11 December 1917, WTUL of NY Papers.

39. Eva Valesh to Mary Dreier, 8 March, 16 April, 1910, NWTUL Papers; Minutes, Special Meeting of the Executive Board, Women's Trade Union League of New York, 30 April 1910, WTUL OF NY Papers.

40. Margaret Dreier Robins to Mary Dreier, n.d. [mid-November 1913], Robins Papers.

41. Melinda Scott to Leonora O'Reilly, 30 April 1909, Leonora O'Reilly Papers, Radcliffe College, Cambridge, Mass.

42. Melinda Scott to Stella Franklin, 27 November 1914, NWTUL Papers.

43. Margaret Dreier Robins to Mary Dreier, 13 November 1910, 4 February 1911, Robins Papers; Katharine Coman, "The Garment Workers' Strike," *Life and Labor* 1 (January 1911):5–15; "Holding the Fort: The Chicago Garment Workers' Strike," *Life and Labor* 1 (February 1911):48–51; "The End of the Struggle: The Chicago Garment Workers' Strike," *Life and Labor* 1 (March 1911):88–89.

44. Mary Dreier to Margaret Dreier Robins, 2 May 1910, Robins Papers.

45. Minutes, Executive Board, Women's Trade Union League of New York, 27 April 1911, WTUL of NY Papers.

46. Sue Ainslie Clark to Margaret Dreier Robins, April 1912, NWTUL Papers.

47. Ibid.

48. Ibid.

49. Minutes, National Women's Trade Union League Executive Board, 17–19 April 1912, p. 14, NWTUL Papers.

50. Helen Marot, "A Moral in the Cloak Makers' Strike," *New York Call*, 7 August 1910, p. 9; Minutes, National Women's Trade Union League Executive Board, 17–19 April 1912, p. 15, NWTUL Papers.

51. Minutes, Special Executive Board Meeting, Women's Trade Union League of New York, 27 May 1913, WTUL of NY Papers.

52. National Women's Trade Union League of America, *Report of the Convention, 1917*, p. 60; Margaret Dreier Robins to Mary Dreier, 11 November 1916, Robins Papers.

53. "Matters Involving Action on the Part of the National Women's Trade Union League," Submitted by the Eastern Leagues' Conference, June 4–5, 1921, NWTUL Papers.

54. "Illustrations of Need of Federal Charters for Women," NWTUL Papers; Ethel Smith, Jo Coffin, and Elisabeth Christman to National Women's Trade Union League Executive Board, 25 August 1921, NWTUL Papers.

55. Raymond Robins to Mary Dreier, 12 November 1913, Robins Papers.

56. Minutes, National Women's Trade Union League Executive Board, 17–19 April 1912, p. 2, NWTUL Papers.

57. Margaret Dreier Robins to Mary Dreier, 23 November 1909, Robins Papers.

58. Elizabeth Evans to Margaret Dreier Robins, 25 March 1912, Robins Papers.

## Chapter 5

1. Helen Marot, "A Women's Strike: An Appreciation of the Shirtwaist Makers of New York."

2. National Women's Trade Union League, *Proceedings of the Second Biennial Convention, 1909*, p. 17; National Women's Trade Union League, *Proceedings of the Interstate Conference, 1908*, p. 21.

3. The investigation's findings were published some years later in Louise Odencrantz, *Italian Women in Industry: A Study of Conditions in New York City*.

4. Ibid., p. 21.

5. State of New York, Factory Investigating Commission, *Fourth Report of the Factory Investigating Commission, 1915*, 4:57–58.

6. Odencrantz, *Italian Women in Industry*, p. 44.

7. Ibid., pp. 38–39, 41.

8. National Women's Trade Union League, *Proceedings of the Third Biennial Convention, 1911*, p. 19.

9. Minutes, Meeting of the Regular Membership, Women's Trade Union League of New York, January 1913, Women's Trade Union League of New York Papers, State Labor Library, New York, N.Y. (hereafter cited as WTUL of NY Papers).

10. Minutes, Executive Board Women's Trade Union League of New York, 27 March 1913; Minutes, Meeting of the Regular Membership, Women's Trade Union League of New York, January 1913, WTUL of NY Papers.

11. National Women's Trade Union League, *Proceedings of the Fourth Biennial Convention, 1913*, p. 47.

12. Mary Van Kleeck, *Artificial Flower Makers*, p. 92.

13. Pauline Newman to Rose Schneiderman, 9 February 1912, in possession of Pauline Newman.

14. Mary Dreier to Margaret Dreier Robins, 26 September 1911, Margaret Dreier Robins Papers, University of Florida, Gainesville, Fla.

15. Melinda Scott to Leonora O'Reilly, 25 March 1910, Leonora O'Reilly Papers, Radcliffe College, Cambridge, Mass.; Mary Dreier to Margaret Dreier Robins, 13 November 1916, 7 February 1917, Robins Papers.

16. Women's Trade Union League of New York, *Bulletin*, December 1911, pp. 2–3.

17. Secretary's Report, Women's Trade Union League of New York, 22 July 1911, WTUL of NY Papers.

18. Pauline Newman to Rose Schneiderman, 9 February 1912, in possession of Pauline Newman.

19. Pauline Newman to Rose Schneiderman, n.d., in possession of Pauline Newman.

20. Mary Dreier to Margaret Dreier Robins, May 1913, Raymond Robins to Mary Dreier, 12 November 1913, Robins Papers.

21. Women's Trade Union League of New York, *Annual Report, 1913–1914*, p. 1.

22. Leonora O'Reilly quoted in a letter from Pauline Newman to Rose Schneiderman, n.d., in possession of Pauline Newman.

23. Rose Schneiderman to Benjamin Schlesinger, 11 December 1915, Schneiderman Papers, New York University, New York, N.Y. For a good discussion of this period in Schneiderman's career, see Gary Endelman, "Solidarity Forever: Rose Schneiderman and the Women's Trade Union League" (Ph.D. diss.).

24. Pauline Newman to Rose Schneiderman, 14 November 1911, in possession of Pauline Newman.

25. Margaret Dreier Robins to Mary Dreier, November 1913, Robins Papers.

26. Minutes, Special Meeting of the Executive Board, Women's Trade Union League of New York, 19 November 1915, WTUL of NY Papers.

27. Leonora O'Reilly to Mary Dreier, 31 August 1915, O'Reilly Papers.

28. Mary Dreier to Leonora O'Reilly, 6 September 1915, O'Reilly Papers.

29. For general biographical information on Leonora O'Reilly's work after she left the league, see Ellen Lagemann, *A Generation of Women: Education in the Lives of Progressive Reformers* (Cambridge, Mass.: Harvard University Press, 1979), pp. 108–12.

## Chapter 6

1. Mary Dreier to Leonora O'Reilly, 16 September 1916, Leonora O'Reilly Papers, Radcliffe College, Cambridge, Mass.

2. Melinda Scott to Stella Franklin, 27 November 1914, National Women's Trade Union League of America Papers, Library of Congress, Washington, D.C.

3. Wage Earners' Suffrage League, New York, "Senators vs. Working Women: Miss Rose Schneiderman Replies to New York Senator," O'Reilly Papers, quoted in Robin Miller Jacoby, "The Women's Trade Union League and American Feminism," p. 135.

4. Women's Trade Union League of New York, Executive Board Minutes, 19 November 1905, Women's Trade Union League of New York Papers, State Labor Library, New York, N.Y. (hereafter cited as WTUL of NY Papers).

5. *New York Times*, 2 December 1909, p. 3.

6. "Little Sis" to Leonora O'Reilly, 27 April 1908, O'Reilly Papers.

7. Rose Schneiderman and Lucy Goldthwaite, *All for One*, p. 121.

8. The best discussion of the suffrage movement's anti-immigrant bias is Aileen Kraditor, *The Ideas of the Woman Suffrage Movement, 1890–1920*.

9. *New York Times*, 3 December 1909, p. 3.

10. Mary Dreier to Margaret Dreier Robins, 27 November 1906, Margaret Dreier Robins Papers, University of Florida, Gainesville, Fla.

11. Margaret Hinchey to Leonora O'Reilly, n.d. [1913?], O'Reilly Papers.

12. See, for example, Alva Belmont's statement to the *New York Times*, 2 December 1909, p. 3: "The Political Equality League recognizes the fact that women must organize politically as well as industrially if they are to permanently secure the benefits of industrial freedom."

13. *New York Times*, 21 December 1909, pp. 1–2.

14. Mary Grey Peck to Margaret Dreier Robins, 21 September 1914, Robins Papers.

15. Mary Dreier to Katharine Dreier, 12 November 1909, quoted in Jane Marcus, "Transatlantic Sisterhood: Labor and Suffrage Links in the Letters of Elizabeth Robins and Emmeline Pankhurst."

16. For excellent discussions of the impact of the English militants on the American suffrage movement and the relationships between American suffragists and the Pankhurst faction, see Marcus, "Transatlantic Sisterhood," and Sharon

Hartman Strom, "Leadership and Tactics in the American Woman Suffrage Movement: A New Perspective from Massachusetts."

17. Leonora O'Reilly to Margaret Dreier Robins, 23 September 1912, Robins Papers.

18. Women's Trade Union League of New York, Executive Board Minutes, 24 April 1913, WTUL of NY Papers.

19. The most complete biographical information on Maud Swartz is contained in David Brody, "Maud Swartz."

20. The best firsthand account of the 1915 New York campaign is Harriot Stanton Blatch and Alma Lutz, *Challenging Years: The Memoirs of Harriot Stanton Blatch*. Despite its anti-suffrage bias, the *New York Times* covered the campaign extensively.

21. Leonora O'Reilly to Margaret Dreier Robins, 23 September 1912, Robins Papers.

22. Pauline Newman to Rose Schneiderman, 26 July 1912, in possession of Pauline Newman.

23. Margaret Hinchey to Leonora O'Reilly, n.d., O'Reilly Papers.

24. Several historians have found it useful to distinguish between *social feminists*, or women who supported suffrage primarily as a means to achieve other social and political reforms, and suffragists such as Harriot Stanton Blatch, Alva Belmont, and others, who looked upon suffrage as an end in itself. See William O'Neill, *Everyone Was Brave: The Rise and Fall of Feminism in America*; Kraditor, *The Ideas of the Woman Suffrage Movement*; J. Stanley Lemons, *The Woman Citizen: Social Feminism in the 1920s*.

25. Leonora O'Reilly, "Appeal to Organized Working Men," *Life and Labor* 5 (September 1915):141.

26. "Labor on Record for the Women," *New York Call*, 24 March 1911, p. 3.

27. Leonora O'Reilly to Electrical Workers' delegate, Central Federated Union, 19 April 1911, O'Reilly Papers.

28. Handbill, "Senators vs. Working Women," and Mary Beard to Leonora O'Reilly, 1912, O'Reilly Papers.

29. Leonora O'Reilly, "Appeal to Organized Working Men," p. 141.

30. Rose Schneiderman, Suffrage Speech, 16 February 1913, Rose Schneiderman Papers, New York University, New York, N.Y.

31. Eva Diamond to Leonora O'Reilly, 18 December 1912, O'Reilly Papers.

32. Women's Trade Union League of New York, Regular Membership Meeting Minutes, 13 September 1915, WTUL of NY Papers.

33. Local 664, International Brotherhood of Electrical Workers, to Leonora O'Reilly, 9 April 1911, O'Reilly Papers.

34. For a breakdown of returns by district, see *New York Times*, 4 November 1915, p. 3.

35. "Mrs. Blatch Pours Out Wrath," *New York Times*, 4 November 1915, p. 3.

36. This conclusion differs significantly from that reached by Robin Jacoby, who argues in her work on the WTUL and American feminism that the league had considerable success in sensitizing suffragists to women workers' needs. See Jacoby, "The Women's Trade Union League and American Feminism."

37. Mary Dreier to Margaret Dreier Robins, 24 September 1916, Robins Papers.

38. Mary Dreier to Dorothea Dreier, 3 August 1917, Robins Papers.

39. *New York Times*, 7 November 1917, p. 1; Mary Dreier, "Ushering in the Suffrage Victory," *Life and Labor* 7 (December 1917); Ronald Schaeffer, "The New York City Woman Suffrage Party, 1909–1919."

# Chapter 7

1. *Feminism* in this study is used to mean any conscious consideration of women as a discrete social minority. By this definition, the WTUL's work for protective

legislation was a feminist effort despite the fact that other feminist organizations did not consider it thus.

2. *New York Call*, 15 June 1915, p. 1.

3. Mary Dreier to Melinda Scott, 14 August 1914, Leonora O'Reilly Papers, Radcliffe College, Cambridge, Mass.

4. Other works have dealt with the increasingly national orientation of American reform during this period. See, for example, James Weinstein, *The Corporate Ideal in the Liberal State* (Boston: Beacon Press, 1968); Robert Wiebe, *The Search for Order* (New York: Hill and Wang, 1967); and David Thelen, *Robert M. La Follette and the Insurgent Spirit* (Boston: Little, Brown, 1976).

5. See, for example, Heidi Hartmann, "Capitalism, Patriarchy, and Job Segregation by Sex," *Signs* 1 (Spring 1976):137–69. There is little historical evidence to suggest that organized labor was the main force behind most protective legislation efforts. This argument relies heavily on one statement by Adolph Strasser, president of the Cigar Makers' Union, in 1879. "We cannot drive the females out of the trade, but we can restrict their daily quota of labor through factory laws. No girl under 18 should be employed more than eight hours a day; all overwork should be prohibited." Quoted in U.S., Senate, *Report on Condition of Woman and Child Wage-Earners*, "History of Women in Trade Unions," p. 94. For an excellent discussion of early twentieth-century protective legislation, see Judith Baer, *The Chains of Protection*.

6. Mary Dreier to Margaret Dreier Robins, 29 May 1912, Margaret Dreier Robins Papers, University of Florida, Gainesville, Fla.

7. National Women's Trade Union League, *Proceedings of the Second Biennial Convention, 1909*, p. 6.

8. National Women's Trade Union League, *Proceedings of the Third Biennial Convention, 1911*, p. 14; Interview with Pauline Newman, 14 March 1970, International Ladies' Garment Workers' Union, New York, N.Y.

9. *New York Times*, 3 December 1909, p. 6.

10. Report of the Legislative Committee, Women's Trade Union League of New York, March 1911, Women's Trade Union League of New York Papers, State Labor Library, New York, N.Y. (hereafter cited as WTUL of NY Papers).

11. Fire Questionaires, Fire file, O'Reilly Papers.

12. Rose Schneiderman to Frances Ecob, 29 May 1911, Rose Schneiderman Papers, New York University, New York, N.Y.

13. State of New York, Factory Investigating Commission, *Preliminary Report of the Factory Investigating Commission, 1912*, 2:294–95.

14. *New York Call*, 15 June 1915, p. 3.

15. State of New York, Factory Investigating Commission, *Fourth Report of the Factory Investigating Commission, 1915*, 1:774.

16. Minutes, Executive Board, Women's Trade Union League of New York, 24 November 1914, 4 October 1915, Minutes, Meeting of Regular Membership, Women's Trade Union League of New York, 6 December 1915, WTUL of NY Papers.

17. "Data on Women Workers," *New York Times*, 16 March 1919, 2:5. "Where Women Supplant Men Because of War," *New York Times Magazine*, 30 December 1917, p. 6.

18. For the WTUL's war work and legislative efforts, see Women's Trade Union League of New York, *Annual Reports, 1917–1918, 1918–1919*.

19. Mary Dreier to Margaret Dreier Robins, n.d., Margaret Dreier Robins Papers, University of Florida, Gainesville, Fla.

20. *New York Times*, 15 May 1919, p. 12.

21. Margaret Hinchey to Leonora O'Reilly, n.d. [1919], O'Reilly Papers.

22. Mary Dreier to Margaret Dreier Robins, April 1919, Robins Papers.

23. For a discussion of the WTUL's view on the Transportation Act, see Women's Trade Union League of New York, *Annual Report, 1918–1919*.

24. Membership figures and patterns taken from Women's Trade Union League of New York, *Annual Report, 1918–1919* through *Annual Report, 1935–1936*.

25. Women's Trade Union League of New York, *Annual Report, 1918–1919*, p. 3.

26. Compare William Chafe, *The American Woman: Her Changing Social, Political, and Economic Roles, 1920–1970*, pp. 70–82; Irwin Yellowitz, *Labor and the Progressive Movement in New York State, 1897–1916;* G. William Domhoff, *The Higher Circles: The Governing Classes in America*, chap. 2. Each of these works deals briefly with the WTUL and concludes that upper-class domination explains the league's shift to legislation.

27. "Calls Labor Safe From Bolshevism," *New York Times*, 18 July 1919, p. 15.

28. Speech by Rose Schneiderman, 1926, p. 6, National Women's Trade Union League of America Papers, Library of Congress, Washington, D.C.

29. National Women's Trade Union League, *Why Labor Laws for Women?* (Chicago: National Women's Trade Union League, 1926), pp. 2–3.

30. Consumers' League survey reported in *New York Times*, 4 April 1920, 2:6. The figures from the New York Industrial Commission quoted in "Women's Wages Half Those Paid to Men," *New York Times*, 20 September 1923, p. 4.

31. "Find Women's Wages Below Cost," *New York Times*, 4 April 1920, 2:6.

32. "Senate Judiciary Hears Arguments against the National Woman's Party Amendment," *Life and Labor Bulletin* 2 (March 1924):3.

33. Mary Dreier to Margaret Dreier Robins, 26 April 1920, Robins Papers.

34. Rose Schneiderman to Franklin Delano Roosevelt, 12 June 1929, quoted in Joseph Lash, *Eleanor and Franklin* (New York: Signet, 1971), p. 439.

35. Quoted in Elizabeth Faulkner Baker, *Protective Labor Legislation*, p. 190.

36. "Women's Work Limited by Law," *New York Times*, 18 January 1920, 3: 4.

37. "Women at Odds on Laws for Them," *New York Times*, 25 March 1923, 2: 15.

38. See, for example, her article "The Third Sex in Industry," *New York Times*, 30 March 1919, 7: 10.

39. "Trade Union Women Challenge Woman's Party to Debate," *Life and Labor Bulletin* 4 (February 1926): 3.

40. Women's Trade Union League of New York, *Annual Report, 1926–1927*, pp. 16, 18; U.S., Department of Labor, Women's Bureau, *The Effects of Labor Legislation on the Employment Opportunities of Women*, pp. xv–xvi.

41. Women's Trade Union League of New York, *Annual Report, 1923–1924*, p. 3.

42. "Trade Union Women Challenge Woman's Party to Debate," p. 3.

43. National Women's Trade Union League, *Why Labor Laws for Women?*, p. 3; National Women's Trade Union League, *Proceedings of the Convention, 1924*, p. 70.

44. Consumers' League of New York, *The Forty-eight Hour Law: Do Working Women Want It?*, p. 5. The Consumers' League surveyed 462 working women in manufacturing and mercantile establishments.

45. "Trade Union Women Challenge Woman's Party to Debate," p. 3.

46. Ibid.

47. U.S., Department of Labor, Women's Bureau, *The Effects of Labor Legislation*, p. xvii.

## Conclusion

1. Eva Wechsler, "Frances Perkins, State Industrial Commissioner," *Life and Labor* 9 (April 1919): 76.

2. Margaret Dreier Robins to Mary Dreier, 6 November 1920, Margaret Dreier Robins Papers, University of Florida, Gainesville, Fla.

3. For works that discuss the persistence of the progressive reform impulse in the 1920s and its relation to women's organizations, see especially J. Stanley Lemons, *The Woman Citizen: Social Feminism in the 1920s*, and Clarke A. Chambers, *Seedtime of Reform: American Social Service and Social Action, 1918–1933*.

4. Mary Dreier, "Expansion through Agitation and Education," p. 165.

5. "Report of Committee on Organization Survey, Committee Appointed by Executive Board, February, 1925," Rose Schneiderman Papers, New York Univer-

sity, New York, N.Y.; Reports of the Organizer, 1926–1927, Women's Trade Union League of New York Papers, State Labor Library, New York, N.Y. (hereafter cited as WTUL of NY Papers); Interview with Sadie Reisch, 6 June 1972, New York, N.Y.

6. Women's Trade Union League of New York, *Annual Report, 1933–1934*, pp. 13–14.

7. Minutes, Meeting of Executive Board, Women's Trade Union League of New York, 21 June 1955. WTUL of NY Papers.

# Selected Bibliography

## Primary Sources

I. *Manuscript Collections*

Cambridge, Mass. Radcliffe College. Arthur and Elizabeth Schlesinger Library on the History of Women in America. Leonora O'Reilly Papers; National Women's Trade Union League of America Papers.

Gainesville, Fla. University of Florida. Manuscripts Department. University of Florida Library. Margaret Dreier Robins Papers. (Microfilm Edition.)

Madison, Wis. State Historical Society of Wisconsin. American Federation of Labor Papers; Raymond Robins Papers; William English Walling Papers.

New York, N.Y. State Labor Library. Women's Trade Union League of New York Papers.

New York, N.Y. New York University. Tamiment Institute Library. Rose Schneiderman Papers.

New York, N.Y. New York Public Library. Manuscripts Division. Rose Pesotta Papers.

Washington, D.C. Library of Congress. Manuscripts Division. National Women's Trade Union League of America Papers.

II. *Public Documents*

State of New York, Assembly. *Report of the Special Committee of the Assembly (Appointed by Resolution, March 13, 1895) to Investigate the Condition of Female Labor in the City of New York.* 2 vols. Albany: 1896.

State of New York, Department of Labor. *Annual Reports*, 1902–1911.

————. Bureau of Statistics and Information. *Trade Union Statistics in 1913.* Special Bulletin No. 60. Albany: 1914.

————. Bureau of Statistics and Information. *Statistics of Trade Unions in 1914.* Bulletin No. 74. Albany: 1915.

————. Bureau of Statistics and Information. *Strikes and Lockouts in 1912 and 1913.* Bulletin No. 66. Albany: 1914.

————. Division of Women in Industry. Bureau of Research and Special Codes. *Women Who Work.* Special Bulletin No. 110. Albany: 1922.

State of New York, Factory Investigating Commission. *Preliminary Report of the Factory Investigating Commission, 1912.* Albany: 1912. 3 vols.

————. *Second Report of the Factory Investigating Commission, 1913.* Albany: 1913. 4 vols.

————. *Third Report of the Factory Investigating Commission, 1914.* Albany: 1914.

————. *Fourth Report of the Factory Investigating Commission, 1915.* Albany: 1915. 5 vols.

U.S., Congress, Senate. *Report on Condition of Woman and Child Wage-Earners in the United States.* "Women in the Men's Clothing Industry." Vol. 2. S. Doc. 645, 61st Cong., 2d sess., 1910.

————. *Report on Condition of Woman and Child Wage-Earners in the United States.* "Wage-Earning Women in Stores and Factories." Vol. 5. S. Doc. 645, 61st Cong., 2d sess., 1910.

————. *Report on Condition of Woman and Child Wage-Earners in the United States.* "History of Women in Trade Unions." Vol. 10. S. Doc. 645, 61st Cong., 2d Sess., 1911.

U.S., Department of Commerce and Labor, Bureau of the Census. *Twelfth Census of the United States, 1900,* Vol. 19.

U.S., Department of Commerce and Labor, Bureau of Labor. *Economic Conditions of the Jews in Russia,* by I. M. Rubinow. Bulletin No. 72. September 1907. Washington, D.C.: U.S. Government Printing Office, 1907.

————. *The Women's Trade Union Movement in Great Britain,* by Katherine Graves Busbey. Bulletin No. 83. Washington, D.C.: U.S. Government Printing Office, 1909.

U.S., Department of Labor, Women's Bureau. *Some Effects of Legislation Limiting Hours of Work for Women.* Bulletin No. 15. Washington, D.C.: U.S. Government Printing Office, 1921.

————. *Proceedings of the Women's Industrial Conference.* Bulletin No. 33. Washington, D.C.: U.S. Government Printing Office, 1923.

————. *Standard and Scheduled Hours of Work for Women in Industry.* Bulletin No. 43. Washington, D.C.: U.S. Government Printing Office, 1928.

————. *The Development of Minimum-Wage Laws in the United States, 1912 to 1927.* Bulletin No. 61. Washington, D.C.: U.S. Government Printing Office, 1928.

————. *The Effects of Labor Legislation on the Employment Opportunities of Women.* Bulletin No. 65. Washington, D.C.: U.S. Government Printing Office, 1928.

————. *History of Labor Legislation for Women in Three States.* Bulletin No. 66–I. Washington, D.C.: U.S. Government Printing Office, 1932.

III. *Proceedings*

National Women's Trade Union League of America. *Proceedings of the Biennial Convention*, 1907–1919.

International Ladies' Garment Workers' Union. *Proceedings of the Convention*, 1900–1913.

IV. *Newspapers and Periodicals*

International Ladies' Garment Workers' Union. *Ladies' Garment Worker*, January 1911–January 1913.

National Women's Trade Union League of America. *Life and Labor*. 1911–1921.

National Women's Trade Union League of America. *Life and Labor Bulletin.* 1922–1926.

*New York Call*, January 1908–December 1915.

*New York Evening Journal*, January 1901–December 1905.

*New York Times*, 24 November 1909–15 February 1910; September–November 1915; May 1917–December 1937.

*New York World*, 24 November 1909–15 February 1910; October–
    November 1915.
United Garment Workers of America. *Weekly Bulletin of the Clothing Trades*,
    July 1902–January 1909.
Women's Trade Union League of New York. *Bulletin*. 1911–1912.

V. *Published Reports*

National Women's Trade Union League of America. *Report of the Interstate
    Conference of the National Women's Trade Union League held September
    26–28, 1908, in New York*. New York: Women's Trade Union League,
    1908.
Women's Trade Union League of New York. *Annual Report*. 1906–1934.

VI. *Books and Pamphlets*

Abbott, Edith, and Breckinridge, Sophonisba. *The Wage-Earning Woman
    and the State*. Boston: Boston Equal Suffrage Association for Good
    Government, n.d.
Beard, Mary Ritter. *The American Labor Movement: A Short History*. New
    York: Macmillan, 1931.
Bernheimer, Charles S. *The Shirt Waist Strike*. New York: University Settle-
    ment, 1910.
Blatch, Harriot Stanton, and Lutz, Alma. *Challenging Years: The Memoirs of
    Harriot Stanton Blatch*. New York: Putnam, 1940.
Bryn Mawr College Class of 1907. *Carola Woerishoffer: Her Life and Work*.
    Bryn Mawr, Pa.: Bryn Mawr College Class of 1907, 1912.
Cohen, Rose. *Out of the Shadow*. New York: George Doran, 1918.
Consumers' League of New York. *The Forty-eight Hour Law: Do Working
    Women Want It?* New York: Consumers' League of New York, 1927.
Dodge, Grace H., ed. *Thoughts of Busy Girls: Written by a Group of Girls
    Who Have Little Time for Study, and Yet Find Much Time for Thinking*.
    New York: Cassell, 1892.
Dorr, Rheta Childe. *What Eight Million Women Want*. Boston: Small,
    Maynard, 1910.
———. *A Woman of Fifty*. New York: Funk and Wagnalls, 1924.
———. *Women's Demands for Humane Treatment of Women Workers in
    Shop and Factory*. New York: Consumers' League of New York, 1910.
Gompers, Samuel. *Seventy Years of Life and Labor*. New York: E. P. Dutton,
    1925.
Harper, Ida Husted, ed. *History of Woman Suffrage*. Vols. 5, 6 (1900–1920).
    New York: National American Woman Suffrage Association, 1922.
Hasanovitz, Elizabeth. *One of Them: Chapters from a Passionate Autobiog-
    raphy*. Boston: Houghton, Mifflin, 1917.
Ladies' Waist Makers' Union. *Souvenir History of the Strike*. New York:
    Ladies' Waist Makers' Union, 1910.
Laidlaw, Harriet Burton. *Organizing to Win*. N.p.: National American
    Woman Suffrage Association, 1914.
Lang, Lucy Robins. *Tomorrow Is Beautiful*. New York: Macmillan, 1948.
Malkiel, Theresa Serber. *The Diary of a Striking Shirtwaist Maker*. New
    York: Cooperative Press, 1910.

Marot, Helen. *American Labor Unions: By a Member*. New York: Henry Holt, 1915.

Nathan, Maud. *How to Organize: A Problem. Resumé of Findings, One Day Institute on Trade Union Organization*. Chicago: National Women's Trade Union League, 1929.

———. *Once Upon a Time and Today*. New York: Putnam, 1933.

———. *The Story of an Epoch-Making Movement*. Garden City, N.Y.: Doubleday, Page, 1926.

Odencrantz, Louise C. *Italian Women in Industry: A Study of Conditions in New York City*. New York: Russell Sage Foundation, 1919.

Pike, Violet. *New World Lessons for Old World People*. New York: Women's Trade Union League of New York, 1912.

Pope, Jesse Eliphalet. *The Clothing Industry in New York*. Social Science Series, Vol. 1. Columbia: University of Missouri Studies, 1905.

Rembaugh, Bertha. *The Political Status of Women in the United States: A Digest of Laws Concerning Women in the Various States and Territories*. New York: G. P. Putnam's Sons, 1911.

Robins, Margaret Dreier. *Margaret Dreier Robins (Mrs. Raymond Robins) to the Enfranchised Women of the United States*. Chicago: Western Headquarters, National Republican Party, 1916.

Schneiderman, Rose, with Lucy Goldthwaite. *All for One*. New York: Eriksson, 1967.

Taft, Jesse. *The Woman Movement from the Point of View of Social Consciousness*. Chicago: University of Chicago, 1915.

Van Kleeck, Mary. *Artificial Flower Makers*. New York: Survey Associates, 1913.

———. *A Seasonal Industry: A Study of the Millinery Trade in New York*. New York: Russell Sage Foundation, 1917.

Willett, Mabel Hurd. *The Employment of Women in the Clothing Trade*. New York: Columbia University Studies in History, Economics, and Public Law, 1902.

Women's Trade Union League of New York. *Story of a Waitress*. New York: Women's Trade Union League of New York, 1907.

VII. *Articles*

Abbott, Edith. "Employment of Women in Industries: Cigar Making, Its History and Present Tendencies." *Journal of Political Economy* 15 (January 1907): 1–25.

———. "The History of Industrial Employment of Women in the United States: An Introductory Study." *Journal of Political Economy* 14 (October 1906): 461–501.

Abbott, Edith, and Breckinridge, Sophinisba. "Employment of Women in Industries: Twelfth Census Statistics." *Journal of Political Economy* 14 (January 1906): 14–40.

Barnum, Gertrude. "A Hungarian Girl's Impressions of America: A True Story Told By a White Goods Striker." *Outlook* 104 (17 May 1913): 111–16.

———. "Women in the American Labor Movement." *American Federationist* 22 (September 1915): 731–33.

Barrows, Alice P., and Van Kleeck, Mary. "How Girls Learn the Millinery Trade." *Survey* 24 (16 April 1910): 105–13.

Beard, Mary R. "The Legislative Influence of Unenfranchised Women." *American Academy of Political and Social Science* 56 (November 1914): 54–61.

Clark, Walter. "Suffrage, a Labor Movement." *American Federationist* 26 (May 1919): 389–92.

Clark, Sue Ainslie, and Wyatt, Edith. "Women Laundry Workers in New York." *McClure's* 36 (February 1911): 401–14.

———. "Working Girls' Budgets: The Shirtwaist Makers and Their Strike." *McClure's* 36 (November 1910): 70–86.

Comstock, Sarah. "The Uprising of the Girls." *Collier's* 44 (25 December 1909): 14–16.

Davis, Philip. "Women in the Cloak Trade." *American Federationist* 12 (October 1905): 745–47.

Dorr, Rheta Childe. "The Women Strikers of Troy." *Charities* 15 (November 1905): 233–36.

Dreier, Mary. "Expansion through Agitation and Education." *Life and Labor* 11 (June 1921): 163–65, 192.

Goldmark, Josephine C. "The Neccessary Sequel of Child Labor." *American Journal of Sociology* 11 (November 1905): 312–25.

Gompers, Samuel. "The American Labor Movement." *American Federationist* 21 (July 1914): 437–548.

———. "Coming into Her Own." *American Federationist* 22 (July 1915): 517–19.

———. "Don't Sacrifice Womanhood!" *American Federationist* 24 (August 1917): 640–41.

———. "Labor and Woman Suffrage." *American Federationist* 27 (October 1920): 936–39.

———. " Out of Our Weakness Strength Supreme." *American Federationist* 17 (February 1910): 132–33.

———. "Should the Wife Help to Support the Family?" *American Federationist* 13 (January 1906): 36.

———. "The Struggles in the Garment Trades—From Misery and Despondency to Betterment and Hope." *American Federationist* 20 (March 1913): 185–202.

———. "Women Workers in War Times." *American Federationist*, 24 (September 1917): 747–49.

———. "Working Women Organize!" *American Federationist* 21 (March 1914): 231–34.

Goodman, Pearl, and Ueland, Elisa. "The Shirtwaist Trade." *Journal of Political Economy* 18 (December 1910): 816.

Henrotin, Ellen. "Organization for Women: Its Necessity in Order That They Shall Meet the Modern Method of Collective Bargaining." *American Federationist* 12 (November 1905): 824–27.

Hutchinson, Woods. "The Hygienic Aspects of the Shirtwaist Strike." *Survey* 23 (22 January 1910): 541–50.

"The Italian and the Settlement." *Survey* 30 (5 April 1913): 58–60.

Kelley, Florence. "Minimum Wage Laws." *Journal of Political Economy* 20 (December 1912): 999–1010.

———. "Women and Social Legislation in the United States." *Annals of the American Academy of Political and Social Science* 56 (November 1914): 62–71.

Kingsbury, Mary. "The Relation of the Settlement to Women and Children." *Charities* 1 (June 1898): 5–7.

Laidlaw, Harriet Burton. "The Woman's Hour." *Forum* 56 (November 1916): 541.

Leupp, Constance D. "The Shirtwaist Makers' Strike." *Survey* 23 (18 December 1909): 383–86.

Littleton, Martin W. "The Legal Aspects of the Strike." *Survey* 23 (22 January 1910): 555–58.

McDowell, Mary. "The National Women's Trade Union League." *Survey* 23 (16 October 1909): 101–7.

Mangano, Antonio. "Associated Life of Italians in New York City." *Charities* 12 (1904): 476–80.

"Many Minds on the Minimum Wage." *Survey* 33 (23 January 1915).

Marbury, Elisaberth. "We Are All Members of the One National Family." *American Federationist* 17 (March 1910): 210.

Marot, Helen. "Revolution in the Garment Trades." *The Masses* (August 1916): 29.

———. "A Woman's Strike: An Appreciation of the Shirtwaist Makers of New York." *Proceedings of the Academy of Political Science in the City of New York* 1 (1910): 119–28.

"The Minimum Wage—What Next? A Symposium." *Survey* 50 (15 May 1923): 215–22.

"New York a Prey to Strikes." *The Outlook* 103 (18 January 1913): 102–3.

Odencrantz, Louise. "The Irregularity of Employment of Women Factory Workers." *Survey* 22 (1 May 1909): 196–210.

"Position of the Trade Union Woman." *Survey* 38 (23 June 1917): 277.

"Protest of the Working Women of New York." *Survey* 31 (14 February 1914): 605–6.

"Report on the First International Congress of Working Women, Washington, D.C., 1919." *Monthly Labor Review* (December 1919): 280–90.

Schneiderman, Rose. "A Cap-Maker's Story." *The Independent* 58 (1905): 935.

"The Shirtwaist Makers' Strike." *Survey* 23 (15 January 1910): 505–6.

Spadoni, Adriana. "Italian Working Women in New York." *Collier's* 49 (23 March 1912): 14–15.

"The Stress of the Seasons." *Survey* 29 (8 March 1913): 806.

"A Strike and Its Remedies." *Outlook* 103 (1 February 1913): 253–58.

"The Strike of the Lady Shirtwaist Makers." *Survey* 23 (8 January 1910): 489–90.

Sumner, Mary Brown. "The Spirit of the Strikers." *Survey* 23 (22 January 1910): 550–55.

Taber, Esther. "Through Trade Union Organization Waitresses Have Secured Marked Improvements in Conditions." *American Federationist* 12 (December 1905): 927–28.

Tarbell, Ida. "The Shirtwaist Makers: A New Solidarity of Society." *American Federationist* 17 (March 1910): 209.

Teller, Charlotte. "Cloth Hat and Cap Makers." *American Federationist* 13 (April 1906): 222–23.

Van Kleeck, Mary. "Working Hours of Women in Factories." *Charities and the Commons* 17 (6 October 1906): 13–21.

Walling, William English. "Field of Organization for Women Workers." *American Federationist* 12 (September 1905): 625–27.

————. "Open Shop Means Destruction of the Unions." *Independent* 56 (12 May 1904).

Walter, Henriette R. "Women as Workers and Citizens." *Survey* 42 (21 June 1919): 465–66.

"The White Goods Workers' Protocol." *Survey* 29 (8 March 1913): 807.

Woodbridge, Alice. "Children and Female Labor." *American Federationist* 7 (April 1900): 103.

Wyatt, Edith. "The New York Cloak-Makers' Strike." *McClure's* 36 (April 1911): 708–14.

Younger, Maud. "Diary of an Amateur Waitress: An Industrial Problem from the Worker's Point of View." *McClure's 28* (March–April, 1907): 543–52; 665–77.


VIII. *Personal Interviews*

Feinbaum, Anna. Flushing. N.Y. 31 December 1971.

Newman, Pauline. International Ladies' Garment Workers' Union, New York, N.Y. March 1970; June 1975.

Reisch, Sadie. New York, N.Y. 6 June 1972.

Rubien, Gerel. Local 62, International Ladies' Garment Workers' Union. New York, N.Y. 16 August 1972.


**Secondary Sources**

I. *Books*

Antonovsky, Aaron. *The Early Jewish Labor Movement in the United States.* New York: YIVO, 1961.

Baer, Judith. *The Chains of Protection.* Westport, Conn.: Greenwood Press, 1978.

Baker, Elizabeth Faulkner. *Technology and Woman's Work.* New York: Columbia University Press, 1964.

————. *Protective Labor Legislation.* New York: Columbia University Studies in History, Economics, and Public Law, 1925.

Baum, Charlotte; Hyman, Paula; and Michel, Sonya. *The Jewish Woman in America.* New York: Dial Press, 1976.

Boone, Gladys. *The Women's Trade Union Leagues in Great Britain and the United States of America.* New York: Columbia University Studies in History, Economics, and Public Law, 1942.

Catt, Carrie Chapman, and Shuler, Nettie Rogers. *Woman Suffrage and Politics.* Seattle: University of Washington Press. 1969.

Chafe, William. *The American Woman: Her Changing Social, Political, and Economic Roles, 1920–1970.* New York: Oxford University Press, 1972.

Chambers, Clarke A. *Seedtime of Reform: American Social Service and Social Action, 1918–1933.* Minneapolis: University of Minnesota Press, 1963.

Covello, Leonard. *The Social Background of the Italo-American School Child: A Study of the Southern Italian Family Mores and Their Effect upon the School Situation in Italy and America.* Totowa, N.J.: Rowman and Littlefield, 1967.

Danish, Max. *The World of David Dubinsky.* Cleveland: World, 1957.

Davis, Allen. *Spearheads for Reform: The Social Settlements and the Progressive Movement, 1890–1914.* New York: Oxford University Press, 1967.

Domhoff, G. William. *The Higher Circles: The Governing Classes in America.* New York: Random House, 1970.

Dreier, Mary E. *Margaret Dreier Robins: Her Life, Letters, and Work.* New York: Island Press Corporation, 1950.

Dubofsky, Melvyn. *When Workers Organize: New York City in the Progressive Era.* Amherst: University of Massachusetts Press, 1968.

Graham, Abbie. *Grace H. Dodge, Merchant of Dreams.* New York: Woman's Press, 1926.

Faulkner, Harold U. *The Decline of Laissez Faire, 1897–1917.* New York: Holt, Rinehart and Winston, 1951.

Henry, Alice. *The Trade Union Woman.* New York: D. Appleton, 1915.

———. *Women and the Labor Movement.* New York: George Doran, 1923.

Joseph, Samuel. *Jewish Immigration to the United States from 1881–1910.* New York: Columbia University Studies in History, Economics, and Public Law, 1944.

Kessner, Thomas. *The Golden Door: Italian and Jewish Immigrant Mobility in New York City, 1880–1915.* New York: Oxford University Press, 1977.

Kraditor, Aileen. *The Ideas of the Woman Suffrage Movement, 1890–1920.* New York: Columbia University Press, 1965.

Lagemann, Ellen. *A Generation of Women: Education in the Lives of Progressive Reformers.* Cambridge: Harvard University Press, 1979.

Lang, Harry. *"62." Biography of a Union.* New York: Undergarment and Negligee Workers' Union, Local 62, International Ladies' Garment Workers' Union, 1940.

Laslett, John. *Labor and the Left.* New York: Basic Books, 1970.

Lemons, J. Stanley. *The Woman Citizen: Social Feminism in the 1920s.* Urbana: University of Illinois Press, 1973.

Levine, Louis. *The Women Garment Workers: A History of the International Ladies' Garment Workers' Union.* New York: B. W. Huebsch, 1924.

Lubove, Roy. *The Professional Altruist: The Emergence of Social Work as a Career, 1880–1930.* Cambridge, Mass.: Harvard University Press, 1965.

O'Neill, William. *Everyone Was Brave: The Rise and Fall of Feminism in America.* Chicago: Quadrangle, 1969,

Pratt, Caroline. *I Learn from Children.* New York: Simon and Schuster, 1948.

Rischin, Moses. *The Promised City: New York's Jews, 1870–1914.* New York: Harper and Row, 1962.

Rodgers, Daniel T. *The Work Ethic in Industrial America, 1850–1920.* Chicago: University of Chicago Press, 1978.

Rowbotham, Sheila. *Women, Resistance, and Revolution.* New York: Pantheon, 1973.

Schauss, Hayyim. *The Lifetime of a Jew.* Cincinnati: Union of American Hebrew Congregations, 1950.

Seidman, Joel. *The Needle Trades.* New York: Farrar and Rinehart, 1944.

Sochen, June. *The New Woman in Greenwich Village, 1910–1920.* New York: Quadrangle, 1972.

Stein, Leon. *The Triangle Fire.* Philadelphia: J. P. Lippincott, 1967.

Stolberg, Benjamin. *Tailor's Progress: The Story of a Famous Union and the Men Who Made It.* New York: Doubleday, 1944.

Taft, Philip. *The A. F. of L. in the Time of Gompers.* New York: Harper and Brothers, 1957.

Tentler, Leslie Woodcock. *Wage-Earning Women: Industrial Work and Family Life in the United States, 1900–1930.* New York: Oxford University Press, 1979.

Thelen, David P. *The New Citizenship.* Columbia: University of Missouri Press, 1972.

Tobias, Henry J. *The Jewish Bund in Russia from its Origins to 1905.* Stanford: Stanford University Press, 1972.

Williams, Phyllis. *South Italian Folkways in Europe and America: A Handbook for Social Workers, Visiting Nurses, School Teachers, and Physicians.* New Haven: Yale Institute for Human Relations, 1938.

Wolfson, Theresa. *The Woman Worker and the Trade Unions.* New York: International Publishers, 1926.

Yans-McLaughlin, Virginia. *Family and Community: Italian Immigrants in Buffalo, 1880–1930.* Ithaca: Cornell University Press, 1977.

Yellowitz, Irwin. *Labor and the Progressive Movement in New York State, 1897–1916.* Ithaca: Cornell University Press, 1965.

Zborowski, Mark, and Herzog, Elizabeth. *Life is with People: The Culture of the Shtetl.* New York: Schocken, 1962.

## II. *Articles*

Brody, David. "Maud Swartz." *Notable American Women*, 3:413–15.

Cohen, Sol. "Helen Marot." *Notable American Women*, 2:499–500.

Conway, Jill. "Women Reformers and American Culture, 1870–1930." *Journal of Social History* 5 (Winter 1971–1972): 164–78.

Cook, Blanche Wiesen. "Female Support Networks and Political Activism: Lillian Wald, Crystal Eastman, Emma Goldman." *Chrysalis* 3 (1977): 43–61.

Davis, Allen F. "Margaret Dreier Robins." *Notable American Women*, 3:179–81.

———. "The Women's Trade Union League: Origins and Organization." *Labor History* 5 (Winter 1964): 3–17.

Dewey, Lucretia. "Women in Labor Unions." *Monthly Labor Review* 94 (February 1971): 42–48.

Dubofsky, Melvyn. "Gertrude Barnum." *Notable American Women*, 1:93–94.

———. "Organized Labor and the Immigrant in New York City, 1900–1918." *Labor History* 2 (Spring 1961): 182–201.

Filler, Louis. "Rheta Childe Dorr." *Notable American Women*, 1:503–5.

Flexner, Eleanor. "Maud Younger." *Notable American Women*, 3:699–700.

Freedman, Estelle. "Separatism as Strategy: Female Institution Building and American Feminism, 1870–1930." *Feminist Studies* 5 (Fall 1979): 512–29.

Gettleman, Marvin E. "Charity and Social Class in the United States, 1874–1900." *American Journal of Sociology and Economics* 22 (July 1963–October 1963): 313–29, 417–26.

Jacoby, Robin Miller. "Feminism and Class Consciousness in the British and American Women's Trade Union Leagues, 1890–1925." In *Liberating Women's History: Theoretical and Critical Essays*, ed. Berenice Carroll, pp. 137–60. Urbana: University of Illinois Press, 1976.

———. "The Women's Trade Union League and American Feminism." *Feminist Studies* 3 (Fall 1975): 126–40.

Kenneally, James. "Women and Trade Unions, 1870–1920." *Labor History* 14 (Winter 1973): 42–55.

Kessler-Harris, Alice. "Organizing the Unorganizable: Three Jewish Women and Their Union." *Labor History* 17 (Winter 1976): 14–28.

———. "Where Are the Organized Women Workers?" *Feminist Studies* 3 (Fall 1975): 92–110.

Kerr, Thomas J. "The New York Factory Investigating Commission and the Minimum Wage Movement." *Labor History* 12 (Summer 1971): 373–91.

Lemons, J. Stanley. "The Sheppard-Towner Act: Progressivism in the 1920s." *Journal of American History* 55 (March 1969): 776–86.

———. "Social Feminism in the 1920s: Progressive Women and Industrial Legislation." *Labor History* 14 (Winter 1973): 83–91.

Marcus, Jane. "Transatlantic Sisterhood: Labor and Suffrage Links in the Letters of Elizabeth Robins and Emmeline Pankhurst." *Signs* 3 (Spring 1978): 744–55.

Nash, Roderick. "Carola Woerishoffer." *Notable American Women*, 3: 639–41.

Rischin, Moses. "The Jewish Labor Movement in America: A Social Interpretation." *Labor History* 4 (Fall 1963): 227–47.

Schaeffer, Ronald. "The New York City Woman Suffrage Party, 1909–1919." *New York History* 43 (July 1962): 268–87.

Schwartz, Judith. "Yellow Clover: Katharine Lee Bates and Katharine Coman." *Frontiers* 4 (Spring 1979): 59–67.

Shively, Charles. "Leonora O'Reilly." *Notable American Women*.

Smith-Rosenberg, Carroll. "The Female World of Love and Ritual: Relations between Women in Nineteenth-Century America." *Signs* 1 (Autumn 1975): 1–29.

Strom, Sharon Hartman. "Leadership and Tactics in the American Woman Suffrage Movement: A New Perspective from Massachusetts." *Journal of American History* 62 (September 1975): 296–315.

III. *Dissertations*

Berman, Hyman. "The Era of the Protocol." Columbia University, 1957.

Buhle, Mari Jo. "Feminism and Socialism in the United States, 1820–1920." University of Wisconsin, 1974.

Conway, Jill. "The First Generation of American Women College Graduates." Harvard University, 1968.

Endelman, Gary Edward. "Solidarity Forever: Rose Schneiderman and the Women's Trade Union League." University of Delaware, 1978.

McCreesh, Carolyn Daniel. "On the Picket Line: Militant Women Campaign to Organize Garment Workers, 1880–1917." University of Maryland, 1978.

Walker, Claire Brandler. "A History of Factory Legislation and Inspection in New York State, 1886–1911." Columbia University, 1969.

# Index